The Budget Backpacker

The Budget Backpacker

How to Select or Make,
Maintain and Repair Your Own
Lightweight Backpacking
and Camping Equipment

L. A. ZAKRESKI

WINCHESTER PRESS

NEW YORK

Library of Congress Cataloging in Publication Data

Zakreski, L   A
   The budget backpacker.

   Bibliography: p.
   Includes index.
   1. Backpacking—Equipment and supplies.   2. Camping—Outfits, supplies, etc.   3. Handicraft.   I. Title.
GV199.6.Z24   688.7′6′5   77-8349
ISBN 0-87691-189-0

The charts on pages 21 and 42 are reprinted from LIGHT WEIGHT CAMPING EQUIPMENT by Gerry Cunningham and Margaret Hansson with the permission of Charles Scribner's Sons. Copyright © 1976, 1959 Gerry Division, Outdoor Sports Industries, Inc.

WINCHESTER is a Trademark of Olin Corporation used by Winchester Press, Inc., under authority and control of the Trademark Proprietor.

Published by:
Winchester Press
205 East 42nd Street
New York, N.Y. 10017

Printed in the United States of America

Contents

DEDICATION

This book is for Donna; she got it started.

ACKNOWLEDGMENTS

Thanks to Cliff and Lorne, the CADS of C.A.D.S. Manufacturing, for advice, materials, and support; without them there would have been no book. Many thanks also to Phyllis for the countless hours of typing from my scribbles, and to the folks at Fresh Air, who patiently allowed me to fondle all their expensive merchandise, while never buying any.

Introduction

The Budget Backpacker is intended to be used primarily as a do-it-yourself guide for the construction of sturdy and light-weight backpacking and camping equipment. It contains illustrated, step-by-step instructions that guide you from raw materials to quality, finished camping gear, suitable for backpacking. If you wish to diverge from the plans I have presented, it also provides enough additional information to enable you to design your own gear. With patience, care, and the information in this book, you can make such items as packs, tents, clothing, and sleeping bags, and you can have a lot of fun while doing it.

This book also tells you how to evaluate, choose, and acquire the lightweight camping equipment that best suits your needs; how to use, maintain, and repair that equipment—to get the most out of your gear once you have it—and most of all, how to save money on the equipment you need to enjoy backpacking. As the title implies, this is a book about low-cost camping—how to get the equipment to go backpacking, while on a budget.

The Budget Backpacker is not an introduction to camping or backpacking. Neither is it a complete guide to the selection, construction, or design of camping gear. It would have to be thousands of pages long if it were. What this book is, is merely a distillation of information, ideas, and techniques that I have found to be most useful to the home builder.

If you're a beginner, or a do-it-yourself addict not yet experienced in camping, I suggest that you read some books and learn a bit about camping before you start in with the make-it part of do-it-yourself camping. Using borrowed or rented equipment, go out on a few short trips. Such trial runs can be extremely valuable to a beginner; they ensure that your investment will be worthwhile—that you really will enjoy camping; they familiarize you with your individual equipment needs—so that you can choose intelligently which items to take along; and they provide actual field experience with various types of equipment—which will be useful when you start buying or making your own. For now, don't worry about any lack of do-it-yourself abilities; you will be guided by step-by-step, illustrated instructions, and all necessary skills may be easily learned as you go along.

You may be skeptical now, but with patience, care, and proper information even a beginner can make backpacking and camping gear equal or superior to commercial equipment. Once you've tried it, you will find that making your own gear is not as difficult as you had thought it was. Prior to my involvement with do-it-yourself camping, my sewing experience was limited to buttons and blue jean patches. With a borrowed sewing machine and a lot of enthusiasm (and also a great deal of ignorance), I started making my own gear. Since then, I've managed to outfit myself with a respectable amount of top-quality equipment with a minimum outlay of cash, and I've learned a lot along the way.

If you're already an experienced camper and enthusiastic do-it-yourselfer, you really don't need any sales pitch from me to get you started. You already know that making and using camping gear can be rewarding. If you are an experienced camper, but are not familiar with homemade camping gear, then you may be skeptical about do-it-yourself as a source for quality, reliable camping equipment. I hope to persuade you to change your mind.

Do not, however, underestimate the work involved. While you can save a substantial amount of cash by making your own, realize that this savings comes from an expenditure of your time. You must balance your time against the money saved—and the other benefits—to decide if making your own is worthwhile for you. Personally, I have found that making my own camping gear is a very practical way to stay within my tight budget. For me, do-it-yourself camping is the best way I have found to spend my recreational time and money.

Remember, I cannot tell you everything, or do anything for you; after all, this is a book about do-it-yourself. What I will do is supply you with certain necessary information, but you will have to add your personal contribution—your own enthusiasm, perseverance, ingenuity, and hard work.

The Budget Backpacker

1

Why Make Your Own?

If you are like most people, concerned about saving money, then you are probably interested in finding some form of low-cost, enjoyable recreation. Camping, and particularly do-it-yourself camping, is one of the best bargains around today. Consider it from a strictly practical point of view: for only a small investment you get to enjoy a satisfying, interesting, and immensely rewarding activity. After a reasonable initial investment for equipment, your expenses and upkeep are small; food, transportation, and an occasional repair bill are all that are needed to keep you camping. When you also consider that well-maintained camping gear can last a lifetime, and that quality equipment keeps a high resale value throughout its long life, then you must agree that camping is a fantastic recreational bargain.

When patience and ingenuity are used to acquire the necessary equipment, camping becomes an even greater bargain. With patience, your initial investment can be spread out by buying only what is absolutely necessary for the present trip. You can start out on short, easy trips with a bare minimum of gear, and still enjoy camping. Later, as your budget allows, you can add the extras and the nonessentials that increase your range and comfort. You may even discover that it is possible for you to enjoy camping without many of these extras. If so, you can greatly reduce your major expense, which is for equipment.

With ingenuity, your initial investment can be cut even further. By scrounging, by bargain hunting, and most important of all, by do-it-yourself, you can cut your equipment costs significantly. Remember, patience and ingenuity can often replace cash; with them it is possible to enjoy camping while on the tightest of budgets.

Why Do-It-Yourself Saves Money

If a tight budget is your main incentive for considering do-it-yourself as a source for camping equipment, then make sure you realize that there are other alternatives. Scrounging or bargain hunting may often prove to be faster and cheaper sources for satisfactory gear; Chapter 8 goes into this in greater detail. You will usually find, however, that do-it-yourself will produce a greater cash saving than any other method of obtaining top-quality gear—barring theft, inheritance, or gifts. Since you rarely get something for nothing, the money you save by making your own backpacking and camping gear must come from somewhere. An understanding of why quality, lightweight equipment costs so much will help you understand how and why you can save money by making your own.

Many people feel that the retail prices for quality, lightweight camping gear are a rip-off. Actually, when you go into it in detail, you can see how these large price tags *might* be justified. To begin with, you must realize that a manufacturer is in business for one main reason: to make money. He must make a profit on his products or he will not survive. This is a simple fact of life. At the same time the manufacturer must pay for expensive, specialized materials and skilled labor for every single item that he makes. To this add the overhead, necessary to pay for the development, testing, tools, facilities, and wastage encountered in production. The sum of materials, labor, and overhead gives us a figure I call the manufacturer's basic cost, or MBC. To the MBC we must add manufacturer's profit; after all, he is not in business just for the fun of it. Then comes manufacturer's tax, shipping, wholesaler's costs and profit, retailer's costs and profit, retail sales tax, duty, and so forth. Obviously, with all these people handling the item and expecting their cut of the final purchase price, there is a lot of room for saving money.

As a home builder, however, you have different goals, and can afford to have different priorities. You will be producing a small volume of equipment for use by yourself, or your close friends, and you rarely expect to make a profit. To you, material costs and labor are irrelevant; you work for fun, and are primarily interested in turning out the best equipment you can. You count costs and profit as secondary—if you count them at all. This means that what is uneconomical or impractical for the manufacturer may be feasible, or even ideal, for you, the home craftsman. You are not worrying about profit margins, or extra labor, or that the item is not readily suitable for mass production. In fact, the home builder can afford to experiment with many excellent and different ideas, designs, and materials that are too expensive or too impractical for the manufacturer, but which may lead the amateur to superior equipment. In short, you can afford to pursue your hobby in many cases where a businessman cannot afford his business.

Also, you may find that it often costs you less to make an item than it does the manufacturer. The MBC consists of labor, materials, and overhead. Since you don't have to pay for expensive production tools and facilities, your overhead will usually be less than the manufacturer's. All of the items presented in this book can be made with basic, inexpensive tools that are common to most home workshops; and all testing and development has already been done for you. Nevertheless, you won't really save much on overhead; it is a relatively small fraction of the MBC.

Next, consider your materials. The manufacturer—if he is conscientious—will buy only the best materials available. To ensure an adequate supply of these materials, he will usually buy direct from the producer in bulk. Due to these bulk purchases, the manufacturer gets a discount on material costs that is not available to the small buyer. You will not usually be able to buy direct from the producers; they deal in thousand-yard lots or greater. You will have to order from some other source that is willing to sell by the yard. This means that there are middlemen between you and the producers; and these middlemen all want to be paid for handling the materials. Unless you are exceptionally lucky or resourceful, you will not be able to beat the manufacturer's material costs. And don't try to save money here by using inferior quality materials; this is false economy. For do-it-yourself—where material amounts are small—using the best materials costs only a few pennies or dollars more per item.

Labor, then, is the main source of the savings from do-it-yourself. The manufacturer must pay, and pay well, for his labor. His skilled and experienced workers, using heavy-duty equipment and streamlined, mass-production techniques, can easily produce finished camping gear much faster than you can at home, with your do-it-yourself tools and techniques. However, you do not have to compete with them. You are not being paid by the hour; your payoff comes from the money you do not have to spend to get the quality camping gear you want.

Realizing this, you should compute your labor costs at a different rate than the manufacturer's. In fact, you can figure in your time at x dollars per hour, if that is what you feel your spare time is worth to you. However, if you consider do-it-yourself as a hobby, or as a recreational activity, then another set of values comes into play; you must usually pay for your recreation. If you enjoy do-it-yourself, you can almost consider that you are being paid to have fun—the money you save on quality camping gear is your pay, and the time spent at making your gear can certainly be fun.

Although the idea of being paid to have fun is attractive, it is of course only a fiction; you cannot put this pay in the bank. Nevertheless, by making your own you save real money, which is still around to be spent. This represents a tangible increase in your purchasing power, if not in your bankbook.

How Much Can You Save?

Figures often are misleading, but here are some showing what it might cost you for finished equipment, materials, or kits. Remember, these figures reflect local conditions in my area. If you are really serious about doing a more relevant comparison, shop around in your own area for your own figures.

In computing the times I have given very rough approximations, which I feel are reasonable. Anyone experienced at sewing should be able to do better, but there will be many beginners who will need twice as long. If you are enjoying your work, it really shouldn't matter how long it takes; your main savings come from your time, which costs you nothing, so use as much of it as is necessary to do the job carefully and properly.

In computing the material costs I have used local (Canadian) prices. Usually the materials were bought at retail prices, and no real attempt was made to look for bargains. You may be able to do better, especially if you are American (Canadian duty varies, but it runs around 30 percent for most of the materials). Local sources will almost always be the cheapest, but check out what the mail-order people are charging. Don't forget to include the hidden extras such as shipping and tax, when figuring out where to buy.

The prices I give for the kits may seem grossly inflated to those of you who have

HOW MUCH CAN YOU SAVE?

| Item | Do-It-Yourself | | Kits | Commercial Gear |
	Time	Cash		
Day Pack	3 hours	$ 7.75	$ 17.00	$ 30.00
Mountain Parka	8 hours	$16.00	$ 31.00	$ 65.00
Down Vest	4 hours	$12.50	$ 19.00	$ 35.00
"A" Tent	2 days	$62.75	$108.00	$170.00
Sleeping Bag	2 days	$52.00	$ 92.00	$100.00

looked in a catalog lately, but they represent what I would actually have to pay for these items. When you add in the Canadian duty, insurance, shipping, and the highly desirable air freight charges (otherwise you wait forever), the competitively priced kits are no longer competitive. If you live in the States the kits will cost less, but do-it-yourself from scratch will still save you the most.

INTANGIBLES

After our short lesson in economics, you should understand exactly how and why do-it-yourself camping can save you money on your recreation. Obviously, saving money is a valid reason for making your own, but there are other reasons that may not be as obvious or seem as practical. These are the intangibles.

Intangibles are difficult for a person to evaluate objectively. I know that I find it difficult to place a value—in economic or practical terms—on all of the rewards that do-it-yourself camping has to offer. Nevertheless, I am going to list some of these intangible reasons. Of course, these are subjective evaluations, based on personal values you may not share. Everyone can appreciate that achieving a perfect custom fit can be important and practical, but not everyone can appreciate some of the other rewards available. You should consider these rewards from your own personal point of view. When deciding whether or not to do-it-yourself, stress the ones that you feel are most appropriate.

Do-It-Yourself Can Be Fun

For me, the most influential reason for making my own camping equipment is that I find this almost as much fun as using the finished products. I must admit, however, that I did not always feel this way. Initially, I began making my own camping gear entirely for economic reasons; I just could not find cash to pay for the top-quality gear I wanted.

I had been enjoying camping for some time, and was getting quite serious about backpacking, when I began to realize that my equipment—mostly scrounged, well worn, and of doubtful quality—just wasn't suitable. I knew what kind of equipment I wanted—the expensive kind—but I did not know how I could afford it. In desperation, I attempted to make some of those specialized, lightweight, and expensive, items for myself. I soon discovered that I could make good, lightweight camping equipment at home, and at a fraction of the retail cost. Somewhere along the way, I also discovered that I enjoyed making the gear almost as much as I enjoyed using it.

For me, making my own camping gear has become an enjoyable, independent hobby, as well as a valuable supplement to my camping. Lately, I have even been adding to my income by custom making equipment for friends, and in a small way for retail. In fact, I have occasionally been passing up some perfect camping weather to stay at home with my sewing machine. I enjoy it that much.

Of course, you don't have to carry it this far. You may have turned to do-it-yourself as a last resort, and may hate the idea of time spent indoors, away from camping. Even so, there is no reason why you cannot enjoy the time you spend making your camping gear. You will find that making your own gear is the perfect solution for those rainy weekends, or for those long, boring winter months that are too often spent poring over catalogs, planning trips, and wishing that you were camping. If you do-it-yourself during your otherwise wasted spare time, making your own gear need not subtract at all from your camping time, and it can add considerably to your camping pleasure.

Quality Control

Another excellent reason for making your own camping gear is the control you will then have over its quality. Most experienced campers are very careful about choosing their gear, and with good reason; their experience has taught them that good equipment contributes a great deal to their enjoyment of camping. They know that only the best, most reliable equipment can be depended on in really rugged terrain, and they may have doubts about how well homemade gear can stand up to the outdoors. Equipment failure may not seem important in town, where repairs, parts, and service are readily available for a few dollars, but in real wilderness, equipment failure can be much more serious; in certain situations, it can even be fatal. Even under more normal conditions, a pack or boot failure can ruin what otherwise could have been a pleasant outing. When you realize this, it becomes obvious that using anything but top-quality gear is an unnecessary gamble. You are staking your comfort, and possibly a lot more, on your equipment, so use the best. The quality that goes into your equipment during construction always pays off later—in comfort, durability, reliability, and security.

If you are a mountain climber, a winter camper, or a backpacker who ventures into hostile terrain, remember that you may literally be staking your life on your equipment. If you are not confident of your ability to turn out equipment that will be of the best quality, then buy your gear from one of the many reputable dealers who specializes in quality equipment. On the other hand, if you're the type of person who believes that the best way to get something done right is to do it yourself, then making your own gear is for you.

By making your own, you will be assured that your gear has been made with all the care and attention to detail possible, that it was made from the best materials available, and that it is designed to be suitable for the conditions you anticipate. In short, you will know that you can really depend on it, that it is the best you can get.

Dissatisfaction with Commercial Gear

For those of you who are dissatisfied with the selection of commercial equipment available, for whatever reason, then do-it-yourself is the logical answer. After all, there are many valid reasons for being unhappy with commercial camping gear; perhaps the selection carried by your local retailers is limited; perhaps import duty and other markups have increased to the point where your pocketbook, or your principles, rebel; perhaps you are 4′8″ or 6′10″, and no one manufactures the items you want in your size; or perhaps none of the gear you have seen has all of the features you want. By making your own camping gear, you can solve all of these, and many other, problems. With do-it-yourself, you end up with the gear you want, not the gear a manufacturer—who doesn't even know you—wants you to purchase.

Homemade gear has a distinct advantage over commercial equipment in meeting your exact, individual, and personalized equipment requirements, especially if they are at all unusual. Take packs, for example. With do-it-yourself and a little forethought you can choose a design that will be as versatile or as specialized as you desire, the exact design that is best for the specific type, or combination of types, of camping that you anticipate. Since there is no such thing as one pack design that is "best," what you want to do is choose the design that is best for you and for the conditions you are expecting. Then, with do-it-yourself, you are able to custom tailor your choice to fit your individual needs and your personal style of camping. The ski-touring buff can add on special ski straps to his favorite, comfortable touring pack design—to hold his skis when they are off his feet. The photographer can add on or design special-equipment pockets—to perfectly fit and protect his fragile photo gear. The

mountain climber can fit a removable ultralight summit bag to a sturdy frame.

New Ideas May Be Profitable

If he is really ingenious, the home builder may occasionally come up with new, unique, and worthwhile designs that are not available commercially—yet. While the manufacturers do have an advantage in experience, they definitely do not hold any monopoly on fresh, innovative ideas. If you should come up with a genuinely new idea for some improvement or innovation in this field, it could be valuable.

It is a long way from an idea to a practical, and profitable, piece of equipment, which you can patent, copyright, or market, but do-it-yourself offers you the perfect way to evaluate, test, develop, refine, and perfect your "dream" until it is a marketable reality. Of course, very few of you will ever manage to cash in on this particular pot of gold, but who knows—with luck and determination you could be one of them.

Perfect Fit

There are several other—perhaps more practical—reasons for taking up do-it-yourself camping. Doing it yourself, for yourself, offers you the perfect chance to achieve something important, and rare, in camping gear—a perfect fit.

One of the worst shortcomings of commercial gear is that it is designed to fit everyone—and therefore rarely fits anyone perfectly. Quality gear is usually offered in various sizes, or it has a wide range of adjustability, to fit as many people as possible. Such gear will usually fit the average person fairly well, but if you are not built like Mr. Average Camper—or if you are not satisfied with fairly well—do-it-yourself can help. When making gear for yourself, you don't have to worry about fitting a wide range of body types; you can concentrate all of your efforts into achieving the best possible fit for the one person who really matters—yourself.

Craftsmanship

Another valid reason for do-it-yourself is the pride you will feel in something you have hand crafted. Sadly, craftsmanship and quality are fast disappearing from our modern, mass-produced world. The values and character traits learned from craftsmanship are not to be taken lightly. Self-respect, patience, attention to detail, caring, and a feeling of personal accomplishment are all valuable to any person's character. You can take pride in doing something "just a little bit better than you had to," and this in itself is sufficient reason for making your own.

There are many who feel that homemade gear is in some way inferior to commercial gear, that it's not as chic or as stylish as is bought. I won't argue with anyone who dislikes homemade gear for this reason. After all, this is a personal judgment. I would like to point out, however, that for all practical purposes homemade gear can be as good as the most expensive commercial gear, and it can—with care and ingenuity—even be as stylish. Of the many experienced campers I have met, the majority were more concerned with how well their equipment performed, rather than how it looked, or how stylish it was, or how much it cost, or what someone else thought of it.

Equipment Evaluation

Finally, making and using your own equipment is probably the best practical way there is to become an expert judge of commercial gear. By making your own, you will know exactly what must go into the gear—materials, labor skills, design features, and construction. An experienced camper who makes and uses his own gear picks up knowledge concerning general construction principles, materials, designs, etc., that will allow him to make fairly good evaluations of commercial gear. This is perhaps the only practical way an individual can learn enough about the generalities involved to become a decent equipment evaluator.

As you can see, there are many good reasons—both tangible and intangible—for making your own backpacking and camping equipment, and I am certain that you will find do-it-yourself camping a rewarding and worthwhile endeavor if you will just give it a try.

2

What to Take Camping

For the beginner, and sometimes even for the expert, one of the most difficult parts of a backpacking trip is deciding what gear to take along. I've seen several books on camping and backpacking that attempt to help out by giving exhaustive lists and detailed advice, but I'm not sure if these are more of a hindrance or a help. The beginner could use the advice, but gets confused by the lengthy lists, while the expert already has his own deeply ingrained opinions and prejudices, so he is not too likely to listen anyhow. Whether beginner or expert, however, trip planning is important, equipment is important, and if you don't have a photographic memory, lists can be important, especially when you are in a hurry to get it all packed and get going. Here are several of my lists for use as a reference when making up lists of your own.

EXAMPLE #1: A short backpacking trip of two days' duration—leave Friday after work, return Sunday evening—easy terrain, expecting good weather. Such a trip could be handled by an informed begin-

ner, but perhaps a few day trips, with no overnighting, might be a good way for the novice to acquire his initial experience.

Equipment List #1	Weight	Cost
1. Fresh air day pack (with slight modifications)	14 ounces	$ 7.00
2. Lightweight sleeping bag (1-pound down, sewn through)	37 ounces	13.00
3. Ensolite sleeping pad (with stuff sack for bag)	7 ounces	5.00
4. Poncho (for tarp tenting, ground sheet, rain wear)	16 ounces	7.00
5. Canteen (full, with canteen cup)	54 ounces	2.00
6. Backpacker's grill	3 ounces	2.00
7. Knife, fork, spoon set, and G.I. can opener	3 ounces	1.00
8. Knife (single blade, folding)	4 ounces	10.00

9. Flashlight (compact, alkaline batteries)   3 ounces   2.00
10. Miscellaneous (matches, toilet paper, lypsyl, insect repellent, premoistened towelettes)   4 ounces   2.00

Clothing to Wear

11. Boots (Wallabee crepe-soled moccasins)   36 ounces   —
12. Socks (thick, wool)   3 ounces   —
13. Underwear (cotton shorts and T-shirt)   4 ounces   —

A weekend's worth of equipment spread out.

The numbers identify the equipment. See the list for a short description.

14. Pants (blue jeans)	22 ounces	—
15. Shirt (cotton flannel or wool, depending on weather)	16 ounces	—
16. Wind/rain jacket (breathable nylon)	8 ounces	6.00

Clothing to Carry in Pack

17. Extra socks	3 ounces	—
18. Balaclava (wool, just in case of cold)	2 ounces	2.00
19. Handkerchief	—	—
20. Nylon swimsuit/underwear	2 ounces	5.00
21. Sweatsuit (synthetic, 2 piece, for pajamas, long underwear, lounging outfit, extra shirt)	28 ounces	8.00
22. Food (stored in two plastic garbage bags): 3 large meals (freeze dried, assorted)	12 ounces	8.00
2 small meals (trail snacks)	8 ounces	2.00
2 breakfasts (Granola, powdered milk)	6 ounces	—
Goodies (powdered soup, lemonade, candies)	8 ounces	1.00
23. First-aid kit (see page 15 for details)	10 ounces	8.00
24. Survival kit—optional (see page 15 for details)	52 ounces	30.00

If you are not following a plainly marked trail, you should also carry a map of the area and a compass, which you know how to use. If this is to be your first trip, you should have at least tried out your boots, sleeping bag, and pack around home, to make sure there is nothing drastically wrong with them. Also, it would be helpful for you to read up on backpacking before you start out.

Total weight of all equipment is 22 pounds, 13 ounces. Subtracting from this figure the weight of the clothing you will wear—total 5 pounds, 9 ounces—gives you the weight of your pack. Subtracting the weight of equipment you may prefer to carry in your pockets—knife, flashlight, miscellaneous, your trail snacks and goodies (total 1 pound, 11 ounces)—you are left with 15 pounds, 9 ounces in your pack. You will notice that some of the items in the survival kit (see page 15) may not be needed on a short trip. It does duplicate several of the items you are already carrying. Leaving out the survival kit drops another 3 pounds, 4 ounces off the total weight to give you in the pack 12 pounds, 5 ounces for the weekend (includes your water supply).

Total cost of the whole outfit is around $120. This assumes that you will be making your own pack, sleeping bag, and poncho, or else that you will purchase items in this general price range. I bought my sleeping bag on sale for $13, and it is possible to find packs suitable for day trips for under $12, so these figures won't be too far out.

If you need to save money, you can substitute plastic sheeting for the poncho (saves about $5), and you can substitute kitchen utensils for the pocketknife and eating tools (saves $11). You might be able to make do without a canteen (use plastic not glass, saves $2), the swimsuit (saves $5), and you don't have to use freeze-dried foods (saves $11).

By economizing in these places you can

save around $34. And if you don't invest $30 for the optional survival kit, your total cash outlay to outfit yourself for a weekend of backpacking, from scratch, can be as little as $60. Then, on later trips, all you'll have to pay for is your food, and perhaps for the extra gear that extends your range and comfort.

EXAMPLE #2: A weekend to a week in genuine wilderness, moderate terrain, praying for good weather, but prepared for the usual snafu. This type of trip is the most popular and probably accounts for the vast majority of actual hours spent backpacking.

A week's worth of equipment spread out.

The numbers identify the equipment. See the list for a short description.

1. Freedom weekender pack

2. Mediumweight sleeping bag (2-pound down, triangular baffles, semirectangular design)

3. Ensolite sleeping pad (with stuff sack for tent, bag in lower pack compartment; you also might consider a sleeping bag cover, a pillow, and an air mattress—on a trip of this length good sleep is important and worth the extra weight)

4. Poncho

5. Canteen (full)

6. Stove

7. Pots, pans, and utensils (canteen cup most useful, but supplemented with rectangular cook set—French Army Surplus, 14 ounces, $3)

8. Knife

9. Flashlight

10. Tent. On a trip this long you can get by without a tent. However, some campers make it a practice *always* to carry a small, lightweight tent on a weekend or weeklong trip. This is something you'll have to decide for yourself.

11. Clothing to wear: The usual items in Equipment List #1.

12. Clothing to carry in pack: The usual, in Equipment List #1.

13. Food: On this kind of trip you can get by with cold meals, but I think the boost a warm meal gives is worth the weight and hassle. On anything over a weekend, freeze dried is the only way to go—unless you are Hercules himself. I had been sort of putting up with freeze-dried foods until I discovered Mountain House. Their food is fantastic—good taste, good selection, and best of all, a minimum of hassle preparing and serving (add boiling water, wait, and eat out of the wrappers). You can leave the foil wrappers at home, but don't take them off till just before you leave. There are other good brands, so experiment—at home, not on the trail—and find the ones you like. I seal everything into a plastic freezer container, and this is a good way to go. It adds a few ounces, but the security, organization, and freshness are strong selling points for such containers.

14. First-aid kit (see page 15 for details).

15. Survival kit—optional (see page 15 for details). On trips this long the survival kit is always with me, usually carried on my belt.

The main concern on a lengthy trip is with weather reports, maps, and advice on local (unfamiliar) conditions. The camper who attempts such trips will usually have enough experience to look out for the zillion other things he should know.

EXAMPLE #3: An extended trip into rough country—any conditions, any weather—is where the real action is, but if you need me to tell you what to take, you aren't ready for it yet. Get a few more week trips in varied conditions under your belt before you try one of these. Make sure you have adequate experience for the conditions you might encounter, and get in shape yourself before you go—not with a 60-pound pack on the trail.

If you are experienced enough to be serious about expedition camping, you probably have your own lists, and you definitely have your own opinions. But for those of you who like to compare lists, here is what I keep around the house. According to conditions, terrain, length and purpose of trip, I choose and trim until I come up with the gear list I feel is appropriate.

Luggage

1. Pack pockets/belt packs—survival kit case (8×6×3 inches)
   —1 small (12×6×4 inches)
   —2 large (16×6×4 inches)
2. Fresh air day pack—accessory straps
3. Freedom weekender pack
4. Rear-loading frame pack bag—triangular slat frame
   —tubular frame
   —padded shoulder straps
   —padded hip belt
   —2-inch web waist belt
5. Assorted stuff sacks
6. Sports bag (16×10×8 inches—add to frame pack for immense loads)
7. Duffel bags—large canvas (surplus) (36×18 inches)
   —small hand (24×12 inches)
8. Plastic airtight boxes and baggies
9. Rigid rec pac/grub box (16×24×8 inches with web harness)
10. Bicycle panniers/dog pack

Clothing

11. Rain gear—poncho/bivouac
    —rain chaps
    —waterproof rain jacket
12. Cold-weather clothing—insulated parka
    —insulated jacket
    —insulated vest
    —insulated pants/bivouac bag
    —shell + liner mitts
    —shell + liner mukluks
13. General clothing—mountain parka
    —water-resistant jacket/windbreaker
    —shirts (wool and flannel)
    —pants (surplus, jeans, wool)
    —sweatsuit
    —net underwear
    —socks (wool; thick and thin)
    —underwear
    —swimsuit (light nylon), cutoffs/hiking shorts
    —headwear (balaclava, sun hat, hoods)
    —gloves (orlon liners, leather outers)
    —belts (1-inch web, money belt)
    —boots (camp shoes, lightweights, mediumweights, heavy
    mountaineering)

Shelter

14. Lightweight single-wall tent
15. Expedition tent with fly

16. Accessories—poles, pegs, line, shock cord, repair kit, stuff sack

Sleeping Needs

17. Sewn-through down inner bag
18. Sewn-through fiber inner bag
19. Baffled down outer bag
20. Accessories—pads, cover, hammock, stuff sacks, hood

Accessories

21. Knives—pocketknife
    —sheath knife
    —cooking knife
22. Canteens —G.I. with nesting cup
    —G.I. 2½ quart, folding
    —2 gallon, plastic
23. Cook set—stoves (butane, gas)
    —pots
    —utensils
24. Food (freeze dried, Gerry squeeze tubes)
25. Compass
26. Flashlights—2 small
    —1 large
27. Camera
28. Fishing tackle
29. Survival kit (see page 15 for details)
30. Toiletries
31. Spare glasses (1 pair photogray for glare)
32. Repair kit (see Chapter 9, Repairs)

Travel Equipment

33. Snowshoes
34. Cross-country skis
35. Skin-diving gear
36. Inflatable kayak
37. 10-speed bicycle
38. Dirt bike
39. Dune buggy
40. V.W. van (camperized/modified for off road)

Extended trips are usually for some reason other than pure pleasure, so expect to work hard carrying all of the gear you will need. This special gear must find a place on top of all the many things required to stay alive and healthy on an extended tour in real wilderness. Spend a little extra time making up your list, and decide at home that you really don't need those seventeen extra lenses for that special shot and trim, trim, trim. But don't trim in the survival gear; it's more important here than ever.

Every outdoorsman should have his own survival kit, be it as simple as an extra box of matches and a chocolate bar, or as elaborate as the one detailed here. Actually, survival depends more on attitude and knowledge than it does on equipment. The best way to get the proper attitudes and knowledge is through experience, so I recommend you try a trip or two with nothing more than your survival kit. This will familiarize you with your equipment and will give you confidence that will be invaluable in a genuine survival situation.

A survival kit that is too large gets left someplace else when you need it most, so spend a little time and effort to ensure that your personal survival kit is compact, light, and convenient. Here is what I keep in my belt survival kit:

SURVIVAL KIT

Information
1. Personal identification
2. Traveler's checks
3. Pen
4. Survival manual

Food and Water
5. Vitamin supplements
6. Foil
7. Can opener
8. Soft canteen
9. Halazone tablets

Tools
10. Knife
11. Rope
12. Cord
13. Sewing kit
14. Ripstop tape
15. Wire saw
16. Pliers

Rescue Equipment
17. Mirror
18. Compass
19. Flashlight
20. Flares
21. Maps

Miscellaneous
22. Matches
23. Space blanket

First-Aid Kit
24. First-aid manual
25. Spare glasses
26. Assorted bandages
27. Q-tips
28. One-inch surgical tape
29. Alcohol
30. Razor blades
31. Scissors
32. Tweezers
33. Antiseptic
34. Antibiotic
35. Pain killer
36. Gravol
37. Stimulant
38. Oil of cloves
39. Salt tablets
40. Prescription drugs for any special problems

EVALUATION

To some extent, any book will reflect the experience and prejudices of the author. I'm primarily a backpacker, and it will become obvious to you—as you study the equipment recommendations I just gave you, and my designs and advice throughout the book—that I am writing primarily for backpackers; all my advice, equipment, and do-it-yourself plans are slanted toward this specific form of camping. However, if you are not a backpacker, you will find that most of what I say applies to all forms of camping. After all, backpacking is nothing more than a specialized form of camping; a backpacker is merely a camper who transports himself and his gear on foot.

A backpacker keeps his camping gear to a minimum, and all of his gear must be durable, efficient, and light. Durability, efficiency, and lightness are highly desirable features for all types of camping gear. This means that good backpacking equipment often will be suitable for other forms of camping, except when extra comfort or convenience is desired.

While it definitely would be desirable to have specialized equipment for each activity, in my situation I find it more efficient and more economical to have a small selection of versatile gear, which may be adapted to suit whatever activity I am planning—be it camping, fishing, canoeing, skiing, or any other form of recreation I choose. Therefore, the equipment I prefer and the equipment I recommend in this book is versatile and adaptable. So when evaluating camping equipment for my own use, my priorities are—in the order of their importance to me—durability, efficiency, versatility, lightness, and adaptability. Of course, each of these factors should not only be considered individually, but you must also consider how they will combine and interact, or how they balance off.

There must always be some compromising, but in good camping equipment you won't notice it too much; it will be a balanced compromise, and these factors will combine without sacrificing or overemphasizing any one thing. However, this is sometimes difficult to achieve. In those cases where something absolutely had to be sacrificed, I consistently rated comfort, convenience, and economy as least important. You may find that getting your equipment as durable as you would like means sacrificing lightness or that efficiency at one specialized task means a sacrifice in versatility. Only you can make these decisions. I would suggest that you make up your own personal set of priorities—and prejudices—in whatever order you feel is appropriate, and use this list as a guide when evaluating equipment.

3

Do-It-Yourself:
Materials, Tools, and Procedures

This chapter deals only with the basics and covers only the generalities; for more specific coverage of individual articles and for step-by-step construction details, refer to the individual chapters that follow.

MATERIALS

For the average do-it-yourselfer, a detailed technical study of all the materials available would probably be more confusing than informative. All the average reader needs is an understanding of the basic materials most commonly used in lightweight camping equipment—the more conventional ones that have already proved themselves in the field, the materials that are most suitable for the home builder. However, since a major part of equipment design is matching the right materials to the demands of the job, a thorough knowledge of materials is the first step to becoming a competent designer. Some of you will be interested in designing your own, and for this reason my coverage will be as thorough as is feasible, but I will try to keep it simple. If you want more expert technical information, get in touch with the following companies:

Fabrics. Howe & Bainbridge is very active in the field of specialized fabrics for the outdoors, and a lot of their products are designed specifically for this field. They have clear, concise, informative promotional material available, and a letter to them is a good place to start learning about fabrics.

Down. Everybody seems to have their own opinions about down, but I have found that the catalogs put out by North Face say a lot that I agree with. Check out their catalogs or the catalogs of other reliable users or suppliers of down.

Fibers. You might try MAKIT and EMSKIT for propaganda on the fibers, since they use them in their kits.

Zippers. YKK is the biggest supplier of zippers for outdoors use, and their large Delrin and nylon-coil zippers are the standard.

Aluminum. Any local shop using or selling aircraft-quality aluminum tubing is a good source for information on the various specifications and characteristics of this material.

FABRICS AND FIBERS

I recently received a sample booklet from a supplier specializing in fabrics for outdoors equipment. There was nylon, and Dacron, and cotton, and cotton/polyester blends; there was ripstop nylon, and nylon taffeta, and nylon oxford; there was ¾-ounce ripstop nylon, and 22-ounce Cordura nylon. In fact, there were over fifty different kinds of fabrics listed in that one book. And this was only a partial listing, from one supplier.

With the vast assortment of fabrics available today, and with manufacturers working constantly to discover new materials and improve the old ones, selecting the proper fabric for use in lightweight backpacking and camping equipment can be a confusing job for anyone. An understanding of exactly what goes into a fabric will take you a long way toward understanding exactly what you can expect to get out of it.

Very simply, fabric is made by twisting fibers into yarns that are woven together. Once a fabric has been woven, it may be ready for use as is, or the manufacturer may subject it to various treatments, which modify the fabric in some way. All fabrics are similar in one respect; the simplest homespun and the most exotic miracle fabric come from fibers that are woven and then treated. Always keep these similarities in mind when considering fabrics.

Cotton. Because cotton is a natural product from a plant, there can be a great range in the quality of the fibers themselves. The best-grade cotton comes from plants that produce long fibers, such as the Egyptian or American pima.

The processing these fibers receive on their way to becoming finished fabric has a lot to do with the quality of the finished cloth. Before being spun into thread, natural fibers are carded, to remove any foreign matter mixed in with the fibers. Quality cotton fabrics come from fibers that go through an additional process known as combing, in which the long fibers are separated from the short. Cotton threads made exclusively from such long fibers have proved to be stronger, and of course make up into stronger fabric. In general, when selecting cotton fabrics look for some indication that the fibers used were long, or combed, or that they came from Egyptian or pima plants.

Advantages of cotton fibers:

• Cotton can be woven into a very tight fabric. Cotton fibers don't have much stretch, so they can be packed tightly. Ventile is a trade name for a cotton fabric that has been woven into a very tight, wind- and water-resistant type of cloth. Such a fabric is one of the best available for parkas and outerwear.

• When cotton threads get wet, they swell. A tightly woven cotton fabric will be almost perfectly water repellent. When it rains the fibers will swell up and close all the holes in the weave. At the same time, such a fabric will still allow air to pass through.

• Cotton fibers are absorbent and will soak up liquids quite readily. This means that treatments penetrate right into the fibers and stay there.

• Cotton is a pleasant fabric to the touch; it absorbs sweat and doesn't feel clammy.

• Cotton is not too expensive. This may not continue to be true, as the price of cotton fluctuates depending on such things as what kind of crops came in, the world political situation, and so forth.

Disadvantages of cotton fibers:

• Cotton is weaker than most synthetics, which means you have to use a heavier weight of cotton fabric to do the same job.

• When cotton fabric gets wet, it shrinks. In a cotton tent, when it rains you have to loosen off on the guy ropes or seams may be torn apart. I also have had a few T-shirts that started out as size large, and eventually became size too small.

• Cotton fibers are absorbent. Leave an untreated cotton tent out in the rain for a while and it soaks up a lot of water, which adds weight, and it takes a long time for the cotton to dry out.

• Wet cotton is cold. If you have ever worn wet blue jeans, you know exactly what I am talking about. When cotton gets wet it provides nearly zero insulation.

• Cotton is subject to rotting and mildew. I've got the remains of a cotton tent in my backyard to remind me of what happens when a cotton tent is rolled up wet and thrown into the trunk of a car for next time. In this case, next time never came; the tent fell apart first.

Wool. Wool is hair shorn from a sheep. Like cotton, wool is a natural fiber and, also like cotton, there can be a wide range in the quality of the raw fibers. The quality of those fibers depends on such factors as the breed of sheep, the climate, when it is shorn, and especially how the wool is processed after it is shorn. In general, if you end up paying a lot for it, it is probably the good stuff.

When selecting items made from wool, look for a label that identifies exactly what fibers went into the fabric. One hundred percent virgin wool is the best you can get. However, you will often find that nylon or some other fiber has been blended in with the wool—for example, 85 percent wool, 15 percent nylon. These blends may be just as suitable as pure wool for some items.

Those other fibers have not always been added to save on the cost of wool; they are often put there to help overcome some of the disadvantages that wool has as a fiber. Blends can be great, but watch out for bargains that use reprocessed wool, or a blend of wool and unidentified fibers, or wool that was not properly processed (has lumps in it).

Advantages of wool fibers:

• Wool is a soft, bulky fiber. Wool fibers are fuzzy; socks made of wool provide a cushion to feet; sweaters made from wool are thick and warm; anything made from wool is soft and comfortable (to some people anyhow). Wool clothing dries quickly on the inside, from your body heat, and wool wicks moisture away from the body.

• Wool retains much of its loft and insulating power when wet. This factor is very important to winter campers. Down—and some other insulations—lose a lot of insulating power when wet, so wool makes reliable clothing for cold and wet conditions.

Disadvantages of wool fibers:

• Wool is weak, and relatively heavy, and wet wool is weaker still. Wool is a soft, stretchy fiber that is nowhere near as strong as the synthetics in tensile strength or abrasion resistance. It must get extra care when washing—items can stretch or shrink completely out of shape, and can easily mat.

- Some people find wool very uncomfortable, even irritating. I must wear a cotton T-shirt under my sweaters, but I have no problem with wool socks or smooth-finished shirts; however, some people can't wear wool in any form (they are actually allergic to it). For them, one of the synthetics, such as orlon, would be better.

- Moths attack wool. Hang your wool sweater up in a closet and see if this is really true. Personally, I have never found a moth hole in any of mine, but it could be that I'm just lucky.

Nylon. Nylon was introduced to outdoors equipment about thirty years ago, and things have never been the same since. When it first arrived, nylon caused a revolution in lightweight camping-equipment design. For the first time, lightweight camping could really live up to its name. The use of nylon in sleeping bags and tents made possible an amazing reduction in equipment weight, and with no sacrifice in equipment durability.

At its introduction, nylon was hailed as the miracle fiber, and it is still one of the toughest, strongest, and most useful fibers available. Ordinarily, nylon is made as a continuous filament yarn, a solid elastic rod drawn out to a fine diameter, and used as is for weaving.

Since it is a man-made fiber, nylon can be tailored to some extent. The filaments can be spun together into heavier threads, made larger for greater strength (as in heavy-filament nylon cloth for packs), the cross section may be modified (flattened to more closely resemble cotton), or the

molecular formula can be changed slightly, giving somewhat different properties (nylon comb, for example).

Advantages of nylon fibers:

- Nylon is strong, the strongest of the fibers in common use today. This means that a fabric from nylon can be lighter than a fabric made from any other fiber, and it will still be as strong. Also, because of its nature, nylon filament has excellent abrasion resistance.

- Nylon can be woven into a very light, tight fabric. Nylon taffeta and ripstop nylon provide the ultimate in lightweight wind protection. Such fabrics are the best for extralight wind and rain clothing. These tight weaves are breathable, and mildly water repellent.

- Individual nylon fibers are not absorbent; because of this nylon will not soak up liquids and is quick to dry.

- Nylon is a pleasant fabric to the touch; it is smooth, nonirritating, and nonallergenic. When used as a sleeping bag shell, it has less tendency to soak up body heat than cotton, and it will not cling to you like some other fabrics.

- Nylon is completely mildewproof and very rotproof; not only is this important in itself, but it also means that you can pack up wet nylon when in a hurry. (It is not recommended that you pack any item away wet for more than a short time, no matter what it is made of.)

Disadvantages of nylon fibers:

- Nylon is slippery; unless the fabric receives special treatment—calendering or heat setting—nylon filaments make up into a very sleazy fabric (sleazy means not very tight). This doesn't matter to the home builder—weaving the fabric is not his job—but because of the slipperiness of the individual fibers, nylon ravels very easily. This means that all edges must be finished in some way, and this matters to the home builder very much.

• Nylon fibers are not absorbent; the treatments applied to the fibers never do penetrate as they do with cotton. These treatments, such as water repellents, stay on the surface where they eventually wear off. Since nylon is basically a sleazy fabric, and since the fibers do not swell to fill the gaps in the weave when wet, untreated nylon will not make a good water-resistant fabric. In addition, because the nylon fibers do not absorb the rain, it stays on the surface where it may be easily shaken off—onto you.

• In some cases, nylon is an uncomfortable fabric; because the nylon will not absorb perspiration, tight clothing can feel clammy if worn in warm weather.

• Nylon is stretchy. Nylon fibers are elastic and proper manufacturing techniques must be used to pack them tightly. Again, this is not the worry of the home builder, but where the home builder is concerned is with sewing threads made from nylon. These threads are the strongest available, but this stretchiness often causes feeding problems on a home sewing machine.

Dacron. Dacron is another synthetic that is fairly useful for lightweight equipment. While it has not caught on as well as nylon, in some instances its special properties make it superior to nylon.

Advantages of Dacron fibers:

• Dacron is strong, almost as strong as nylon and stronger than most of the other commonly used fibers.

• Dacron is much less elastic than ny-

TABLE OF COMPARATIVE TEXTILE
FIBER PROPERTIES*

Fiber	Nylon	Dacron	Orlon	Cotton	Wool
Tensile strength in gms/denier	6.8	6.1	4.5	3.9	1.4
Elongation before breaking	22%	12%	16%	5%	30%
Effect of heat	melts at 482°F	melts at 480°F	sticky at 455°F	scorches at 500°F	scorches at 400°F
Effect of sunlight and weathering	loses strength	loses less strength	very resistant	loses strength	loses strength
Resistance to moths	wholly	wholly	wholly	wholly	none
Resistance to mildew	wholly	wholly	finish may be attacked	very poor	good

* From *Light Weight Camping Equipment and How to Make It* (Fifth Edition) by Gerry Cunningham and Margaret Hansson (New York: Scribners, 1976).

lon. Dacron may be woven into very tight fabrics that are ideal for tents. At least one major tent manufacturer recognizes the advantages of this fabric and makes their tents from it. In addition, Dacron and Dacron-core cotton-wrapped threads are excellent for sewing.

• Dacron is slightly more weather resistant than nylon. Almost all fabrics deteriorate from exposure to the elements. The most important factor is ultraviolet radiation, which at high altitudes can weaken a tent very quickly. Jan Sport makes their tents from 1.9-ounce ripstop Dacron, and they seem to be standing up very well.

Orlon. Orlon is stronger than cotton, but not as strong as the other synthetics.

Advantages of orlon fibers:

• Orlon has excellent resistance to weathering. All other fibers lose some of their strength with exposure to the elements. By far the biggest factor in this deterioration is ultraviolet radiation. Tests have shown that a year's exposure to strong sunlight will reduce the strength of nylon fibers by about 90 percent. This comes from a weakening of the intermolecular structure inside the fibers, and is only a real problem in lightweight fabrics. Orlon is the most weatherproof fiber commonly in use today.

• When the fibers are chopped up and spun, orlon makes up into yarns very similar to wool. Clothing made from such orlon fibers may have many of the advantages of wool, and will be nonallergenic, stronger, and have better resistance to abrasion.

Construction

Yarns. Such terms as yarn, thread, filament, strand, and fiber are often used interchangeably by the nonexpert. To the fabric experts, each term has its own distinct meaning. For the purposes of this discussion, yarn is the term used to refer to the individual threads used for weaving. These yarns may be made from continuous filaments (look at a piece of monofilament fishing line for an overgrown example) or they may be made up from shorter fibers that have been twisted together (look at some knitting yarn). If you have ever watched someone at a spinning wheel, you know exactly how these short fibers may be spun into long threads.

The size of a thread, for sewing or for weaving, is usually given in denier, which refers to the diameter. In weaving, the yarns used may be of different sizes. If two

Spinning thread from wool fibers by hand.

A small hand loom for weaving fabrics.

or more threads are twisted together and used as a yarn, this is referred to as two-ply or three-ply construction. For example, two-ply, 6-ounce nylon pack cloth is a heavy cloth in which two nylon threads were twisted together and used as yarn. Or heavy filament 7.5-ounce pack cloth is a heavy cloth in which the individual yarns (filaments) used were larger than normal.

Weaving. Weaving refers to the process whereby the individual yarns are criss-crossed with each other to make a fabric. If you have a woven wicker basket in the house, you can see exactly how fabric is made, though on a much larger scale of course. In basket weaving each individual strand of wicker is threaded over/under/over the strands perpendicular to it.

The manufacturers use the same basic principles when weaving fabrics, only the speed and the scale of the operation have changed. Machines thread the individual yarns over/under/over the perpendicular yarns, just the same as you would do with wicker and a basket. These individual

yarns are designated as warp or fill, depending on whether they run lengthwise or across the fabric.

The type of fiber has a large effect on the finished fabric's characteristics, but the way in which these fibers are woven together may have just as great an effect. Thread count (number of threads per square inch) is one of the ways in which the tightness of a weave may be expressed. Generally, a fabric with a high thread count (tight weave) is tougher, less porous, and has better tear strength. Look at the difference between nylon taffeta and nylon netting; both are made from nylon

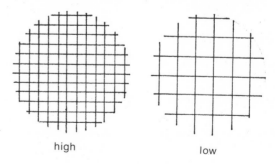

high   low

Thread Count: High = Tight; Low = Loose.

filaments, but the properties and characteristics of the two fabrics are otherwise dissimilar. This is due to the different ways they are woven.

Types of Weaves. There are a great many types of weaves available, but we are interested only in the ones most suitable to lightweight camping equipment.

Plain weaves are the most common and the simplest weaves. One fill yarn is threaded over and under each warp yarn. Taffeta, broadcloth, and muslin are the best-known examples. This weave produces the tightest fabrics—least porous, highest thread count per square inch—but because of the sharp angles the yarns must take, the tear strength of such weaves is not as high as some others.

The most common variation of plain weaves used is ripstop, in which two heavy twisted threads are woven as one every one-quarter inch. This forms a reinforcing grid readily apparent on the surface of the cloth, and greatly increases the tear strength of the basic plain weave. A ripstop weave will have about three times the tear strength as the same weight of similar nonripstop fabric; however, it will

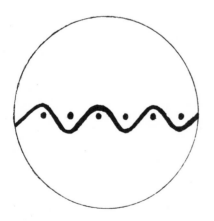

A plain weave.

have slightly less abrasion resistance. Other common variations are oxford weave, in which two parallel yarns are woven as one; duck, in which two warp yarns are woven as one; basket weaves, in which many parallel threads cross each other loosely; and poplin, which has heavier threads running in one direction and a ribbed texture to its surface. One of the most recent variations on a plain weave is Cordura nylon, which uses bulked filaments with discontinuous fill yarns. This gives the fabric a somewhat fuzzier look, and excellent abrasion resistance. Cordura is one of the strongest and toughest fabrics used in lightweight outdoors equipment today.

Diagonal weaves are weaves in which each thread passes over two or three yarns, on an alternate basis. This results in a surface that appears to have diagonal ribs—hence the name—and thus has better abrasion resistance. Examples of diagonal weaves are twill, ripcord, drill, and denim. Look at your blue jeans to see what is meant by diagonal ribs.

Most fabrics consist of a lot of yarn and very little space between them. Obviously, the more threads per square inch, the tighter the fabric. Sleazy is the term used to describe a fabric that is not tightly woven, and netting is basically supersleazy because it contains more spaces than yarns. With only a few threads per square inch to take up any strain, open weaves have a much lower tear strength than most fabrics. For this reason, use only nylon or Dacron netting. There are various other types of netting, but for outdoors equipment only these two are strong enough.

Marquisette netting (sometimes referred to as leno weave) is similar to a plain weave netting, but each warp yarn gets twisted between each fill yarn and this leads to a much more suitable finished product. Marquisette netting is used quite a bit for tent screening and sleeping bag baffles, and is fairly good. The only competition to marquisette netting is a nylon knit, such as nylon tricot, which in some ways is better (and more expensive). Nylon knits are stretchier, they resist strain better, and the best ones "remember" their original shape and return to it when the strain is removed. Marquisette netting keeps out most bugs, but if you need protection from no-see-ums, only the knits are fine enough.

Knits. The fiber most commonly used for knitting is wool, with fuzzy, chopped synthetics a close second. Both these fibers make up into warm, useful articles. Tight knits are reasonably wind and water resistant, and will keep their insulation value when wet. However, for the average do-it-yourselfer, such tight knits are usually beyond his abilities. Most knit clothing made at home is loosely knit, and is very bulky (warm) but also very porous. Such loose knit clothing is still useful if worn under a light, windproof outer shell, such as an untreated nylon parka.

Blends. Blends are an attempt to combine the most useful characteristics of two different fibers into one fabric. Cotton/nylon 60/40 cloth received a lot of publicity as the perfect fabric for outerwear. This cloth has the water resistance and breathable characteristics of cotton, and the abrasion resistance and strength of nylon—in theory anyhow. It also has some of the drawbacks of both fibers, and some unique ones of its own, but cotton/nylon 60/40 is especially suitable for breath-able, water-repellent, light and tough outerwear.

Wool is commonly blended with nylon or another fiber to increase the abrasion resistance of the fabric. Again, a blend can combine the best of both; wool/synthetic blends are very warm and are more resistant to abrasion. In most cases they are considerably less expensive than 100 percent pure wool.

There are two different ways to make up a blended fabric. First, one type of fiber may be used for the warp and another for the fill. This is the most common way of blending two fibers, but it has one important disadvantage: the tear strength in one direction is greater than the tear strength in the other. This is the way most cotton/nylon blends are made, and if specifications are given, the great difference in warp and fill tear strengths will mark them as the first type of blend.

The second type of blend is known as an intimate blend; the individual warp and fill yarns are themselves blends and are identical. This is the type of blending that is used in the wool/synthetic blends, because the wool/chopped synthetic fibers may be spun together into "intimate" yarns with very little extra trouble. This type of blend has recently become available in 50/50 or 65/35 cotton/polyester cloth. This cloth is tightly woven, breathable, water repellent, drapes well, and does not feel clammy. This is one of the very best outerwear fabrics available; look for it to become more popular in the near future.

Types of Treatments

There are several types of treatments available, which are intended to modify the characteristics of the basic fabric. Keep in mind the characteristics of the different types of fibers when considering treatments: Cotton mildews—so there are treatments for protecting cotton fibers from mildew. Nylon is slippery—so there are treatments to overcome the undesirable sleaziness of fabrics made from this fiber. Cotton is absorbent—so the treatments for cotton are meant to be absorbed into the fibers. Nylon is not absorbent—so the treatments for nylon are meant to be coated on, and perhaps are intended to be renewed as they wear off.

Calendering. Calendering is a process involving heated rollers, which actually melts the surface of the fabric slightly. This results in a very smooth, shiny surface texture, and the fabric is made downproof and much more sturdy; the individual nylon fibers have been welded (heat set) together, greatly increasing their resistance to raveling. Several calenderings result in the wet look so popular in ski wear.

Downproofing. Down has the annoying habit of working its way through the smallest of holes, and when you try and remove that one annoying piece of fluff by pulling it all the way through, it likes to bring along a lot of company. This is why fabrics used for down-insulated equipment must be tightly woven, and downproof. If the fabric weave is tight enough, no further downproofing is needed, but such tight weaves are hard to find. Therefore, several treatments have been developed to seal in the down (but not the air; down must breathe). Kendown, from Kenyon Dye and Fabrics, is probably the most popular downproofing treatment, and it is also somewhat effective as a water-repellent treatment.

Dyeing. When fabric comes off the loom it is either raw fabric that still has to be dyed, or the weaving may have been done with yarns that were individually dyed. Most commonly, if the fiber is nylon, the raw fabric is washed with a detergent, bleached, and then acid dyed. If the fiber is cotton, it will be vat dyed; and if the fiber is wool, the individual yarns will have been dyed before the article was knit or woven. Most of the modern dyeing processes are very colorfast, which means they don't bleed off when washing and don't fade too much from exposure to the weather. But when making repairs on old equipment, it will be readily apparent that no dye processing is perfect; the abuse the outdoors gives out will fade all dyes somewhat as time goes by.

Flameproofing. Many people can vividly imagine themselves trapped in a burning tent or smoldering sleeping bag, but in reality this rarely happens. There are standards for flame resistance that the reputable manufacturer has always met; now, with all the interest in consumer safety, the United States and Canada will soon have standards that are enforceable by law. If you are concerned, look for some indication that the fabrics used "meet C.P.A.I.-84 standards for flameproofing." People who try to smother fires with their sleeping bags, or cook inside their tents and kick over the stove, get scant sympathy from me, however.

Flameproofing is presently available as a desirable option on most of the quality backpacking tents that can be purchased ready made, but when making your own you do not have to conform to governmental standards; the laws will affect only tents made for retail.

At this time, Sierra Designs is the only

firm I know of that supplies flame-resistant ripstop, netting, etc., in the small quantities needed by the home builder, but I'm sure that there will be others. If you are worried about fire, then contact them, but remember that fabrics that meet C.P.A.I.-84 standards for flame resistance will burn if exposed to open flame long enough. The important thing is, don't use gas lanterns or stoves too close to your tent. And whatever you make your tent out of, watch out for sparks from a camp fire. Your tent might not burn up, or even catch fire, but sparks can burn or melt pinholes everywhere. Ventilation in a tent is important, but this is not the way to go after it.

Mildewproofing and Rotproofing. These are chemical treatments used in cotton, which greatly increase resistance to mildew and rot. The treatments may be absorbed into the fibers or painted on, but in either case no cotton fabric is absolutely impervious to mildew or rot. These treatments are very effective, but not perfect—so use normal precautions. For that matter even nylon can rot if packed away dirty and wet for long periods of time, so clean and dry all fabrics before storage.

Printing. Printing involves patterns stamped onto the basic fabric with various colored dyes. It can provide an exceptionally attractive or useful finish—camouflage prints in brown and green, for instance. I prefer camouflage prints above all others for my equipment. I like to blend in with the environment, but there are some who prefer a bright yellow or orange because it is the most visible color available—an important survival and rescue consideration. So far, I have never lost my tent (green camouflage), but when winter camping I would recommend using an orange fly to increase visibility.

Water Repellents. The best-known commercial treatment is DuPont Zepel, which gives good stain repellency and fairly good water repellency when used on tightly woven fabrics. Most often a water-repellent treatment is one of the silicone types that may be sprayed on at home (not so good, but ideal for doing small items not previously treated) or factory applied (much better). This type of treatment is very popular on breathable fabrics, and may also be used on equipment made of coated material when the coated side is to the inside, and a nonabsorbent outer side is desired. Scotchgard is a good example of a spray-on treatment that is applied at home. Many dry cleaners will do a cheap and effective job of treating or renewing water repellency, and this may be easier and better than doing it yourself.

Water Repellents for Cotton. Because of the nature of cotton fabrics, water-repellent treatments for cotton take two forms: wax finish (also known as semidry) and dry finish.

The semidry finishes are usually less expensive, less durable, and less effective. They are applied after the fabric has been woven, and are intended to coat the fibers and clog pores. They can rub off (but may be cheaply renewed) and are recognized by a stiffer, heavier, sometimes tacky or powdery feel to the fabric. Paraffin finishes on canvas are very burnable; these are the ones to worry about.

The dry finish consists of a chemical treatment that is given to the individual yarns before they are woven. This type of treatment is both light and durable—it is inside the fibers—but it is also more expensive. It may be somewhat less flammable than the semidry finishes.

No cotton fabric is totally waterproof—unless it is given a coating of some waterproof substance—but, as mentioned, cotton fibers swell when wet and do a very good job of keeping you dry. On steeper tent walls, cotton sheds water just as effectively as a coated fabric, and is breathable as well.

Waterproof Coatings. There are several types of coatings that may be applied to the fabric to make it completely waterproof and impermeable to air. These coatings are intended to close off the tiny gaps found in even the tightest weaves. In addition, coating does other things to the fabric: it raises the weight; a light coating concentrates strain on only a few threads, significantly decreasing the tear strength of a fabric; it affects the abrasion resistance; it affects the opaqueness, or degree of light, that can get through, which is an important consideration in tents; it gives a different texture to the surface, or surfaces, of the fabric.

Coatings also have some peculiar characteristics of their own. They may burn, sometimes they can peel away from the fabric, they may crack in the cold, the coating may wear off and leave you with nonwaterproof spots, and the coating may affect the stiffness of a fabric.

There are a bewildering number of waterproof coatings available, each with its own specialized properties. The do-it-yourselfer should use the materials that the reputable equipment manufacturers are finding most suitable. The urethane–polyurethane coatings are the most popular today, especially in the field of light-

weight outdoors equipment. They have replaced the older, heavier coatings of rubber and synthetic rubber that were common to the equipment of the past. The urethane coating family is fairly large, and consists of several modifications to the basic urethane compound. The most common urethane coating is Kenyon's K-Kote, which is available with several basic differences:

Light K-Kote—light coating for water resistance.

Super K-Kote—clear heavy coating for maximum water resistance.

K-Kote FR—flame-resistant Super K-Kote.

Temper Kote—sometimes referred to as urethane polymer, or just polymer. It is a special waterproof coating designed to give added tear strength to extremely lightweight fabrics. Gives a softer drape, with more suppleness and less stiffness, than the ordinary urethanes, and is very useful in tent flys, tent floors, etc.

Frostflex—special low-temperature waterproof coating.

Ken-Lox—very light coating for stability, ravel control, with some water resistance.

Klay Kote—a heavy coating for maximum water resistance, combined with maximum opaqueness; you cannot see through it like you can with some of the other coated fabrics.

Heat Sealable K-Kote—a coating that is waterproof; it may be welded into "seamless" ponchos, parkas, etc., that will have no leakage through seam stitch holes.

Met-L-Chine—metallic surface combined with an urethane coating. The metallic surface substantially cuts down on heat loss through radiation.

Though there are many other compounds—neoprene, imitation leather, vinyl—all of these show some undesirable characteristics for use in durable, lightweight, outdoors equipment. They are not suitable, so don't use them. The proper materials are readily available from the retail mail-order outfits, so don't bother with the substitutes. If you hear of some new compounds that I have not covered, make sure that they are thoroughly tested before you try them.

Miscellaneous. There are a great many other treatments that are interesting to a specialist, but are not too important to the average do-it-yourselfer. One of the most useful of the specialty treatments is the bonding of some form of insulation to a fabric. Foam—urethane, in various thicknesses—is available with a fabric backing (such as nylon tricot), and such materials may have a place in outdoors equipment. These insulated fabrics would be suitable for cold-weather clothing.

The search goes on for the perfect water repellent/breathable fabric, which will keep out the water and still allow clothing and tents to breathe. To date, the most promising development has been Gore-Tex, a laminate consisting of two layers of ordinary woven fabric with a microporous film of PTFE (Teflon) sandwiched between. The two outside layers of fabric give strength and abrasion resistance, while the PTFE film provides breathability and water repellency. Gore-Tex is available in several combinations of fabrics, suitable for tents, clothing, and sleeping bags. At this time, only Early Winters in Seattle sells Gore-Tex in small yardages (about $10 per yard), and there definitely is no surplus. This situation should improve as more manufacturers become aware of the potential of this fabric, and supplies catch up with the demand.

Evaluations

Suit the Materials To the Function. The fabrics used to make lightweight camping equipment are highly specialized, and should be carefully matched to the specific job requirements. You should not make a pack out of 1.9-ounce ripstop nylon, even if this fabric is one of the strongest and lightest fabrics around. While packs could be made, and have been made, from 1.9-ounce ripstop, such items have a very short life expectancy because the strength of the materials is not sufficient for the function these materials are expected to perform. Therefore, equipment failure.

Lightweight equipment calls for light materials. When evaluating materials, consider all of their characteristics, not just weight. For example, 4-ounce fabric means 4 ounces per square yard. This figure tells you only the weight of the cloth.

If you decide to make a tent floor out of 4-ounce untreated cotton, instead of 4-ounce coated nylon, which is mildew resistant, waterproof, and more abrasion resistant, you would soon regret your decision. Remember, you walk on floors, you sometimes have water under your tent, and you occasionally will have to pack your tent while it is still wet. Don't get too concerned about any one factor when considering materials for lightweight camping equipment; instead, try to evaluate all of a material's characteristics and judge its usefulness for the job on a total basis.

For a more detailed study of exactly what characteristics a fabric for a tent—or a parka, or a sleeping bag—should have, see the chapters related to these specific articles. Here, we'll simply cover some of the points that must be considered when trying to match a fabric to a job.

Weight. Though the fibers and the weave have much to do with the weight of a fabric, the treatment it receives may also have a significant effect. For example, 400 denier DuPont nylon pack cloth weighs 5.7 ounces per square yard in its greige state, but 9.7 ounces per square yard when both sides are polyurethane coated. In general, the greater the weight of the fabric, the more durable, stronger, and stiffer the fabric. Weight is expressed in ounces per square yard, or in ounces per running yard of a given width.

Durability. The durability of the fabric is very hard to measure objectively; there are too many factors involved to make exact comparisons in the lab. Ultraviolet deterioration, weather, and how it is used, all have an effect on how long a fabric will hold up. But the fabrics being used today will often outlast the owner of the equipment, if they have been properly chosen to suit the requirements of the job.

The biggest component of durability for such items as tent floors, packs, and climbing outfits is abrasion resistance, which again is hard to measure objectively. The best way to judge durability and abrasion resistance is to see what the reputable manufacturers are using, and copy their materials. The top manufacturers use the most durable materials they can find, and their extensive experience will usually be the most reliable guide.

Strength. Strength is described in terms of *tensile strength*, the strength of the individual fibers that make up the fabric; *bursting strength*, which is very closely related to tensile strength, and which is concerned with how much force it takes to burst through the fabric; and *tear strength*, which is a measure of how much force is required to continue a tear that has already started.

Tear strength is of great concern to the outdoorsman, for it is very important to know how much force a snagged tent or sleeping bag can take without ripping. To measure tear strength, cut a slit along the edge of a piece of fabric and measure the force needed to continue the cut. This is usually referred to as the "tongue test," and is the most commonly used procedure. Do so in both directions, across both the warp and fill yarns, to get the tear strength of the fabric.

Stiffness. Stiffness is described in terms of "hand"—soft hand drapes easily; firm hand is stiffer and not quite as suitable for clothing but somewhat nicer for tents.

Porosity. Porosity is very dependent on the tightness of the weave. It is measured in terms of the air that gets through under set conditions and is expressed in cubic feet of air per minute. Porosity is one of the most important, and least understood, of the factors involved in choosing the right fabric for a certain job. It is directly related to the breathability and comfort of such items as rainwear, general clothing, tents, wind clothing, sleeping bags, and to some it is even a consideration in fabrics for packs. Each of these articles has certain specific and different requirements in terms of porosity, and the proper balance between ventilation and warmth, breathability and wind resistance, etc., is a complicated matter.

Basically, the main problem arises from the fact that the human body gives off moisture, in the form of perspiration, which must get out to keep us from drowning in our own sweat. The fabric can be completely impermeable to air (not porous), and if proper ventilation is present, the ventilating air currents will draw off the water vapor (when sweat evaporates it becomes water vapor) without too much problem.

If the fabric is too close to the source of the moisture (as with clothing) or if no excess ventilation is desired (tents, sleeping bags in the cold), then the problem becomes more complicated. In cases such as these, the fabrics themselves must supply the necessary ventilation, so they must be breathable to some extent. Of course, if water and air can get out then air and water can get in, and that is why the proper balance between breathability and impermeability is so important and sometimes so hard to achieve.

Water Repellency. It is important that some water, in the form of water vapor from perspiration, be allowed to get out. Of course, it is also important that rain does not get in, but the perfect balance between waterproof/breathability is hard to find. Coated fabrics are totally waterproof, and at the same time impermeable to the water vapor that must get out. Breathable fabrics are water repellent, and most of them will allow some rain to get in. In general it makes more sense to use the breathable fabrics; you can't get rained on all the time, but you can always rely on your body giving off about one to two quarts of water a day.

Fabric Comparison Chart. The chart on page 32 attempts to simplify the selection of the right fabric for the job. This chart will not tell you everything, but it will be a useful guide for comparison. Make sure you read through the proper chapters on these individual items to pick up more information on just why these

fabrics are recommended for these items.

If you want to compare the tear strengths, porosity, and permeability of any fabrics not listed, there are several rough tests that are suitable for the home craftsman. Tear strength is measured with a pull scale, the "Fisherman's Witness." Hook the scale up to the fabric and see how much force is required to continue a cut. Porosity may be compared by holding the fabrics tightly against your mouth and exhaling. Accuracy is not fantastic, but rough comparisons may be made. Permeability to water can be compared by stretching a sample tightly over a bowl and slowly pouring a set amount of water onto it from a set height. The more water in the bowl, the less water repellent the fabric. Again, not too accurate, but suitable for rough comparisons.

Insulation

To most people insulation is a mystery and the average person gives it little thought until he gets pneumonia from sleeping out in a cheap sleeping bag, or washes his expensive down jacket in a machine and has to go out and buy a new one. Then he notices, but it is usually much too late.

The greater the extremes of the environment, the more aware of insulation you should be. If you are a winter camper or a mountaineer, you should know everything there is to know about insulation; for you it literally may be a matter of life and death. If you restrict your camping to pleasant weather and low altitudes, then you are not too concerned about insulation; the environment will generally keep you comfortable enough.

The technicalities of insulation may seem complicated for the average camper

Commonly Used Name For Fabric	Fibers	Thread Count	Weight	Tear Strength	Abrasion Resistance	Water Repellency	Porosity	Treatments	Applications
Ripstop —the most commonly used cloth where lightness is main concern	nylon	95/95 in 1.9 oz.	¾ oz. –2.4 oz.; usually 1.9 oz.	9/9	good	poor	2 c.f.m. —fairly comfortable	Zepel Kendown	tent walls, down clothing, sleeping bags
Supernyl taffeta —smooth, tight weave used where ripstop is, but considered better by some for down items	nylon	160/90 in 2 oz.	1.1 oz. –2.3 oz.; usually 2 oz.	11/8	good	fair	less than ripstop	Zepel Kendown	sleeping bags, clothing, tent walls
Coated ripstop —most common light, waterproof fabric, for use where strength and light weight are important	nylon	95/95 in 1.9 oz.	1.4 oz. –1.9 oz.; usually 1.9 oz.	9/9	good	100%	none	polymer coating —one side	tent fly, ultralight rain gear, ultralight tent floor
Coated taffeta —strong, abrasion resistant, and still pretty light	nylon	106/88 in 3 oz.	2 oz. –4 oz.; usually 3 oz.	15/16	very good	100%	none	polymer coating —one side or both	tent floor, sturdy rain gear, ultra-light pack
Storm cloth, 60/40 —cotton/nylon or cotton/polyester, either intimate blend or woven; excellent breathability, good strength	blend	176/64	2.5 oz. –5 oz.; usually 2.5 oz.	13.5/6.5	very good	very good	very comfortable	water repellent	best rain wear, some tent walls, best wind clothing
Ventile cotton —100% cotton, very tight weave, good cloth for outerwear	cotton	very tight	varies; usually 2.5 oz.	not as strong as nylon	good	excellent	very comfortable	water repellent	clothing, outerwear, frostliners
Nylon pack cloth —heavy filament, or two ply; may be had coated or uncoated	nylon	62/44 in 6 oz.	5 oz. –8 oz.	50/50	excellent	poor or 100%	—	Zepel, or urethane coating	packs, anything needing good strength
Cordura —the ultimate in toughness; I use the 10 ounce for all my packs	nylon bulked filaments	56/56 in 10 oz.	8 oz. –10 oz.	70/70	fantastic	poor or 100%	—	Urethane, or water repellent	strongest packs, soles for booties, pack floors

and backpacker; however, much useful information can be obtained from catalogs and pamphlets provided by the major manufacturers, such as North Face, Recreational Equipment, Inc., Eastern Mountain Sports, and Frostline. One of the best is a clear and concise fifteen-page pamphlet entitled "How To Keep Warm" by Gerry Cunningham, a backpacker and expert on man and the cold. It is available from Gerry, or Gerry dealers, free of charge. You can also pick up good information from various books on the outdoors.

How Insulation Works

Contrary to popular misconception, insulations do not create heat. All an insulation will do is slow down the rate of heat transfer. Insulations work both ways; not only do they slow down heat loss (keep you warm in the cold) they also slow down heat absorption (keep your ice box cold). Here, we are mainly interested in the ways the human body loses heat to the environment. These sources of heat loss are convection, evaporation, conduction, and radiation.

Convection is heat loss directly to the air. It occurs when your skin comes in contact with the air that is all around us. It is important to remember that heat loss through convection is very small in immobile air, and very large in air that moves (windchill) and this is a most significant factor in outdoors clothing, sleeping bags, and tents.

Evaporation is the change from a liquid to a gas. This is what happens to the water that leaves your body as liquid sweat or the water vapor you exhale.

We all know that when we work harder we sweat more. This is one of the body's ways of maintaining a constant temperature—homeostasis—and this

sweat carries away a significant amount of heat with it when it goes. The more skin-level evaporation taking place, the more dangerous the conditions. (Wet skin freezes at a temperature about 8°C. higher than dry skin.) Controlling the amount we sweat, by controlling activity and ventilation, is the best way we have to control our body's comfort.

Conduction occurs from direct contact. The percentage of the heat lost through conduction is not as great as the percentages of the heat lost through other sources, but conduction is still quite important in practical terms. Sit on a park bench in the winter, and you will quickly agree. It will be very noticeable in those parts of your anatomy that come in direct contact with that park bench.

For campers, the most important loss of heat through conduction occurs when your weight compresses the insulation in your sleeping bag to a negligible amount. Thickness is warmth, and cold creeps upwards from the ground into the no-longer-thick sleeping bag, and from there into you. To eliminate those cold spots under your back, shoulders, and hips, where the insulation gets compressed the most, and to get a comfortable sleep, use a thick pad under your bag. Ensolite pads are more efficient as an insulator, but polyurethane foam is softer and more comfortable.

Radiation is the transfer of heat without any medium—the sun heats us through a vacuum by radiant heat. Radiation plays a somewhat negligible part in heat loss from the body under normal outdoors conditions, but it should not be ignored by those dedicated to getting the most warmth out of their equipment. To the camper, the most significant factors are the facts that clear nights are colder, and that the larger the area of the radiating surface, the more heat radiated. In theory at least, this means that gloves can never be as warm as mitts, that arms and legs need more insulation than torsos, and that tall skinny people will be colder than small people.

Thickness/Warmth. The best generalization that can be made about insulations, in practical terms, is that thickness is warmth. Of course, we must be very specific about what kind of thickness we use to keep us warm. How warm is "comfortable" is a tricky personal question. For example, I sleep with the window wide open in any weather, be it 30° below or what. I know for a fact that I am a warm sleeper. When you also consider that activity, level of fitness, and food intake have a great effect on warmth, making generalizations about comfort/warmth levels gets pretty "iffy"; however, here are some general guidelines that are fairly useful as a starting point.

Take notice of the wind chill chart; it gives you an indication of how important convection and porosity can be to tents, clothing, sleeping bags, and survival. These charts were originally compiled to give an indication of how much exposure unprotected skin could take before frostbite set in. This is one thing you are better off learning from a chart, rather than from experience. With an outer wind shell that is effective—tight breathable nylon is one of the best—heat loss from convection is not quite as high as these scales would indicate, but don't be foolish and try and test them yourself.

Thickness/Weight. To a backpacker, and to every sane camper, weight is a major concern. So, when considering what kind of thickness should be used to provide warmth, look for the lightest available.

The lightest, and all around best insula-

EFFECTIVE TEMPERATURE AND INSULATION THICKNESS-COMFORT

U.S. Army research has established data to determine the thickness of insulation needed for comfort at various temperatures and levels of activity. Actual Temperatures must be converted to Effective Temperatures by using the Wind Chill Chart. To use this Wind Chill Chart, find the estimated or actual wind speed in the left-hand column and the actual temperature in degrees F. in the top row. Effective temperature is found where these two intersect. For example, with a wind speed of 10 MPH and a temperature of −10° F., the Effective Temperature is −33° F.

Wind Chill Chart—Effective Temperature

Actual Temperature °F.

Wind Speed MPH	40	30	20	10	0	−10	−20	−30
	Effective Temperature °F.							
10	28	16	4	−9	−21	−33	−46	−58
20	18	4	−10	−25	−39	−53	−67	−82
30	13	−2	−18	−33	−48	−63	−79	−94
40	10	−6	−21	−37	−53	−69	−85	−100

Greater wind speeds have little added effect.

Use Chart at right for Thickness-Comfort.

U.S. Army—Thickness-Comfort Data

Thickness of Insulation Required for Comfort (in inches)

Effective Temperature °F.	Sleeping	Light Work	Heavy Work
40°F.	1.5''	.8''	.20''
20	2.0	1.0	.27
0	2.5	1.3	.35
−20	3.0	1.6	.40
−40	3.5	1.9	.48

These figures are approximate but are a good base for an average healthy person.

---

tion is air that has been immobilized. "Dead" air is used to keep you warm, no matter what system is used to keep that air dead—down or cement blocks. Studies show that there is a fairly large drag on air in contact with any surface. This effect extends out about ⅛ inch, so if the air can be broken up into pockets of less than ¼ inch, the drag effect will provide dead air, the perfect insulator.

Good quality down provides the ultimate in lightweight insulation. It also has other features that make it an ideal insulating material for campers: compressibility, durability (the number of times it can be compressed and returned to its expanded state), and breathability (provides the proper balance between dead air and porosity, insulation and ventilation).

In outdoors equipment, the thickness of an insulated article is usually referred to as loft. The fill power of an insulating material is examined in terms of how much of a material is required to achieve a certain loft of dead air. Fill power is expressed in terms of cubic inches fill/ounce, and can be as great as 700 cubic inches per ounce in top-quality goose down. Unfortunately, there are no universal standards for measuring the fill power of an insulation, and this is what causes quite a bit of the controversy. Temperature, atmospheric pressure, humidity, and shell construction all have an effect, and while there are certain standard tests, Manufacturer A may use one, while Manufacturer B uses another, which gives a different reading in cubic inches/ounces. Obviously, standardization in this important area is much needed.

As a generalization, the insulation with the highest fill power is usually the best, but realize that there are other factors involved.

Compressibility/Expansion. A good insulation must provide both compressibility and expansion with a maximum amount of resilience, or durability. Down is a superior insulating material for camping because it may be compressed to a fraction of its original volume, which is important when you are trying to stuff your 5-pound down sleeping bag into a manageable bundle.

Just as important as compressibility is expansion, which is what the insulation should do after the pressure is released. When raw down is plucked, before it is processed it gets compressed for shipping. This compressibility is not available in any other material known; at least not in one that can then be expected to expand to somewhere near its original volume.

Down also has tremendous durability, and will keep on expanding and contracting for a long time. Good quality down loses very little of its fill power through the years. Open-cell foams, such as polyurethane, will eventually squash down to a certain extent, and with the closed-cell foams, such as Ensolite, this happens even sooner.

Breathability. Sweat must get out, so the insulation must be porous. The fact that the human body gives off water is a major concern for all camping-equipment designers. And this is most true when you are working with sleeping bags and insulated clothing. The line between adequate insulation and too much is sharp; there is only a limited area where we are comfortable. When we are overinsulated we lose heat through excess sweat, which is to be avoided like the plague. For this reason flexibility of insulation is of prime importance. Flexibility is best achieved by removing or adding insulation (the layer system), or through ventilation (your zippers, storm flaps, etc.).

The conventional insulating materials are all porous, which aids considerably in the ventilation, but not all are absorbent—the fibers themselves may not absorb water. Down is porous and absorbent, and this absorbency is its greatest defect as an insulation. When down gets really wet, then it mats and loses almost all of its loft, which means most of its warmth. This is serious; people have died from exposure because of this characteristic of down.

The biggest advantage the quality synthetic fiber fillings have over down is that they are porous, but the fibers themselves are nonabsorbent. This is very important in cold and wet conditions, fall canoeing, for instance. It means that you can get your insulation soaking wet, and if you merely stop and wring it out, much of the insulating power is still there. This is a very strong selling point for nonabsorbent PolarGuard and Dacron Fiberfill II (and when properly used, absorbent polyurethane foam) as insulating materials in sleeping bags and clothing. Ensolite is a closed-cell foam and it is not porous or absorbent, so it is used mainly as an external pad where it doesn't cause breathability problems.

Usefulness. While down is one of the best theoretical and practical insulations around, it is also very messy to work with. The fibers, and even polyfoam, have the advantage when ease of construction is important.

Different techniques are used for down and the fiber battings, but both are intended to provide maximum loft and truly dead air spaces. Since down consists of a multitude of tiny down pods, it can shift, leaving you with cold spots. To keep the down in place we must resort to heavy baffles to prevent down shift. With Fiberfill II, we need only a backing for efficient use, but with the newest fiber Polar-Guard, which is a continuous filament batting with high stability, we can eliminate the baffles altogether. This cuts into the margin of superiority that down has always had over the synthetics. Also, both fibers and foam provide even insulation, which eliminates those cold spots.

In actuality, however, the efficiency of the designs that utilize down is greater than the efficiency of the designs that use fibers and foam. Down has been around a lot longer than the newer synthetics, so of course more effort has been expended in designing articles with it as the insulation. I predict that the shortage of quality down will soon drive a lot of manufacturers to the synthetics, and with more emphasis on these newer materials, more efficient designs utilizing them should become available. In any case, as a do-it-yourselfer, there is no reason to stick to the established designs with these newer materials; you have just as much chance of stumbling over the "perfect" design as do the manufacturers, although they do have more time and money on their side.

A point to remember is that down has a somewhat better drape to it than do the synthetics. This means that down will conform to your body shape a lot better, which is important in eliminating cold air currents inside the bag. This can be a problem with foam, though the problem is partially resolved with a series of drawstrings—something like bootlaces—that you tighten after you get in.

Down

What is down? If this question could be answered satisfactorily, most of the confusion about down-insulated articles would disappear. My dictionary tells me that down is "the fine soft plumage of birds under the feathers, especially that on the breast of water birds." The legal definition is given as "the undercoating of waterfowl consisting of light fluffy filaments growing from one quill point but without any quill shaft." You would think that this would be specific enough, but, no, there is more to come.

In the United States, by law, the term down has been limited to those mixtures that have the following composition: down, 80 percent minimum; waterfowl feathers, 18 percent maximum; residue, 2 percent maximum. By law, the mixture can be labeled goose down if it meets these standards: down—80 percent, of which 90 percent must be goose down; the remaining 20 percent, feathers or feather fiber. Until 1971, by law, down could have up to 40 percent feathers and miscellaneous. You are better off not knowing what "miscellaneous" could consist of.

The question of goose down versus duck down is one of the most confused and controversial topics in the whole realm of outdoors equipment. The proponents of goose down question the longevity of duck down and note the fill-power superiority of top-quality goose down over top-quality duck down when both are similarly processed. Those who prefer duck down claim this down lifts better and costs less than goose down.

North Face, a reliable manufacturer, in 1976 used goose down in every down

product, primarily because of "the demonstrated superiority in fill power" but also because "duck down that has received special high-loft harvesting and processing tends to lose a greater percentage of loft over time."

On the other side of the argument, quite a few manufacturers are using large quantities of duck down, and many of them are very happy with the loft/cost relationship that duck down has, and most of them are passing this savings on to the customer. There are many who admit that duck down is not as good as goose down, and point to the very convincing loft/cost argument as justification for their use of duck down. Personally, I have used a good quality duck down sleeping bag for years and have been more than satisfied with the service it has given. The reason for using duck down is normally a price consideration.

Down Quality Varies. Because down is a natural product, there is a lot of variation in the quality. Here are some of the factors that influence down quality.

Maturity. The older the bird, the larger the bird, up to a point. Mature birds have larger, and therefore better, down pods.

Climate. The colder the climate the bird was raised in, the better the down. This is why the down from the Arctic eider duck is credited with magical, mystical powers. There is some doubt as to the quality of the duck down imported from warm-climate Asian areas, such as Taiwan.

Diet. Somewhere or other I heard a rumor that the Taiwanese feed their ducks on fish meal, which causes the down to give off a fishy odor when wet. I have doubts about this rumor, though I have owned one cheap bag, labeled feathers and down, which did have this disgusting odor. This was more likely caused by the processor not properly cleaning the down to remove some of the excess oils, which can cause such smells.

Processing. There are methods of processing down—known as high-loft processing—that do increase the fill power of the down quite a bit. The question is, "How long will this high loft last?" To date there has been some controversy.

Grading. We have already gone into this in detail, but I'll add two additional points to confuse you even further. There is garment grade down—8 to 12 percent feathers—and there is bag grade down—12 to 20 percent feathers. There are several people who use only garment down (more expensive but slightly better fill—Holubar is one), and then there are those who maintain that some feather content is necessary to maintain the fill resiliency and the durability.

For the most part the suppliers and manufacturers all use around 15 percent feathers and pick out their own names for their blends. There is Northern, Prime Northern, Prime, 100 Percent Pure Down, White, Gray, etc., and all of this means only that this is what the manufacturer or supplier chooses to call it.

Blends. Goose down may have a certain percentage of feathers and duck down in it, and it is still goose down by law—and label. The unscrupulous take liberties with the laws and stretch that percentage an awful long way, while still labeling their articles as pure goose down. There is nothing you can do about this even if you had a microscope and a lot of time.

Don't be afraid of the manufacturers who are honest enough to label their products as blends. Like I said, without a fully equipped lab the differences between quality downs will not be readily noticeable. The manufacturers who are honest enough to admit to using blends are probably honest enough to use quality downs for their blends.

In summary, the principal advantages of down are that down offers the most fill power per ounce of any known substance. Down is the most compressible material known that will still regain its loft when pressure is released (hand pressure will compress 1 ounce of down to as little as 15 cubic inches). And it has a very long life with proper care.

Down is also very efficient to use because it breathes from "bellows" action, drapes itself closely around the body, eliminating convection currents, and there are a number of good designs to choose from.

Down has several disadvantages that the do-it-yourselfer should be aware of: Down compresses too easily for sleeping bag bottoms. It loses a great deal of loft when wet; this can kill you. Some people are allergic to down, or to the dust that clings to down. The quality control of down is a joke. There are no real standards, so get your down from a reputable source. Down is remarkably tough, but it can be ruined by improper care, and proper care can be a pain. Down is also difficult to work with. Down is expensive (good goose down was selling for $26 a pound in 1975), and it's going to get worse, not better.

Fiber/Down. One of the newest innovations in the insulation field is the use of two different kinds of fill for the bottom and tops of sleeping bags. Since down compresses too easily to make an efficient bottom for a sleeping bag, a lot of people are improving performance by using the less compressible, and cheaper, fibers or foams. For example, Trail Tech uses foam on the bottom and PolarGuard on the top. Jan Sport has PolarGuard on the bottom and down on the top. The Jan Sport bag is slightly more compressible, but both are within reason for the backpacker. I think the down top/PolarGuard bottom arrangement makes the most sense of all the designs I have seen, and I am working on such a rig right now for my personal use—in a double separating into two single bags with different fills.

Polyester Fibers

The fibers that are presently accepted as suitable for modern lightweight insulated equipment are all synthetics, and there should be little confusion about their quality—they certainly get enough publicity as "miracles of man's ingenuity." So far, though, nature is a better designer of insulation than man; good down remains the standard by which all others are judged. However, there have been some very competitive new fibers developed recently. For our purposes only the two best quality polyester fibers are suitable—Dacron Fiberfill II and PolarGuard. Both of them are very easy to work with, compared to down, and they have consistent quality, price, and availability on their side. When you add in their superlative insulating power when wet, and their fair weight/loft ratio, plus their nonallergenic

properties, you can see why they are becoming more popular all the time.

I have not had as much experience with the fibers as I would like (I use mostly unpackaged down for the insulated items I make), but I intend to use the fibers more. Perhaps MAKIT (PolarGuard kits) and EMSKIT (Dacron Fiberfill kits) can provide you with more information. I think that the fibers are perhaps the ideal material for the do-it-yourselfer, unless like me you are hung up on weight. For canoeists, kayakers, and where weight is not the main concern, go with the fibers. For discriminating backpackers, stick with the down. For the rich or the do-it-yourselfer, who can also afford to be extravagant, why not get gear with both?

Dacron Fiberfill II. Not to be confused with its older relative, the original Dacron, this second-generation polyester has a lot going for it. In fact, Jim Whittaker, general manager of Recreational Equipment, Inc., and the first American on top of Everest, has tested all kinds of equipment under all kinds of conditions, and as a result carries two sets of gear whenever possible— one with down for dry-cold and one with Dacron Fiberfill II for wet-cold. He advises that if you can carry only one, carry the Dacron.

The people at Eastern Mountain Sports use it in their insulated EMSKITS, and they claim to have considered the alternatives pretty closely before choosing the Dacron II. The reasons they give are ease of construction for the home builder, over down, and the fact that they think the Fiberfill II stands up somewhat better after repeated washings than does PolarGuard or down—plus, of course, the "wetability" of the polyester.

For those of you who will be getting your gear wet and dirty, perhaps this is the best of the lot. While I can't speak authoritatively on the durability of the fibers (they are new to me), I think it very relevant to point out that even the best down will lose some of its loft after repeated washings, or a few improper washings, while both PolarGuard and Dacron II claim to retain loft, or even improve with proper care.

PolarGuard. PolarGuard is a continuous filament polyester insulation batting from Celanese. It differs from Fiberfill II in that the individual fibers are resin and heat cured to provide better stability and somewhat better loft retention than Fiberfill. PolarGuard has at least two distinct advantages over Fiberfill: it doesn't need fabric or cheesecloth to hold it together, and it has a slightly higher filling power. PolarGuard is also flame retardant.

The principal advantages of fibers are the following:

Fibers absorb very little water—less than 1 percent in the Dacron Fiberfill II—so are the only way to go in cold or wet conditions. They may be wrung out and dried in the field, and take less time drying than down. This is the fiber's most significant advantage over down, and it is an important one.

Fibers are cheap—MAKIT, PolarGuard batting in 8 ounces, cost only $4 a pound in 1975.

Fibers are consistent—you know what you are getting.

Fibers are easy to use, and they provide even insulation. Fibers are also durable when they have been properly used and cared for. And caring for them is nowhere near as big a job as with down.

The fibers are nonallergenic and nonodorous. This may seem unimportant to most of us, but it will be the most important thing in the world to a dedicated backpacker with an allergy to down. It can become pretty important also when you are lying in a cheap down bag that gets wet and starts smelling like a fleet of fishermen downwind.

The fibers have some disadvantages, the principal ones being the following:

Neither of the fibers is as effective at filling a bag or garment. The "bounce per ounce" is not up to down; and we are still waiting for designs that will give us theoretical efficiency in the field. EMS handles down and both fiber types, and they estimate (1976) about 50 percent actual efficiency (32 percent heavier bag when finished).

Neither of the fibers compresses as much as down. This is not really a disadvantage on sleeping bag bottoms; in fact, I think the fibers are ideal here. And on bag tops and jackets, the finished gear is still within a backpacker's range of interest (one with a bigger pack).

Although neither of the fibers seems to have a real durability problem, it is possible to destroy them through improper care. Unfortunately, not enough emphasis is placed on this by the people who push them. Fibers are washable—much more so than down—but read the instructions. Miracle fibers they may be, but don't ask them to prove it by abusing them. Do not use an agitator-type machine to wash any sleeping bag; even the ones that use fiber can be torn to shreds.

Which fiber to choose? I like PolarGuard, primarily because of the no-backing, but the choice is pretty close. Concentrate instead on whether you want fibers or down, or if you like the foam idea best of all.

Foams

Foams come in two different types: open (polyfoam) and closed (Ensolite). The open foams are porous, absorbent, bulky, and should be used with a cover. The closed foams are lighter, more efficient, and don't need a cover. Use them under your bag for warmth and comfort, but warmth is usually the most important consideration.

I have used a polyurethane (open-cell) foam mattress for years, and the only complaint I have is that it has settled in the middle a noticeable amount. I have also used several closed-cell foam pads while camping and the reason I ended up using several was that they, too, eventually "die" on you. However, the price is not out of line, and they are practically indispensible items as pads under sleeping bags. Both are good—Ensolite for minimum bulk and efficiency, with no porosity or absorbency; polyfoam for luxurious comfort, more bulk, and absorbency.

Pads. If you get the poly it should be used with a cover or ground sheet, but you can lay out Ensolite right on the ground or snow with comfort. Comfort is relative, but most winter campers use the ⅜-inch Ensolite or the 2-inch poly. These foams are available in different densities and consistencies. The Ensolite comes in M and MH (firmer), and there are several competitive brands that claim superior properties in cold/flexibility/lightness. The polyfoam is available in a wide range of firmness, so try it out for yourself. Some bags might get away without a pad, but with most types your weight will compress the insulation to a negligible amount, so use a pad.

Polyfoam is more than just a sleeping bag pad; it is a basic material for the construction of some really interesting winter gear. I have used Ensolite quite a bit in places like pack straps, soles, and even ugly mukluks, but poly breathes and wicks moisture. This makes it better for sleeping bags (commercially available) and clothing (limited, but interesting possibilities). If you want to create and explore, this field is relatively new and looks fairly promising.

A New System. I had always thought of polyfoam as suitable for nothing more than sleeping bag pads, but the first time I read R. C. Rethmel's *Backpacking*, and discovered the appendix on subzero camping, I was amazed. There were comprehensive directions for a completely new—to me—system of cold-weather camping that utilized polyfoam as the basic ingredient. If you are thinking of starting out in winter camping, before you invest the better part of your fortune on commercial down gear, take a look at Rethmel's book.

Several companies (Ocate, Trail Tech, etc.) are now marketing commercial equivalents so the idea is no longer as radical as it once was. If you would like further information on this system, contact Ocate and Trail Tech. You might like to experiment with this idea a bit; it can be used for bags, mitts, ridiculous looking jackets, great looking mukluks, etc. This is one area where not too much work has been done, so all you nonconformists and innovators might be able to come up with some good stuff here.

On page 42 is a helpful chart from *Light Weight Camping Equipment and How to Make It* by Gerry Cunningham and Margaret Hansson (New York: Scribners, 1976).

TABLE OF SUPPORT OF VARIOUS MATERIALS

Support provided by equal weights per area (.1 gm/cm²) under a loading of .5 kg/cm². This represents the approximate practical weight for a sleeping pad and the pressure exerted by body pressure points.

Material	cm of thickness under load
Spongex 534	.85
Polyurethane Foam	.75
Ensolite M	.70
Virgin wool overlayed with ¼" Ensolite	.67
Polyester foam	.63
Virgin wool batting	.60
Sponge rubber G-200-C	.55
Dacron batting	.50
Dacron pile fabric	.40
White goose down	.32

Compiled by GERRY for USAF Arctic Aeromedical Lab.

Here is what I have been able to dig up on fibers versus down regarding filling power:

Material	Maximum Fill Power
Goose down	550 cubic inches per ounce; some say higher, but this is common. (Snow Lion mentions 725 cubic inches per ounce in their Limited Edition bag.)
Duck down	450 cubic inches per ounce; some say higher, depending on quality.
PolarGuard	375 cubic inches per ounce in the lab; somebody will get rich if he can do as well in the field. (MAKIT claims 13 percent difference between down and PolarGuard.)
Fiberfill II	North Face claims 67 percent of down.

Don't get overexcited by advertised fill power. I would suggest that the home builder concentrate on practicing consistency at filling, rather than worrying about the theoretical filling power of the materials. With care and proper design, all of these fillers do an excellent job.

For those of you who don't believe in labels, the best way to tell good down fill from very cheap down fill is simple: pinch the shell and some down between your fingers and if you feel a lot of quills and lumps, it is cheap. I once turned up a 2-inch pin while doing this. I shudder to think what else might have been in that batch of down.

Webbing

Webbing is an extremely tough, strong, versatile material that is used extensively in modern camping equipment. There are many types of webbing, but for our purposes we are interested only in the flat type, with finished edges.

Webbing is strong:

$9/16'' \times 1/16''$ nylon webbing ...	550 lbs.
$3/4'' \times 1/16''$ nylon webbing ...	750 lbs.
$1'' \times 1/16''$ nylon webbing ...	1,000 lbs.
$2'' \times 1/16''$ nylon webbing ...	6,000 lbs.

As you can see from these figures, even the smallest size webbing will have ample strength for our purposes. And since webbing is generally woven from very coarse, tough threads, its abrasion resistance is also exceptional. This means that webbing will rarely have to be replaced because of rips or abrasion. However, webbing can sometimes be cut (unlikely but possible) and since webbing is a coarse, loose weave, it often frays badly enough to make replacement necessary.

In the narrower sizes (½ to 1 inch), webbing is used for pack harnesses, snow shoes, belts, accessory straps, tent peg loops, reinforcing for stress points, and so forth. In the larger sizes it is useful for load bearing straps. The 2-inch-wide nylon webbing, commonly referred to as seat-belt webbing, is ideal for day pack shoulder straps and nonpadded waist belts.

For joining 2-inch webbing to 1-inch webbing (as for shoulder straps) several arrangements can be used. For attaching webbing to packs, tents, etc., it is important that you consider the strength of the material and the loads the web may encounter. All of the load put on a piece of webbing will be transmitted to the webbing/fabric seams, and if the load is greater than the strength of the seams or the strength of the fabric, it will tear the threads or rip the cloth. Using heavy-duty thread and using the stitch patterns shown should provide adequate strength for the seams.

If the fabric is light (anything but heavy-duty pack cloth), it may be necessary to double or triple layers of cloth under the joint to allow the fabric to accept the strain without ripping. Round patches sewn on are neat, transmit the stress evenly to the surrounding single layer of fabric, and have no corners to peel

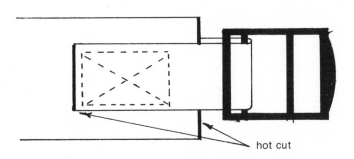

hot cut

Two-inch web, 1-inch web, and a buckle for shoulder straps.

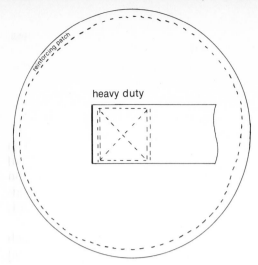

heavy duty

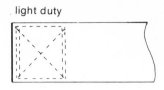

light duty

Attaching webbing to fabric.

up or wear off. (See Chapter 4 for some innovative ways to use webbing.)

Nylon Webbing

Nylon webbing should be used for quality outdoors equipment. It is superstrong, supertough, rot and mildew resistant, attractive, easily available, and cheap. For tent loops it is the only suitable material, as cotton, polypropylene, or folded fabric just does not handle the abuse of sharp pegs and sudden winds as well as does the nylon.

For making straps, webbing made of nylon is remarkably easy to work with. All cut ends must be finished (simply melt them in an open flame). For a neater end, you can do the actual cutting with an old table knife heated up. The knife melts (not cuts) its way through the web, welding the individual fibers together as it goes. This provides an attractive finished end that won't fray or ravel, at least not for a while. Cutting at a slight angle provides a slightly more finished look. Buckles may be attached to the end of such a strap. These make a very useful accessory strap, waist belt, etc.

Nylon webbing in the 2-inch size is readily available from automotive shops or wreckers (seat-belt webbing), and if you

look around you may even be able to find colors that will coordinate with the fabrics you are using, or you can use black, which goes with any color fabric. This webbing is available in several weaves, which may not match up from car to car, so if you are visiting the wrecker for some webbing, take what you need from one car. There is only one disadvantage to using nylon webbing: it frays and ravels like crazy, so all cut ends must be melted. Even so, the melted part can crack in use, and you may have to remelt occasionally. Since all other webbing will also fray badly, this is not too much of a handicap, but it is annoying.

Cotton Webbing

Cotton webbing at one time was the standard, but for modern outdoors equipment, nylon is much better. The cotton is not as strong, not as abrasion resistant (important on adjustable straps that rub against the buckles), and it can rot or mildew. In addition, cotton straps must have the ends finished differently than do the synthetics. Since cotton will not melt, all cut ends must be finished in some other way. This means capping them with metal, or folding them over for a finished seam; all in all, a lot more work, and those caps are always falling off with use.

Other Synthetics

Polypropylene webbing is sometimes used on cheap imported equipment. The poly is not as strong, frays more easily than nylon, and is usually woven more coarsely. It is recognizable by frizzy-looking threads along the edges or elsewhere, and if you burn it and some nylon webbing side by side, the very different smells will give it away. The poly is not as suitable as the nylon.

Folded Fabric

If you ever get stuck for webbing, or perhaps you want to save pennies, then you can make straps that can substitute for webbing out of folded fabric. This is marginally suitable, though a lot more work, but you see it quite a bit on some of the very cheap day packs.

On more expensive packs (even the best) fabric is often made into a tube, which is padded inside with a piece of Ensolite. This arrangement is almost universal for padded straps. This provides the ultimate in shoulder strap comfort, and it is usually plenty strong. Of course, such an arrangement involves a lot more work than chopping off a piece of seat-belt webbing and sewing it on, but for heavy loads it is well worth it. For light loads (10 to 20 pounds), the 2-inch webbing is usually comfortable enough.

Leather

On older packs and some European imports, you will find straps made of leather. These usually have buckles similar to the ones used for leather belts, involving holes in the belt/strap. I dislike leather straps for a number of reasons. The leather straps can stretch, dry out, crack, or tear out those holes, which weaken the strap in the first place; leather in that thickness is hard to sew without proper tools; the design does not allow for universal adjustment of the straps; the buckles can easily come loose if not under tension; and leather requires more care than webbing. I don't recommend it for straps at all.

Cord

The experienced camper will know all about braided nylon cord in the 550-pound-test size (parachute cord) for use around camp. This material is also quite useful in the workshop. I use it for all my drawstrings, tent lines, and wherever cord is required (mukluk laces, lashing, etc.). This size cord works well with most commercially available tent-line tighteners, and fits the cord clamps, too. Two things to remember with this material—knots tied in nylon cord have a tendency to work loose, and all cord ends should be melted in an open flame to prevent raveling. This is useful stuff; stock up on it.

Thread

Sewing thread is somewhat different than the threads used to weave the fabric. Because seams are almost always weaker than the surrounding fabric, thread used for sewing must be as strong as possible. Remember, in the fabric there are many threads, all reinforcing each other, but in a seam there are only a very few threads to take up any strain. And often, because of poor design, strain and stress are focused on the seams and therefore on these few threads. If you want your stitches to stay together, they have to be neat and tight, there has to be lots of them (double or triple stitching is recommended), and the threads have to be the strongest available.

This rules out cotton completely (besides it could rot out), and narrows the choice to nylon, Dacron, or cotton wrapped/Dacron core. Each of these has its own peculiar properties and characteristics that should be considered before you make a choice.

Nylon. Nylon is unquestionably the strongest fiber for sewing threads. Unfortunately, nylon is also an extremely elastic fiber. For commercial sewing machines that can handle the stretchy threads, nylon is the best choice. If you will be sewing by hand, it is also a good choice. Most quality packs are constructed with nylon threads, which are compatible with the nylon threads used for the fabric, so the two wear well together.

However, for the home builder using an ordinary sewing machine, the nylon threads sometimes can pose quite a problem. Some home machines will handle the nylon thread, but you may have to fiddle around with the adjustments to get it to work. Other home machines won't take nylon thread no matter how much you play around; they drop stitches, change stitch tension, and do some other exasperating things. The only way to find out is to try.

Dacron. Dacron has much less stretch than nylon, but it does give up some strength. Dacron is nearly as strong as the nylon, and for those who can't get nylon through their machines, Dacron is a good choice. Some excellent packs are made

with Dacron thread, but the users of nylon thread point out that the Dacron sometimes wears at a different rate than the surrounding nylon fabrics. If you can't use the nylon, the Dacron (polyester) threads should do a good job.

Cotton Wrapped/Dacron Core. This thread is especially popular for sewing tents, ponchos, and rain garments. The cotton wrapping is supposed to swell when wet to close off the needle holes, and the Dacron core supplies the strength. This thread feeds well through the sewing machine. Large sizes for packs, small sizes for ripstop—both seem to do a good job. The cotton wrapping supposedly cushions the harder core from cutting through the fabric. Even though the cotton swells up and keeps out some of the water, I waterproof all seams in any case. The cotton wrapped/Dacron threads also work well for down-insulated items; the fuzzy wrapping clogs the needle holes and helps prevent down loss.

The choice between these three threads is arbitrary; all of them will do the job. The size of the thread and the quality and amount of stitching should concern you more than the differences between these threads. Use whatever your sewing machine prefers, and as a rule of thumb, use the biggest size that will work.

HARDWARE

Much of the hardware used in lightweight outdoors equipment was designed specifically for this field. This means it is sometimes difficult to pick up locally. If you can't find what you need in your local mountain shop, chances are you will have to order it by mail from one of the kit people or from one of the bigger mail-order firms specializing in backpacking. For the hardware that is really hard to find (I am thinking now about fiberglass tent wands), you may have to write directly to the manufacturer for a list of distributors in your area, and then write them.

Zippers

While YKK is not the only company making zippers, it sometimes seems that way. YKK's #5 and #10 Delrin, and their assorted sizes of nylon-coil zippers, find their way into nearly every piece of outdoors equipment using zippers. The reason for this is simple—they work properly, and then keep on working for a long time. North Face prefers the German Optilon coil type (which they say is better than anything), and you occasionally see some equipment with large Lightning "funny looking coils," but in general YKK rules the market.

I use the #10 Delrin whenever I want strength, though it may be a case of over-kill for some items. Frostline tells me the #5 Delrin is plenty strong enough for sleeping bags, but I'll keep using the #10 for things like packs. For applications involving tight corners, the coil zippers seem to take curves somewhat better, and again, in the large sizes, they are reliable. The choice between nylon coil and Delrin is a tough one, but both should do the job. Get whatever is available.

Types of Zippers. There are many different kinds of zippers: metal zippers, nylon-coil zippers, Delrin zippers, etc. Then there are zippers that are closed one end, closed both ends, separating, single slider, double slider, single tab, double tab, open from the middle, and open from

the ends. When designing and constructing outdoors equipment, it is very important that you use the proper style of zipper for the job.

A zipper consists of teeth, tape, slider (or two sliders), and ends (open or closed, separating or nonseparating). The teeth are attached to the tape, and the slider merely pries them apart (opening) or pries them shut (closing). The direction in which the slider travels determines whether it closes or opens the teeth.

The slider has a pull tab, which you grasp to work the slider. If you ever lose this pull tab, you will regret it, because you now end up breaking fingernails. Some sliders have two pull tabs, one on the inside of the zipper, and one on the outside. These are used primarily for tent doors and sleeping bags, so you can get out after you close up the zipper.

A slider with double-pull tabs, and one with single tabs.

For a large pack opening, or perhaps for a tent door or window, it may be convenient to have double sliders, so that you can open just one small section of the pack (or tent window), without having to open up the rest. If the sliders open the zipper traveling from the middle to the ends, then the zipper is an open-from-the-middle, double-slider-type zipper. In this type of zipper the sliders face in opposite directions.

For some applications you would be using the areas near the ends of the zipper

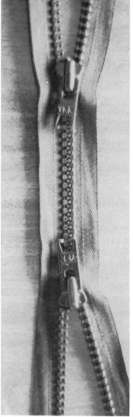

(such as the fly on men's trousers), so we have a closed-one-end type of zipper here. Some zippers will not need to open at either end; they will be used as closures for compartments for which we get in through the zipper opening. These zippers are usually called closed both ends, or sometimes luggage-style zippers.

Zippers that separate completely (such as on a jacket) are called separating zippers. Separating zippers are unique in one respect—one half of a separating zipper can just as easily be zipped to the correct half of another separating zipper.

In addition to how a zipper works, there are some other things to consider when choosing the right zipper. The material that makes up the tape may have an effect on the durability and strength of the zipper. Cotton zipper tapes can mildew and rot, and are weaker than the same weight of nylon tapes; both of these factors are of considerable importance to outdoors equipment. In general, get the nylon taped zippers if they are available.

Left:
An open-from-the-middle, double-slider-type zipper.

Right:
An open-from-the-ends, double-slider-type zipper.

A separating zipper.

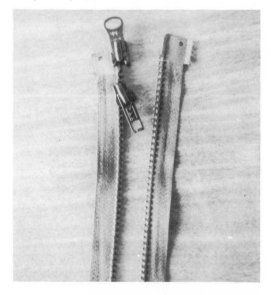

more than you would the middle. For these you would reverse both sliders, which would still meet in the middle, but now you would have an open-from-the-ends, double-slider-type zipper. This type is most commonly found on sleeping bags; it provides access from one end of the zipper (the top) and the bottom can be opened independently of the other slider to adjust ventilation.

Some zippers need only open from one end. The other end may always stay shut

The zipper teeth are the parts that work the hardest in a zipper, and the materials used to make the teeth and the type of teeth are very important. For a long time zippers were made with metal teeth. These had several important disadvantages: they were not reliable; they were weak; they were heavy; they conducted cold; if they snagged on fabric, they usually cut or tore the fabric, and once snagged they often were permanently ruined.

Quality zippers are no longer made from metal. Instead, either nylon coils or cast Delrin teeth are used. Both of these types have none of the disadvantages previously mentioned, but they do have one new one—both of these materials will melt if overheated. With nylon this occurs at about 480°F., and with Delrin at about 330°F. This is a disadvantage only if you intend to dry out your clothing over a heat source that you cannot control (camp fires). For a do-it-yourselfer, this feature is actually a bonus; zippers can be closed off by melting them together with a hot instrument instead of by installing the usual zipper stops. It's cheap, fast, simple, effective, and if done properly, as strong as the rest of the zipper.

The size of the zipper is also an important consideration. Obviously, a larger zipper is stronger and heavier than a lighter one. If strength is the main concern, use #10 Delrin or #7 nylon-coil zippers. If weight is the major concern, use #5 Delrin or #5 nylon coil. In these sizes both styles of zippers have proven their strength and durability in all types of outdoors equipment. Properly installed, and properly matched to the demands of the job, zippers are now quite reliable. If you use them properly, zipper failure is a thing of the past.

Installing a zipper properly will contribute greatly to the life of the zipper and the usability of the item. Here are some points to consider when planning and installing zippers:

1. Tight corners are hard on zipper teeth; keep your zippers straight, or curve them gradually for maximum life. If you must have tight corners, then use nylon-coil zippers; the smaller teeth seem to work better here.

2. Zippers should be installed with flaps wherever possible. The flaps help keep out dirt and water. The illustration shows details for a simple zipper flap.

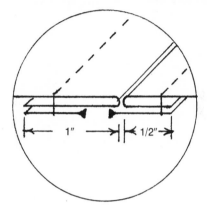

A simple zipper flap.

3. Nylon-coil zippers and Delrin zippers can be cut to size from a "chain," and can be closed at the ends simply by welding the teeth shut with some hot object (a heated table knife, for example).

4. When sewing the zipper in place, don't stitch too close to the teeth or else the stitching may bind the slider.

5. A zipper foot may be helpful.

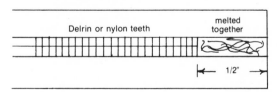

How to make a passable zipper stop with nylon and Delrin zippers.

Buckles

There are literally hundreds of different types and designs of buckles available. However, only a few designs have proven best for outdoors equipment. Such buckles must be secure, strong, light, simple, speedy to operate, and preferably inexpensive.

For quick release and nonslip applications, the undisputed best type of buckle is the ladder or tabler style. For things such as shoulder straps and accessory straps, it is ideal. It is strong, light, simple in design, simple to use, it does not slip, and it costs only pennies.

For semipermanent, nonslip, but still adjustable installations, a simple slider buckle is lighter, more compact, and cheaper still.

For a 2-inch waist belt, which must have quick release, ease of operation, and still be nonslip, the standard has been a grated buckle. However, there have been some recent improvements made in buckles, and better ones may be found. The grated

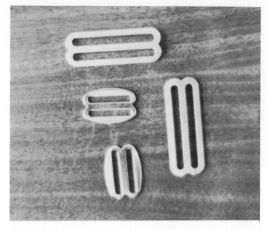

Sliders in 1-inch and 2-inch sizes.

A 2-inch grated buckle for waist belts.

A tabler buckle.

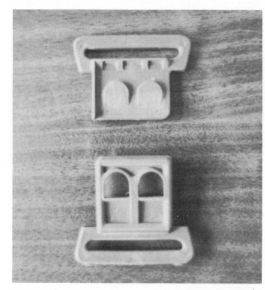

Canadian Army surplus cast plastic buckle for web belts.

buckle was awkward to use, and not totally secure with certain types of webbing (it works well only with very coarsely woven webbing).

The buckle I prefer and recommend is a Canadian Army surplus web belt buckle. This buckle, made of tough cast plastic, is light, totally secure, simple, and quick to use (it provides instant release). If you can find one in a surplus store, it should cost you only a few cents. Used with a web belt of 2-inch seat-belt webbing, it's the best design I have seen.

Of course, buckles are totally useless without the proper webbing to match. There are many important factors involved in matching webbing to a buckle, and you should be aware of them:

Width—always match the buckle to the correct width of webbing or it probably will not work properly.

Thickness—tabler buckles and sliders are designed to be used with a specific thickness of webbing. Webbing is often made available in various thicknesses. Make sure the buckles and the web are compatible.

Material—webbing is made from several different materials. For tabler buckles, which rely on friction to lock them in place, abrasion may be a problem if cheap webbing is used. Use only good quality nylon webbing.

Stiffness—for some applications (lower shoulder straps) limp webbing is desirable. A tabler buckle that works well with limp webbing may not slide or lock properly with firmer webbing.

Weave—webbing that is tightly woven is smoother and therefore more slippery; this matters with some types of buckles.

Check out the webbing and the buckles to make sure they are compatible, and right for the job at hand.

Aluminum

Aluminum is the standard material for use where strength, rigidity, and lightness are desired, and finds its way into many pieces of outdoors equipment. Aluminum, its exact composition, its strength, its hardness, and so forth, is a complicated and technical subject. For detailed advice on the technical aspects ask the people selling it to you; they generally are knowledgeable. Describe your needs, and the use which the materials will be put to, and they should be able to pick out the proper materials for you.

In general, the do-it-yourselfer will be interested mainly in aluminum tubing for tent poles and pack frames. I use 6061-T6 seamless aluminum tubing for these applications. It seems to have the desired compromise needed between hardness and workability, and it is readily available. Of course, there are other formulas that may be better for specialized applications, so quiz the dealer before buying.

O.D. ⅝-inch tubing is the perfect size for tent poles and light-duty pack frames. For heavy-duty pack frames get 1-inch or ¾-inch O.D. tubing. These are definitely quite a bit stronger. For pack stays I like to use ⅛ × 1¼-inch flat aluminum bar stock. This can be softer than the other materials as it will be bent to conform to the back, and may get bent and rebent fairly often.

Small (¼- to ⅜-inch) diameter tubing in the harder, springier alloys is being used successfully by several manufacturers in place of fiberglass for their stressed-skin tent designs; 7001 is the formula often given, but see if it is available before planning to use it. Fiberglass tent wands are also hard to find, but they may be more obtainable than the hard, springy aluminum tubing necessary to replace them.

Snaps and Grommets

Snaps are extremely useful little items for closures. If a weatherproof seal is desired, zippers and snaps (set into a flap over the zipper) do a very good job. If the seal does not have to be completely weatherproof, use the snaps by themselves. When installed with a zipper, the snaps provide a back-up system in case the zipper should fail. In addition, they will help take up any sudden shocks and strains that might otherwise travel directly to a zipper and ruin it. When buying snaps get the heavy-duty "dot" type; the lighter "glove" types just aren't strong enough.

Grommets are necessary for many items you will make (pack bags attach to frames with them, ponchos and ground sheets should have them around the edges, etc.). Commonly, grommets are made of brass, but the best ones are made of stronger stainless steel. Unfortunately, the stainless steel grommets are hard to find. Get the grommets in size #0 (¼-inch hole) up to size #4 (½-inch hole). The smaller or larger sizes are not really useful.

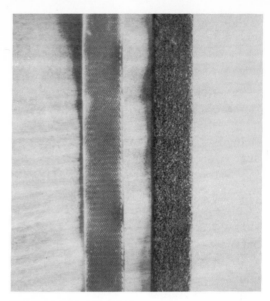

Velcro—hooks and loops.

Velcro

Velcro is an exceptionally useful material for lightweight outdoors equipment, and has almost replaced the traditional metal snaps for closures on many items. The reasons for this are many: Velcro is light—much, much lighter than snaps; Velcro is easier to work than snaps—since the Velcro doesn't have to line up exactly, the way snaps do, opening and closing is easier and faster; Velcro will not conduct cold the way metal snaps do, an important consideration for sleeping bags and insulated clothing; Velcro is strong—it may take only a few pounds of force to separate Velcro in one direction, but in the other directions it will take much, much more; Velcro is easier to install without special tools than snaps.

Velcro tape comes in various widths, and in various strengths. For our purposes the 1-inch and the 2-inch sizes, in the heavy-duty strength, are desirable. You will use quite a bit of the 1-inch size,

Grommets.

which may be picked up locally at nearly any fabric shop, but the 2-inch width will be harder to find. You may have to order it from one of the companies selling back-packing equipment and materials. Velcro tape comes in two different sections, both of which are needed to make a joint. There is the loop side and the burr side; make sure you get some of both.

Miscellaneous Materials

There are quite a few odds and ends of hardware that go into a piece of camping gear. Most of these miscellaneous items could be left out, but often they provide extra convenience, so it may be worth-while to use them, or to jury rig something similar. For example, cord clamps are not strictly a necessity item, but for adjusting draw cords on such things as sleeping bags and parkas, they are much quicker and easier to use than knots.

D rings have many uses—they provide a convenient place to tie or snap things to; two of them can be made into a passable buckle for webbing straps; they can be used in series with a lace as a bootie or pack-adjustment system, etc. If you are going to use D rings for something, get the one-piece type, or the welded type; the style that is merely bent up from wire is not strong enough.

Snap hooks are sometimes useful for at-taching straps that need to be quick re-leased, but which do not need to be quick adjustable. I prefer the tabler buckles for such applications, but some may prefer to use the snap hooks here. Get the heavy-duty spring-loaded types available from harness shops and climbing stores; a snap hook that will open up on you is worse than no snap hook at all.

Pack bags are most commonly attached

Two styles of D rings.

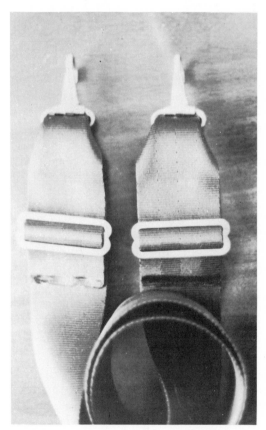

Two snap hooks, two sliders, and some 2-inch web-bing make up into a nice removable shoulder strap.

Pack frame pins; they hold the bag in place.

to frames with a system that uses grommets and light, sturdy aluminum pins. Get them in ¼-inch or ⁵/₁₆-inch diameter, in lengths that will be suitable to the tubing and fittings they will have to pass through. And don't try to save money here by substituting something else. These pins are carefully made from lightweight, hardened aluminum; nothing else will be as light and still wear well. Besides, they cost only pennies and are available almost everywhere.

TOOLS

The do-it-yourselfer does not want to get involved in mass production, as do the commercial manufacturers, so the tools he'll use will be very different from those used by the professionals. The home craftsman will be making only a few items, so the tools involved will be kept to a minimum, they will be cheap, and they will be simple to use and simple in design. This has its disadvantages (it may limit the type of projects the home craftsman should reasonably attempt), but in general almost all backpacking equipment can be made at home, with only a few basic tools.

Basic Tools

The tools needed for measuring and marking include a 16-foot tape measure, an 8-foot straightedge, a carpenter's square (16×24 inches), and a few drafting tools such as a protractor, compass, and triangles. These tools should allow you to lay out your projects full size, with accuracy and ease. Tailor's chalk, a very soft pencil, and grease pencils will come in handy for transferring the pattern markings onto the fabric.

If you sew already, you should have most of what you will need for sewing outdoors equipment. A good pair of scissors is a necessity. They must be sharp or else they will not cut the heavy fabrics cleanly, and you will find that dull scissors even make a mess of cutting lightweight ripstop nylon.

You will need plenty of pins for holding the fabric in place while you are sewing it. I recommend the ones with large plastic-coated heads; they are hard to forget and they are the only ones that you can ram through two or three layers of heavy pack cloth without wearing out your thumb.

Small projects, such as packs, booties, mittens, can be sewn by hand. If you don't have a machine you can still make them, but it will take an inordinate amount of time. Seriously consider borrowing or renting a machine; it will be worth it. Several hand needles in various sizes (and perhaps a curved one) may come in handy for finishing off some items and areas where a machine can't go.

There is no need to go out and buy a more expensive heavy-duty or industrial machine, because your ordinary home sewing machine should be able to handle anything that will come up with these projects. If you are thinking of buying a

A Speedy Stitcher for those tough jobs.

invest in a cheap, simple set of tools like those shown. These do a good job, but they are much slower than the tools used by most small shops.

For working with aluminum tubing you will need a hacksaw, an electric drill, and some files (flat and round), for example. Most do-it-yourselfers will already have most of them.

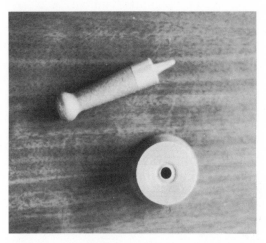

Hand tools for installing grommets. A similar tool is available for snaps.

sewing machine just for these projects, then look for one that has zigzag, reverse, and serging. The zigzag is almost a necessity, the reverse a real convenience and time saver, and the serging will save you hours of flame sealing with all your cut edges in nylon.

For sewing on webbing, and especially for thick leather, some machines may have a rough time. If your machine balks at the heavy stuff, you can still use it by turning the wheel over by hand. If you absolutely can't get through the heavy jobs with your machine, buy a hand awl or Speedy Stitcher from any local leather shop. These little items are designed to work with the thickest leather, and they make handy tools for a field-repair kit.

Miscellaneous Tools

For installing the occasional snap or grommet, the home builder may wish to

A foot-powered heavy-duty tool for installing snaps and grommets.

For bending the aluminum tubing you can use jigs, heavy pipe, or something else to bend around, but this isn't too reliable. For crisp, clean, accurate bends some sort of a conduit-bending tool is best. The cheapest and the easiest to use tool I have seen is one used by electrical contractors to bend electrical conduit. These tools come in various sizes, so try to get the right size for the tubing you will be working with. Although these tools aren't expensive (less than $10), they are hard to find. Try some local electrical suppliers to see if they have one for sale, or if they will rent theirs to you for an afternoon.

For working with down bought in bulk there are two things that are highly recommended. Down should always be portioned out by weight, rather than by volume. Because down is so compressible, it is almost impossible to accurately divide it up by volume. This means that you will need some kind of accurate scale for weighing out down. Postal scales or small kitchen scales may work. If you can find one with a range of 0 to 5 pounds in ¼-ounce divisions, it will be ideal.

The other item that is handy for working with down is the plastic bags sold in most grocery stores for use as sandwich bags. I prefer the Ziploc brand, in the smaller sizes, for parcelling out down in ½-ounce, 1-ounce, and 2-ounce lots. Of course, you will need them only if you buy down in bulk. If you buy down from most retail suppliers, they prepackage their down for you by weight, which is a big plus. If you don't want to get involved with scales, plastic bags, and a messy, boring job, buy your down from the retailers.

PROCEDURES

The procedures and techniques used by the home builder are very different from those used by the commercial manufacturers. To the manufacturers, time is money; they are interested in speedy, efficient techniques suitable for mass production. These may involve expensive heavy-duty tools and special skills that are beyond the home builder's means.

Obviously, the home builder cannot compete with the manufacturers in output or speed, but by using techniques specifically designed for home builders, he can compete in quality and cost. By working a little slower, and by using his ingenuity, the home builder can come up with finished camping equipment that is equal or superior to commercial gear, at a fraction of the cost.

Preparation

Proper preparation and planning is about 50 percent of any do-it-yourself project. Too often, a beginner sees some wonderful project in a book, decides it would be simple to make, and then charges in full speed without understanding what he is getting into and exactly what is involved. He may decide that he doesn't need any help from the instructions and either skims through them or ignores them completely. About half way through he finds that things just aren't working out properly, and he then gives up the whole idea, probably blaming the stupid designer for not making things work out for him.

In addition to the proper tools and the proper materials, you will need the proper information, attitudes, and skills to complete these projects. This book supplies much of the information you will need, but it cannot tell you everything. You will benefit greatly from outside sources such as other books, the advice of experienced campers, and especially, your own experience. Time spent gathering information will not be time wasted; the more you know about some item, the easier it will be to design and build it.

The proper attitudes will aid considerably when making your own gear. First, try to convince yourself that it will be fun. If you enjoy your work it goes faster and much easier. If you don't enjoy working with your hands, concentrate instead on all the money you will be saving. Whatever you do, give yourself some convincing reason for finishing what is often hard work. Second, remember who you are making it for—yourself. You want nothing but the best, so make sure this attitude shows up when you are working. Take pride in doing a good job (craftsmanship is its own reward). Third, have patience. A tent or a sleeping bag is a big job, and you may be tempted to give up (or start rushing things) part way through. Take it slowly, don't try to rush (you get sloppy), and remember, your time costs nothing, so use as much of it as is necessary to do a good job.

The skills involved in making your own camping gear are not really that hard to pick up. If you are an experienced sewer, you already know most of the techniques we will be using, and you already have most of the necessary skills. If you are a complete beginner, the answer is simple— practice, practice, practice, until you are thoroughly familiar with the materials, tools, and procedures. You could practice sewing on scraps of material, but why not put this practice to good use by making some simple, useful, inexpensive item? If you glance through the projects, you will see that they are listed with the simplest projects first, the most difficult projects last. For example, one simple to make, inexpensive project is a belt pack. The materials, tools, and procedures involved are similar to those used for a full-size pack. If you make a belt pack first, you can confine your learning and practice (and your mistakes) to the smaller, less expensive item.

Layout

When it comes to making your own camping gear, one of the first things to think about is a clear, well-lit, convenient place to work. I started on the kitchen table, as no doubt many of you will, but if you are serious about do-it-yourself, sooner or later you will have to find something better.

At present I have one entire room in my basement that is exclusively my work room for planning, designing, and constructing my camping gear. All of my tools are neatly assembled and laid out, with materials, resource books, and finished gear all stacked away for convenience and easy access. This saves me countless hours of packing and unpacking, losing and finding, searching and swearing. If you have a spare room, and if you are serious, think about it. You will definitely need a lot of clear space and a flat, smooth surface for laying out and marking fabric for such large items as tents and sleeping bags; otherwise you cannot get the necessary accuracy. I have to work off the floor, but I dream about someday owning a waist-high 8×16-foot table, which would make layout and cutout simple and fast.

If you set aside a space for working, and organize this space properly, it will aid considerably in the actual construction. For the large items it will be helpful to have another pair of hands. In any case, set things up as best you can before you start; it will be worth the extra effort.

All of the projects are drawn considerably less than life size, so to get a proper full-size pattern you will have to scale them up. Each project has an accompanying diagram that gives all pertinent dimensions. These are cut-out dimensions, which already include the ½-inch seam allowance. I generally draw my full-size patterns on heavy brown paper; it's cheaper than fabric if mistakes or corrections must be made. Take care when laying out these full-size patterns that you accurately measure and mark them; inaccuracies here can ruin a project. Be sure to take the time to double check all measurements before you transfer the pattern to the fabric.

If you are making any modifications, changing any dimensions, or trying for a custom fit, it would be useful if you made a trial pattern or mockup from some cheap fabric. Do all of your experimenting with the paper and cheap fabric, and when you perfect your designs, then and only then transfer them to the expensive fabrics. If you are working out designs for tents, it is impractical to make full-size patterns or mockups. Tents and sleeping bags are generally marked directly on the fabric, without using a pattern, so do it right the first time. When experimenting with tents, one useful trick is to make up scale models from paper. Draw them, cut them out, and Scotch tape the seams, and you get a three-dimensional scale model, which will be much easier to understand than a two-dimensional drawing. With some of these tents the panels are very oddly shaped, and trying to turn three dimensions into two (for cutout) can be difficult. Models can help.

For marking on the fabric you will need chalk, crayon, pencil, or grease pencils. Some fabrics have one good side, and with others both sides are identical. If the fabric has only one good side, make sure you take this into account when marking and laying out. The good side should end up on the outside, so either make all marks on the bad side (inside) or use chalk that will rub off. Crayons, pencils, and grease pencils leave marks that are difficult to remove, and an item with such marks showing on the outside does not look very professional.

You will notice that many of the layout diagrams for projects have short, dark alignment marks indicated. These marks are very helpful when fitting pieces together. If you don't want your project to turn out lopsided, use them.

Sewing

Unfortunately, this book cannot be an introduction to sewing. If you are a complete beginner, I recommend that you pick up one of the many good books meant to serve as an introduction. These books are available at any sewing or fabric shop, or you might even consider signing up for a course on the subject. While such outside help is not strictly necessary, it will simplify matters greatly if you understand what I am talking about when I use some terms common to sewing (seams, serging, bobbin, etc.).

Before you actually begin sewing, there is one trick that will help considerably with keeping your seams straight and where they should be. By pinning every seam before you stitch it, you hold the pieces of fabric in correct alignment to receive the stitches. You'll proceed faster if you don't pin the seams, but the fabric may shift out of place as you sew, causing crooked seams. Some experienced sewers never use pins, but for beginners, pinning all seams before stitching is highly recommended.

I suggest that you pin only to the seam allowance. That way there will be no pin holes in the fabric to leak down or water. Also, when working with down-insulated clothing and waterproof (coated) fabrics, it is important that all stitching be done properly the first time. Stitches put in the wrong place must be removed, which will leave needle holes in their place. Again, these holes can leak down or water, and in coated fabrics they are very noticeable, spoiling the finished look of any item.

For machine sewing, which is the only reasonable way to do things, your machine must be properly set up for the job at hand. The weight of the fabric, whether it is coated or not, the weight and type of thread, etc., are all factors in setting up your machine to sew strong, tight, proper stitching. Remember, sewing machines differ from make to make, model to model, and even from one machine to another of the same model. I have found out what works best with my machine, but my settings may not work at all with yours. So read the owner's manual and experiment with some stitches on the specialized material you will be using.

Here are a few things to watch for when sewing light fabrics: On insulated clothing keep the stitches short (ten to twelve per inch) or you may find down leaking through the seams. Thread tension should be slightly looser than usual or the light fabrics may pucker between stitches. Synthetic thread should always be used for extra strength. I prefer cotton wrapped/ polyester thread in the smaller sizes. The larger sizes are stronger, but will not make neat stitches with such a light fabric.

Most machines will handle the heavier fabrics, but you will have to spend a little more time and effort in setting up for it. Here are the things I have found out about sewing heavy fabrics on a home machine.

For packs and other heavy-duty applications, use the strongest thread possible. This thread is commercial-duty nylon, about size 25 (Koban is one brand name). This thread comes in 5,000-yard spools, so make sure it will work with your machine before spending the $10 or so for a spool. Many home machines will not use this heavy thread. If your machine is one of them, the next best bet is a heavy-duty cotton wrapped/polyester type. I find Talon 50/50 heavy-duty button and canvas thread just right. It is slightly weaker than the Koban, but it feeds better. It is available in 70-yard spools from most fabric shops (70 yards isn't much; get two or three spools for a pack).

To sew with these heavy threads you will also need a heavy needle, such as a size 18 or 19 with the Talon, a size 21 with the Koban. Smaller sizes may work, but they increase the friction on the thread as it sews (they have smaller "eyes"). This may seriously weaken the thread and cause thread breakage. In addition, with the heavy thread tensions necessary to use these threads, the smaller needles may bend, which means missed stitches, or they may strike the needle plate and result in broken needles.

You will have to crank up the thread tension nearly as high as it will go, and you may have to increase the length of your stitches to get decent feeding and stitching. Set your bobbin thread tension and play around with tension and stitch length until you get reliable stitching.

Let the machine feed the fabric. If you pull it you may break needles. Sew slowly and smoothly for best results.

Use only sharp needles; the fabric itself will dull needles slowly, and hitting the needle plate may ruin a needle.

When sewing coated fabrics, which are quite common to outdoors equipment, you may have some problems getting the cloth to feed properly. Most coatings are somewhat stickier in texture than the untreated fabrics. The coatings drag considerably when feeding through the machine, which causes jerky feeding and inconsistent stitch length. Here are some suggestions that seem to improve feeding with the coated fabrics:

If the material is coated on one side only, always sew with the coated side down. This allows the feed teeth to get a better grip on the fabric and move it along properly. If the coated side is to the top, it will drag against the presser foot.

If you plan to do much work with the coated fabrics, or if you are using a fabric that is coated on both sides, then it may be worthwhile to invest a few dollars for a presser foot with rollers. These are designed to work with leather, but they work well with the coated fabrics, too. You might also try the special chisel-point needles (also designed for leather); they might work a little better.

Try loosening off on the presser-foot pressure; this usually improves feeding with all coated fabrics.

Whatever item you are making, it is important that your stitching be neat, tight, and strong. A row of stitching is like a chain; it is only as strong as its weakest link. To eliminate any possible problems with weak spots in the stitching, double or triple stitching is used on all quality outdoors equipment. By doubling the stitching you are assuring that there will be at least one good stitch to stand up to any strain. This is cheap insurance against seam failure; so for all your seams, be sure and double stitch.

If you have a zigzag machine you can run one row of stitches with the needle at the left. Then you can run another row of stitches with the needle set to the right. This will give you a very strong seam; the two rows of stitching reinforce each other, and the fabric itself will usually rip before the stitching. Commercial machines are available with double needles, which cuts sewing time in half, but for home machines double needles work only with the lighter fabrics.

Whenever you start or stop a row of stitching, the ends must be finished in some way to keep the stitching from working apart. With a straight-sew machine, sew back and forth over ½ inch at the end of the stitching (backstitching). If your machine has reverse, this will save turning the fabric around.

If your machine has zigzag, set it for a very tight, medium-width zigzag stitch and use it at the end of the stitching to finish the ends. A tight zigzag will produce a dense, strong stitch that will resist working loose quite well. This dense, tight zigzag is also useful for reinforcing any areas of stitching that may be subject to extra strain (corners, for example). Commercial machines are available that produce a reinforcing stitch known as bar tacking, but for home use a tight zigzag is nearly as good.

If your machine has a serging-type stitch (check your owner's manual; there

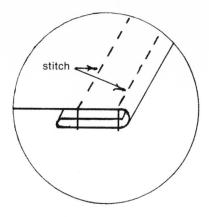

A folded-edge seam. This is known as a finished hem.

are several stitches that may be used for serging), then you can save considerable time. All edges of nylon fabric must be finished, or else the fabric will ravel and fray. This can reduce a fine piece of equipment to a piece of junk in only a few weeks. Serging is a quick and effective way to hold the outer rows of fiber in place, which prevents raveling.

If your machine does not have a serging-type stitch, then you are in for a lot of extra work. Some other method of finishing the fabric edges must be used. Folding the fabric over will give you a finished-edge seam. This seam is quite useful; it can be used as a hem; it can be widened and a drawstring inserted to give you a draw hem; and the seam itself adds strength to the edge of the fabric—important for such things as tent flaps.

If this seems like too much bother, there is an alternative—flame sealing. This is the method used most often by the home craftsman to prevent the edges from raveling. Nylon will melt when heated to 480°F; and edges that have been treated in this manner will not fray—the heat ac-

tually welds the fibers together. An edge that has been treated in this manner should not be used on the outside—it looks ugly—so use this type of finishing only for hidden edges.

A candle with a wide-based holder is the best source of heat for flame sealing. Hold the edge of the fabric firmly between your hands and pass it close (not in) to the flame. Move it along smoothly and fairly quickly so as to just melt the edge. Keeping the fabric in one place for too long, or holding it too close to the flame, may cause it to burn. With light fabrics continue to hold the fabric taut for a few seconds after it has heated. This allows the melted nylon to cool into a straight edge. Otherwise you may find the edges curling.

Flame sealing the edges of nylon fabric to prevent raveling.

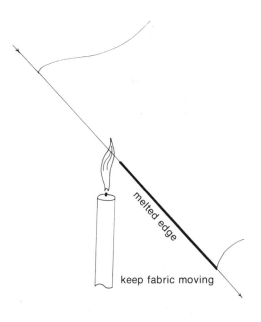

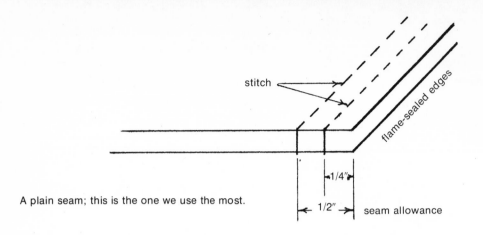

stitch

flame-sealed edges

1/4"

1/2" seam allowance

A plain seam; this is the one we use the most.

Avoid breathing in any fumes from the melted nylon. Avoid getting any of the sticky melted nylon on your hands—it can cause a bad burn.

To join two pieces of fabric together, the most commonly used seam is the simple plain seam. To make such a seam match the edges to be joined, good sides together, then stitch along the edge about ¼ inch. Stitch a second time about ½ inch from the edge (½-inch seam allowance) for a double-stitched plain seam. This seam is used only where the wrong side will not be exposed, or for packs where the heavy fabrics prevent a more finished seam. If used with flame-sealed edges, this seam will be adequate for most of your needs.

For items where both inside and outside will be exposed (tents, clothing, etc.) the

seam should present a finished appearance on both sides. The common flat-felled seam is best here. To make such a seam match the edges to be joined, then stitch once about ¾ inch from the edge. Determine which direction you want the flap to fold (important for horizontal seams in tents) and trim the underneath flap to half its width. (If the fabric is light, there is no need to bother with trimming.) Fold the wider flap around the narrower flap so that no rough edges are exposed, then sew down with two rows of stitches. This gives a very strong, good looking seam.

For sewing around curves, and for making corners, there will often be excess fabric, which will bunch up and make a lumpy or uneven seam when folded and sewn. To eliminate this problem simply

A flat-felled seam—finished appearance on both sides.

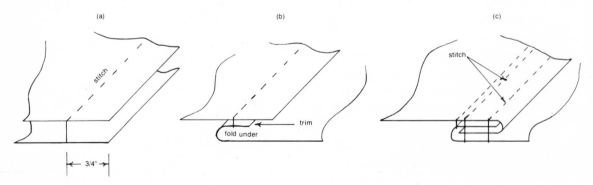

(a)

stitch

3/4"

(b)

trim

fold under

(c)

stitch

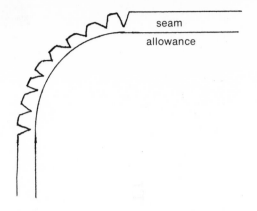

seam
allowance

Notching curves so they will lay flat when folded.

(a)

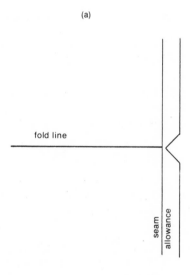

fold line

seam
allowance

(b)

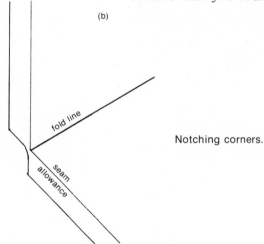

fold line

seam
allowance

cut notches in the fabric to help it lay flat around these curves and corners.

I generally give recommended weights of fill for my designs for insulated items. (Down should always be portioned out by weight, not by volume. Because down is so easy to compress, accuracy is possible only with weighing.) You may be tempted to overstuff things in an attempt to gain extra warmth. Don't do this. Stuffing in extra down will merely compress the down and add weight; it will not add warmth. If the compartments are filled as suggested, you will get good loft. If you want thicker insulation, though it's not really necessary, you will have to change the dimensions of the down compartments to allow the down to loft more. This is complicated, so think about it before you decide it is necessary.

If you have difficulty sewing webbing, or any thick material such as leather or several layers of heavy fabric, you may have to turn the machine over by hand instead of with the motor. The gears and mechanisms inside the machine are usually strong enough to handle the heaviest loads, but many machines are underpowered. Sewing this way will seem very slow, but it will still be much faster than trying to sew with a needle. And the machine will produce neater and better stitches than you could by hand.

Notching corners.

4

Packs and Other Baggage

With dozens of different manufacturers turning out hundreds of different pack designs, some system of organizing and classifying packs is needed, if only to avoid being overwhelmed by the number of different choices available. Here are the names most commonly used to describe and classify the different types of packs: belt packs (fanny packs and belt pockets), day packs, weekender packs (frameless, semiframed, and framed), and frame packs (rigid frame, semirigid frame, and wraparound frame).

There are several ways to go about designing a good pack for yourself. The easiest way is to browse through catalogs and shops until you find the pack that seems just right for you. Then copy it. As long as you are not making these items for resale, it isn't illegal to pirate designs and ideas. In fact, even at the commercial level, ideas are "borrowed" with nobody seeming to raise any serious objections.

Perhaps you already have an old pack that is worn out beyond repair. In this case merely take it apart to use as a pattern for cutting out a new one. By copying established commercial designs, you avoid many of the pitfalls and trials of designing your own. And you end up with good outdoor equipment at about one-third the retail price.

If you are harder to please, and can't find any one commercial design that seems to have everything that you want, then you can take the best ideas from several different designs and blend them all together. The ideal frame from one designer, the right suspension system from another, and the bag that pleases you most can be combined into your idea of the perfect pack, with no really new and unproven features.

By adding or subtracting the features that you want, you can come up with a truly unique and practical design that suits your style of backpacking perfectly. You can also come up with a real monstrosity, especially if you don't understand the basic principles involved, so be careful, use discretion, and try to achieve a practical, coordinated blend.

If you are really interested in designing your own, based on a completely new idea, then you are letting yourself in for a lot of extra work. But of course you may end up with some new and innovative design that could revolutionize backpacking—again. The Gerry teardrop climbing pack, the Kelty two-piece waist belt, the Camp Trails one-piece padded hip belt, and the wraparound hip-suspension system were all better ideas that "revolutionized" backpacking. And there is still room for new innovations that could do so again, but it will be up to you to test, develop, and prove your ideas, without the help of established designs.

BELT PACKS

Belt packs are the small packs worn on a belt around the waist. There are actually two different types of belt packs, the fanny pack and the belt pocket.

Fanny Packs

Fanny packs are belt packs with a belt permanently attached. They are usually contoured to fit around the body. Good ones are comfortable, unobtrusive, and should have interior partitions to help organize your gear. These packs are popular with skiers, who use them to carry ski wax, sandwiches, and sunburn cream instead of stuffing them into their pockets. Capacity is around 5 pounds (fanny packs should be kept small; the large ones are just too uncomfortable when loaded to full capacity). When used alone they offer an excellent way to carry small, light loads, and when combined with another larger pack on the back, they provide a convenient place to carry those small, often used items that are always getting lost in a large pack.

One idea you might want to consider is a combination fanny pack/padded waist belt for your frame pack. At least one manufacturer makes them, and I think the idea has merit. It can serve as your office on the trail, organizing trail snacks, insect repellent, sunglasses, and other often used items into a convenient reached spot. Just don't place pockets over the frame attachment points.

Belt Pockets

Belt pockets are nothing more than pockets or pouches that slip onto your belt. These can be made as simple or as complicated as you desire. Belt pockets have several unique advantages over fanny packs. The main advantage is versatility. When on a belt they are nearly as comfortable and have most of the characteristics of a fanny pack; off the belt they may be used as cases for your first-aid, toilet, or survival kits. This way they can be stored efficiently in your pack, where they organize these items into convenient little bundles.

In addition, you can make a belt pocket detachable, and in combination with the 2-inch web ski straps, you can attach it to your pack and use it as a regular pack pocket, which also comes off and attaches to your belt. Or you can attach a shoulder strap to your belt pocket to turn it into a shoulder bag, camera gadget bag, purse, or whatever. I make all my belt pockets detachable, for use as pack pockets, and I always make them to fit my packs. I prefer the rectangular shape (rectangular fits well inside and outside the pack), and I keep mine small.

Plans for a belt pocket are offered in

A small detachable belt pocket. Note the Velcro flaps; only detachable pockets may be used as removable pack pockets.

or strap and turn them into purses, shoulder bags, or small hand bags. Remember to keep the belt loops high up on them or else they will sway and bounce around quite a bit. This can get very annoying on a long hike.

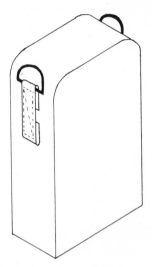

Belt pocket with two D rings; use with snap-on web shoulder strap for a small shoulder bag.

Project 4-1. I highly recommend the unique detachable Velcro flap belt loops that allow you to remove and attach the pocket without undoing your belt; these loops are necessary if the item is to be used as a removable pack pocket. You will find this arrangement far superior to any of the commercial removable pack pocket designs; it can be used as a belt pack, it is stronger and less prone to loss, and it can be used with skis in the ski straps.

Feel free to experiment with different styles, sizes, and shapes of belt packs. They are cheap and are excellent practice for the larger packs. You can make them to fit specific items of gear, with internal partitions, loops, or pockets. You can even add on provisions for attaching a handle

Another way of providing for a detachable shoulder strap; this one provides a convenient handle.

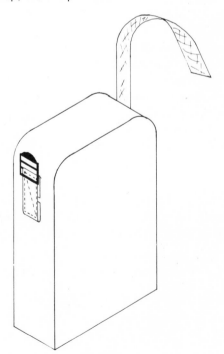

DAY PACKS

Day packs are small, simple, frameless packs that are limited to casual packing and day trips. They will carry between 800 and 1,200 cubic inches of gear weighing between 15 and 20 pounds. These frameless packs have conventional shoulder straps, only a few pockets, and perhaps a nonweight-supporting waist belt. The weight will hang directly from the shoulders, but such packs will be comfortable, convenient, and all the casual camper needs.

The day pack is probably the most useful and certainly the most popular type of pack. When used for general-duty hauling, one-day camping trips, and even occasional spartan overnighting, it will be

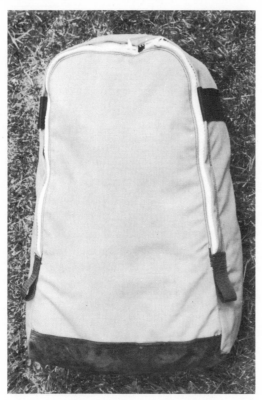

A tapered day pack—top is 8 inches, bottom is 12 inches.

the best pack for most campers. Experienced backpackers on extended trips will often carry an extra day pack in their frame pack, for use on those side trips when a frame pack is a nuisance.

Day packs are also being used now by many people who have never been camping. Many nonbackpackers are finding out what backpackers have known for a long time—that loads are best carried on the back, leaving the hands free. Housewives use them for shopping, students use them for books, bikers use them to carry everything, and joggers often carry their gym clothes to their workouts in them.

The simplest day pack design is little more than a sack with shoulder straps. A rectangular-shaped insert bottom helps such a pack retain a more comfortable shape when stuffed. A wraparound bottom also helps a pack retain its shape, and in addition gets the weight a little closer to the wearer's center of gravity. If overstuffed, all of these designs will tend to bulge out into a cylinder, which is very uncomfortable on the back.

The top closure is usually a simple drawstring, with an oversize flap over the hole for weather protection. Some variations have one to five external pockets to help organize the gear and to help the pack retain its shape. In light materials this is the cheapest pack made (it sells for 98¢ to around $10). Carefully made, of heavy materials, and with loops for accessories, this type of pack is known as a climber's rucksack. Since it is the simplest design, it is often the most reliable for the climber, who will be abusing it by dropping it, hauling it up a line, or rubbing it against rocks. Any of these activities could tear open a zipper and spill the contents down the mountain.

The next simplest design is basically a

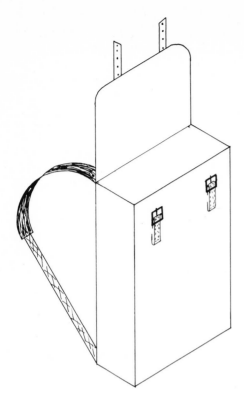

A rectangular day pack of the Scout design.

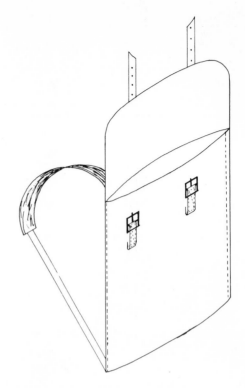

A simple, easily made pack of the Duluth style. This is the best design for an emergency pack.

rectangular fabric pouch or box with shoulder straps. The pouch style is called a canoe pack or Duluth pack. The box-shaped bag is known as a Scout pack or Yucca pack. The top closure is again an oversize flap, usually without the drawstring. The side seams on these designs are fairly effective in keeping the bag from turning into a cylinder if overstuffed; however, the large opening at the top is rarely weatherproof, and gear can get lost in a fall. Both of these designs are out of date, but if you ever need an emergency pack, a Duluth can be easily made out of nearly anything. Keep the loads in such packs small or they will be murder on your back.

The first major improvement over the simple sack, pouch, or fabric box comes from modifying the shape of the pack. The rectangular shape, while efficient for stuffing, is sometimes found to be constricting around the shoulders. Climbers and skiers will notice it the most. Gerry Cunningham developed a modification called the teardrop pack, which is simply a day pack narrow at the top for comfort. The thickness of the pack is kept to a minimum, and the tapered shape combines with this to give a pack with far less capacity. This decreased capacity forces the wearer to carry much lighter loads, which are more suitable for the frameless designs anyway. This is the type of design I favor for my day packs.

The next improvement is really simple;

A pack with a partition. The arched zipper gives better access than a straight design, and is somewhat stronger. Bottom compartment holds three-season sleeping bag. Back pocket fits down jacket. Make the pockets and compartments to fit the gear they will carry. This pack has a detachable floor, which allows it to be converted into one immense compartment for carrying oversized items. A good idea.

all that is involved is placing a partition across the bag. This may not seem like much, but it does three desirable things: it helps hold the pack in shape and keeps it from bulging out into a cylinder; it prevents weight and gear from shifting, allowing you to pack the bag efficiently, with the weight where you want it; and it allows convenient access to the usually hidden and hard to get to gear at the bot-

tom of the bag. However, it also has the disadvantage of having a small compartment when you want to pack a large bulky object.

In the day packs I don't feel a partition is necessary, but in the weekenders one or several is often desirable. If making your own pack, it would be simple to plan and install a partition (don't forget an opening for the bottom), but I feel it is not worth the extra work in a small pack. You can get the same access to the bottom by using an extra-long zipper, and the light loads involved should not really require careful packing.

When the loads get heavier (15 to 20 pounds) a day pack with wide, padded shoulder straps will be more comfortable than the identical pack and load without them. Padded shoulder straps can be made quite easily from fabric sewn into a tube, stuffed with Ensolite. The time involved is about three-quarters of an hour and the expense is minimal. Design and construction details for making and attaching such straps may be found on pages 92–93.

A day pack really won't benefit much from a wide waist belt, but a simple 1-inch web strap used as a belt can still serve a worthwhile purpose. Climbers, skiers, and joggers will appreciate such a belt, which doesn't carry any weight, but which does keep the pack secure against the back, where it can't shift and perhaps cause a change in the wearer's center of gravity at a crucial moment.

There are a number of other very useful modifications and accessories that might be desirable in a day pack, but don't get carried away with the fancy stuff here; a day pack should be simple, and the simpler, the better. Sleeping bag loops, ski straps, and a double bottom can increase the usefulness of your day pack, but too much will clutter it up. For a list of several options, accessories, and modifications that you can add to many packs, see pages 88–93.

If you are interested in making your own day pack, I recommend the Fresh Air Day Pack plans in Project 4-2. Carefully made of proper materials, this day pack is the equal of any similar item on the market. A lot of thought and development went into this item—it was my first attempt at do-it-yourself camping gear— and it has been refined considerably over the years.

WEEKENDER PACKS

It is often difficult to distinguish between large day packs and small weekender packs; there are many day packs that could be used for spartan weekending, and there are many so-called weekend packs that don't live up to their names. Concentrate on what a pack will do, not on what someone chooses to call it. If you can stuff in everything you need for a weekend, and still carry that pack comfortably, then, for you at least, it is a weekender pack.

When I talk about a weekender pack, I am referring to any pack that will easily carry enough gear for comfortable weekends, or perhaps trips of up to a week. It must be able to carry a tent, a mediumweight, three-season sleeping bag, adequate food, and plenty of other gear. Such bags will generally have a capacity of between 1,600 and 3,000 cubic inches, and will comfortably carry between 20 and 30 pounds, with some of them capable of carrying over 40 pounds if the backpacker knows how to pack his gear properly. Weekenders really are a

The Venture Pack, a weekender, from Frostline; available in kit form. Note the use of ski slots. (Photo courtesy Frostline Kits)

separate class of packs, different from day packs and different from frame packs.

There are three principal types of weekender packs: frameless, semiframed, and framed.

Frameless Weekender Packs. Through efficient pack strap design, the use of contoured compartments to keep the bag's shape, a contoured wraparound shape to keep the weight as close to the body as possible, one or more partitions to keep the bag in shape and to control weight distribution for efficient carrying, and well-designed, proper fitting, wide, padded shoulder straps a frame is eliminated altogether (Jensen, Ultima, Thule, etc.).

In addition, a well-designed weekender frameless will always have a wide,

70 / THE BUDGET BACKPACKER

weight-supporting waist or hip belt. A wide belt can support quite a bit of weight, and it relieves the shoulder muscles considerably by transferring this weight to the sturdy pelvic structure. Of course, soft packs without the rigid frame to transfer the weight directly to the belt cannot really put a weight-carrying belt to efficient use. However, if the bag is firmly stuffed, the fabric bag itself will transfer a significant amount of the weight to the belt. While this is nowhere near as efficient as with a frame design, it is a noticeable improvement.

There are several other important factors to consider when designing a frameless weekender pack:

Size. Keep the frameless weekender as small as is practical. When soft packs are made too large, the gear tends to accumulate loosely in the bottom of the compartments, and the bag pulls backwards. Unless such bags are loaded with light, bulky gear, such as winter sleeping bags and down clothing, it is also very easy to overload them.

Shape. In addition to the wraparound bottom another useful way to keep the weight close to the back is slanting the bottom so that the gear tends to slide in closer. But remember not to get the pack too wide at the top or you may find it constricting at the shoulders. Also, don't get it too wide at the bottom or it may interfere with the free swing backwards of your elbows, which is important to a natural style of walking; 12 inches for the top and 16 inches for the bottom is maximum.

If the depth of the bag is too great, heavy objects carried near the back of the pack will exert greater leverage against the wearer, causing a most uncomfortable backwards pull. Keep the bag between 5 to 8 inches for frameless designs. Many packs are tapered in this area also, with a deeper bottom tapering to a shallower top. Just remember to stay over 5 inches or you may not be able to fit in such bulky objects as stoves.

The length of the bag is also fairly critical, and the spacing between the shoulder straps and the waist belt is important. You want the belt to accept its proper share of the load, which it won't do if the distance from belt to straps is too short. In addition, if the waist belt is too high, it fits around the chest instead of the waist, and it causes difficulty breathing when tightened up enough to carry much weight.

On the other hand, if you make the distance from shoulder straps to waist belt too great, the belt supports most of the weight, with the shoulder straps not accepting their proper share. This causes the pack to fall away from the shoulders, requiring an excessive, uncomfortable forward lean to correct. Or you will have to wear the belt too low on your hips, which forces it against the muscles that you use to walk with, causing constriction and possibly cramping.

Partitions and Pockets. These should be designed with two points in mind—the gear you will be carrying, and where you want to store that gear for maximum comfort and carrying efficiency. Obviously, if you have already collected all of your other equipment, it will be much easier to plan for the proper size pack compartments. Otherwise you may end up trying to stuff a 5-pound winter sleeping bag into a compartment that is too small. The right size compartment is important for best usage of the pack's internal volume. Plan your pack around the rest of your equipment, if this is at all possible.

In addition to this, there are certain principles of efficient packing that can make a heavier load feel lighter and much more comfortable. The art of properly packing a soft pack is not one that can be learned overnight, but here are a few hints that can help you plan and achieve a comfortable soft pack:

1. Heavy objects should be stored as close to your back as possible and as high up in the pack as possible.

2. The sleeping bag and other light, bulky gear such as down clothing should be carried in the lower part of the pack where they will keep the heavier objects in their proper place—up high.

3. Hard, sharp objects such as stoves or cans should be kept away from the back by a layer of padding (clothing perhaps).

4. The most used items should be kept on top, or in an outside pocket for easy access; you don't want to empty the whole pack just to get to the toilet paper.

5. Unless gear is kept in fitted compartments, or else is tied to something, it will always shift around in your pack, ruining all of your efforts at efficient, comfortable packing.

Partitions are also important because they give shape and support to the whole pack. For this reason the more complicated soft packs have lots of them—at the bottom a contoured, wraparound compartment for a sleeping bag, plus several horizontal or vertical partitions to compartmentalize gear and to provide built-in rigidity and support to the frameless bag. The main drawback to these types is if you want to carry some large bulky object, too big for any compartment, or if you want a versatile pack instead of such a specialized, fitted one.

Caribou adjustable depth weekender pack; as your load gets smaller you tighten the drawstrings to keep the pack in shape and the load close to your back. Another good idea.

The author's design for a simple weekender pack. This bag could be made with drawstrings along the sides, with ski straps and detachable pockets, with or without some kind of frame, in whatever size is best.

Semiframed Weekender Packs. In these packs the frame is kept to a minimum for flexibility and light weight and often it is removable to convert the bag into a frameless model. Almost any material that is light and strong can be used for a frame. Excellent ones have been made from plywood, slats of wood, fiberglass, plastic moldings, tubular aluminum, and flat aluminum. You are limited here only by your imagination and what is available.

One of the best and most common semiframed designs is made of nothing more than two aluminum strips running the length of the bag, and bent to conform to body shape. Those strips or stays may be sewn inside the bag, sewn on the outside, attached to the harness independent of the bag, or made removable, for when you want a frameless sack or for storage. These stays can hook up to a weight-supporting waist and hip belt for good weight transfer; they are light, cheap, and easy to make. The design I favor for this type of semiframe can be used with any of the bag designs given to increase the comfort (use a weight-carrying waist belt, too).

Framed Weekender Packs. The framed weekender type of packs uses a heavier, more complicated frame than the semiframe to give the desired support, and also to hold the bag in shape, to protect the back, and to provide ventilation. Since the objectives of a weekender frame are different from those of a full-size frame pack, to be most effective the weekender frame should not be merely a scaled-down version of the larger frames used for frame packs. Most weekenders are flexible, light, and not as bulky as a frame pack. These packs are meant to perform as intermediates between the day packs and the frame packs, making them quite useful. If you are interested in overnight ski touring, mountaineering, bushwhacking, or just hitchhiking or hosteling, some form of weekender may be ideal for you. But make sure you try before you buy. These are specialized packs with many features that you may or may not want. Make sure that the pack will fit in with your idea of a weekend, not someone else's.

The frame may be almost any light, strong material, ranging from tubular aluminum to reinforced plastic sheeting. The frame may be removable to allow the bag to become frameless. These designs have less capacity and are less bulky than a regular frame pack. A perimeter or insert frame made of light tubular aluminum seems to provide everything needed in a frame design, with the minimum of complications or undesirable characteristics.

To get a semirigid frame some kind of fittings must be used for the joints. This is actually not a handicap for the home builder; these fittings are cheaper and easier to install than conventional welded joints. I like and recommend Jan Sport fittings and ⅝-inch aluminum tubing for this type of perimeter frame.

If you don't like this particular design, or if you can't get the necessary parts, a fairly good frame can be made by adding one other strip of aluminum to the bottom of the simple stay-type semiframes discussed earlier. By putting this extra strip across the bottom (roughly a triangle), you can turn the stay semiframe into a flexible, light, well-ventilated frame that gives good weight transfer and fair protection. Unfortunately, it cannot provide the tension along the outside of the bag as does a perimeter frame, so the bag will lose its shape when overstuffed or understuffed. Still, for the person desiring lightness, simplicity, and ease of construction, this is a very good design.

Whatever style of frame you decide on—stays, perimeter tubing, or triangular—I highly recommend that you make it removable. This way you can use the bag without it if desired, and the weekender can be stored in a minimum of space when not in use (perhaps in your frame pack, for use as a large day bag or summit pack).

FRAME PACKS

For extended backpacking trips in clear, level terrain, the best pack for the job is the frame pack with a separate fabric bag. Today, most frames are made of aluminum tubing. Such a frame, with the corresponding large bag and a modern shoulder harness and waist-belt suspension sys-

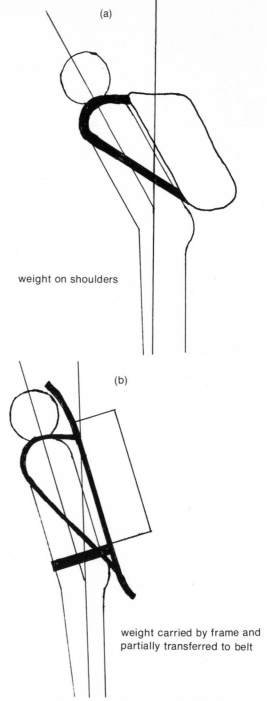

(a)

weight on shoulders

(b)

weight carried by frame and partially transferred to belt

A properly designed frame aids considerably in carrying heavy loads by transferring weight to the sturdy pelvic structure, and by eliminating much of the forward lean.

tem, is significantly better at carrying heavy loads for long distances than any other system yet discovered. The frame supports the load carried by the sack and transmits this load to the carrier in a much more manageable and comfortable way. In some designs the waist belt supports over 75 percent of the weight. The frame packs also carry the load higher, and closer to a person's vertical axis, therefore eliminating some of the forward lean that is so tiring. So if you are looking for one pack suitable for all your backpacking needs, the frame pack is the best choice. Though there are specialized packs that will be more suitable for certain activities, the frame pack can be used for nearly anything: climbing, skiing, or as a day pack.

If you can afford two packs, a day pack and a frame pack make an excellent combination—the frame pack for the heavy loads that the day pack just couldn't handle, and the day pack for when the frame pack would be a bulky, heavy nuisance. Or for the absolute ultimate in pack efficiency, you might make your frame pack bag removable (convertible) for use as a large day pack, or perhaps, with the addition of an aluminum stay frame, for use as a comfortable, flexible weekender.

Frames

The frame is usually the most important part of a frame pack. The main considerations are durability, lightness, and efficient design. The present standard for durability is a rigid tubular aluminum ladder frame with welded joints. This type of frame has proven itself through the years, under all types of conditions. The tubing should be ¾ to 1 inch for the outside frame rails, and ½ to ¾ inch for the crosspieces. For the do-it-yourselfer, 6061-T6 seamless aluminum aircraft-quality tubing is usually available and works well. If you are planning sharp bends, talk to the supplier about wall thickness and degree of hardness desirable. High-quality heli-arc welding provides the most acceptable method of joining the tubing.

Lightness depends on materials and design. Using the suggested sizes of aluminum tubing, and any one of the many standard designs, you should end up with a sturdy but fairly lightweight frame. Lighter frames could be made from magnesium tubing (slightly stronger and lighter than the aluminum, but harder to weld), or smaller diameter tubing (some frames are made with ½-inch tubing throughout), or less tubing (without any extra bracing), but these designs all sacrifice durability to some degree.

Efficient design is difficult to pin down; it seems we all have our own opinions on just exactly what is efficient. When it comes to which is the most efficient design for you, you will have to make up your own mind. The simplest and the best way to choose a frame is to try out a few on your own. Most shops have rental facilities; try a few until you find the frame you like best. In general, frame designs made from aluminum tubing conform to three main variations: rigid, semirigid, and wraparound.

Rigid Frames. This is the most popular frame pack and is the standard by which all other packs are judged. In this style the tubing is formed into a ladder-shaped arrangement by welding, by soldering, or by some form of nonflexible fitting. The ladder is curved slightly into a shallow "S" shape vertically. Most of these designs

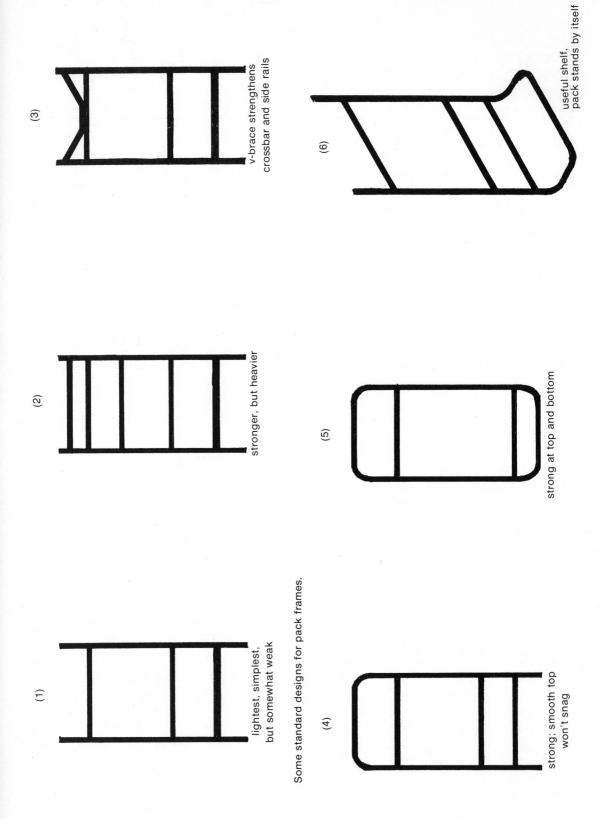

(3)

v-brace strengthens
crossbar and side rails

(6)

useful shelf,
pack stands by itself

(2)

stronger, but heavier

(5)

strong at top and bottom

Some standard designs for pack frames.

(1)

lightest, simplest,
but somewhat weak

(4)

strong; smooth top
won't snag

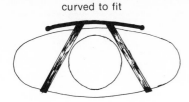

curved to fit

The crossbars should be curved to match the contours of your back.

feature crosspieces that are curved to comfortably fit the contours of the body. The number of these crossbars is not too critical; three will give a lighter, weaker frame, and four or five a stronger, heavier frame.

The crossbars can themselves be reinforced by several thin braces of aluminum tubing about ¼ to ⅜ inch in diameter. These braces add considerable strength, with little extra weight, and they help a great deal in keeping sharp objects away from the back, and by tipping the top forward, they allow the heavy items carried

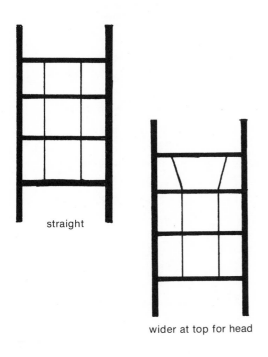

straight

wider at top for head

Bracing the crossbars.

up high to get directly over the wearer's center of gravity.

It is often difficult to find any real difference between the various bends, with some preferring one style and others preferring another. If making your own, I would suggest that you leave the side rail straight. You can always add some bends later, if carrying the pack for a while proves it necessary. Since the pack touches the back only at the upper and lower backbands, these are the only critical areas for side rail design.

Once you have settled on the right design, start thinking about the right size. Pack frames, just like people, come in various sizes, and it is important that the frame properly fits its wearer. Here are some basic guidelines for sizing a frame. But the final criteria for choosing a frame should always be how it feels with a load, not what some chart or salesman recommends.

The vertical distance is the distance between the bottom and the top shoulder strap attachment points. The vertical distance can be increased by attaching the top shoulder straps to the top of the crossbar. This distance should be about 2 inches longer than the distance from your

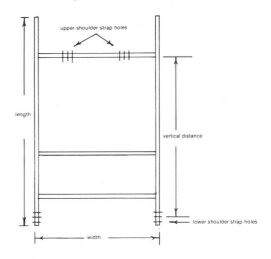

upper shoulder strap holes

length

vertical distance

lower shoulder strap holes

width

How to determine vertical distance.

SIZING A PACK FRAME

| Height of Wearer | | Dimensions of Frame (approximately) | | |
Men	Women	Length	Width	Vertical Distance
Less than 5'3''	Less than 5'4''	27''	14''	18''
5'3''–5'7''	5'4''–5'8''	29''	15''	20''
5'7''–6'	5'8''–6'	31''	16''	22''
Over 6'	Over 6'	33''	16''	23''

waist (top of your pants) to your shoulders (the big bump on the back of your neck). Note that the frames can be made slightly adjustable by drilling several holes at the shoulder strap attaching points, instead of just one. Three holes spaced about 1 inch apart should give you all the range of adjustment you will need if you have picked the proper size frame.

Semirigid Frames. This is similar to the standard rigid style except that the joints are made flexible. Fittings of some kind are used to provide adequate strength and rigidity, but at the same time allowing the frame to flex just enough to improve walking comfort. These types are very popular for skiing, where the rigid frames seem to interfere with some people's balance and rhythm.

There are many ingenious designs that offer flexibility, support, and lightness, but the most popular type is the ladder frame of aluminum tubing, joined with flexible fittings. Jan Sport is one of the best known manufacturers that handles this type, and they offer their fittings for sale at many retail outlets. The fittings, which take ⅝-inch O.D. tubing, are tightened into place by a very large screw (coin operated for field adjustments) that does a good job of holding things together. The smaller diameter tubing and the play around the fitting provide the desired flexibility, with lightness, strength, and dependability.

The big advantages of the flexible frame are low cost, ease of construction, and adjustability of frame. A major part of a welded frame's cost comes from the labor (skilled welding cost $12 an hour last time I checked). Fittings eliminate this entirely. The fittings may be installed with a minimum of inexpensive tools. This makes them ideal for the home craftsman. In addition, several designs feature an adjustable frame, in which the crosspiece that holds the upper shoulder straps may be moved up or down to fit the wearer. This is the ideal setup for a growing child's pack, or for a pack that will be used by many people (family pack).

Wraparound Frames. The most comfortable frame pack I have ever used with heavy loads was one of the wraparound types. With this pack 60 pounds felt like 40 pounds in one of the standard frames. This is the style I favor above all others for my framed designs. In the standard-style frame the transfer point between the frame and the waist belt is well behind the vertical axis of the wearer. The wraparound (sometimes called Hip Carry) frames move the transfer point forward along the waist belt until it corresponds with the wearer's vertical axis. The transfer point on these rigs is just about directly over your hips (and your arches), so with a properly set up wraparound little forward lean is necessary, even with heavy loads. Some experts claim that shifting the transfer point forward will cause the pack to fall away from the shoulders, requiring a forward lean to correct. I have found this to be true only with an improperly set up harness. When I adjusted the harness, this was no longer a problem.

Good wraparound designs are available from Alpenlite (available from Frostline without bag for those who prefer to make their own) and from Jan Sport, who will sell you the fittings so you can take a stab at bending up your own frame. A few manufacturers even offer kits to convert your standard design into a wraparound. Since proper fit is critical with a wraparound frame, be prepared for a lot of "cut and try" engineering if designing your own, or else copy a commercial design that feels good. The flexible wraparound style from Jan Sport is a good design for home craftsmen to copy; it uses fittings (cheap, easy to install, strong, flexible), it is not beyond the average skills of most do-it-yourselfers, and it is adjustable for proper fit. All in all it's an excellent wraparound frame design.

The frame alone is merely one part of the total frame pack; there is still the harness and the bag to consider, both of which are of major importance to the complete system, so don't ignore them. The various harness arrangements and varieties of bags will be covered more thoroughly in the following sections.

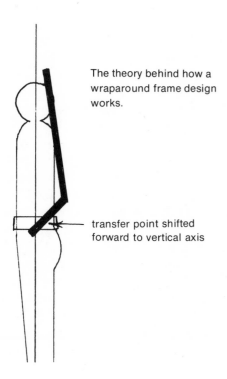

The theory behind how a wraparound frame design works.

transfer point shifted forward to vertical axis

Harnesses

The harness is the part of the pack that joins the camper to his load. An improperly designed or fitted harness can make that load feel awkward, twice as heavy, and painful to carry.

A good pack harness will do several things:

1. It will spread the load over a large area of the backpacker's body, so that

weight will not be concentrated on any one spot. Older designs, without a weight-carrying waist or hip belt, concentrate all of the load on the upper shoulders; the result is sore muscles in the neck and shoulders.

2. It will transmit the load to the carrier in an efficient manner. A heavy load suspended from the shoulders is mechanically inefficient; the carrier must lean forward to support it, causing a rather stooped, unnatural walk, poor posture, and sore muscles in the upper and lower back.

3. It will comfortably hold the pack firmly in place, while still allowing freedom of movement. Some harnesses are too loose, allowing the pack to shift and sway as the hiker walks, which can be annoying. Others are too tight, requiring the wearer to lace them up like a straightjacket, forcing him into a rigid, constricted style of walking.

In general, the harness designs now available commercially seem to do a very good job, if properly fitted to the wearer. Here are some points to consider when choosing or designing a pack harness.

Shoulder Straps. These are usually the most important component of the harness. What they are made of, how they fit, and how they are attached determine the comfort of your harness and of your pack.

Width. The wider the shoulder strap, the more area the load is spread over; 2 inches is a practical minimum for light loads and 3 inches about maximum. For day packs, or any pack restricted to loads under 15 pounds, a good set of shoulder straps can be made from 2-inch nylon seat-belt webbing. For medium loads (15 to 30 pounds), straps made from nylon

fabric stuffed with Ensolite work well. (Details for construction of such straps are included on pages 92–93.) For heavy loads (30 pounds and up), you might make the straps slightly wider. I use 2½-inch-wide straps of Ensolite (type MH) inside a fabric tube for my frame pack shoulder straps and for my larger weekenders.

Length. It is important that the upper shoulder straps do not chafe the armpits when walking. If you make them too short they will. Make your shoulder straps long enough to clear this area, and place the buckles where they will be convenient to operate. This will differ from person to person.

Buckles. I use only the 1-inch tabler buckles with 1-inch nylon webbing in this critical area. The buckles must be nonslip and easy to operate, and nothing I have seen comes close to the tablers.

Attachment. There are several ways to attach shoulder straps to the back of your pack bag or to your pack frame. Each of these designs has its good and bad points. For light loads and frameless designs, the style shown is good. You might sew the straps on lightly (basting) to try for a proper fit, then really tie them down with triple stitching when the proper position is found. If you have any doubts about the strength in this area, be sure to double the fabric under the attaching point. Two layers of Cordura, triple stitched to the straps, will hold.

For attaching shoulder straps to a frame, the most commonly used design is the two-point system as shown. This style is simple to make, provides fairly good comfort, and if extra holes are drilled in the crossbar at the upper attachment points, it

The one-point attachment system for upper shoulder straps; suitable for light loads and frameless designs.

can be adjustable for width. I find 7 inches about right, but this will depend on your build (shoulder muscles, neck size). Use only good quality pins here, and if making your own be especially careful when installing the grommets because they have to take a lot of weight. This is one of the most common failure points on a frame pack (the grommets rip out).

The three-point system for attaching shoulder straps provides slightly more comfort (the straps follow the natural shape of the body where they meet at the back) and a much greater range of adjust-

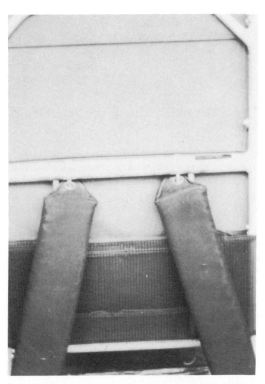

The two-point attachment system; simple, fairly comfortable, the most common way to attach shoulder straps to a frame.

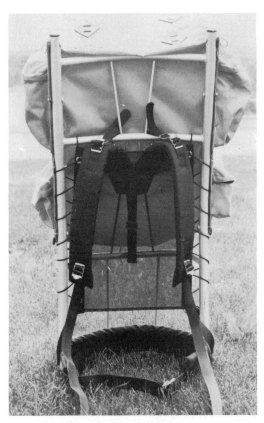

The three-point attachment system; more comfortable, wider range of adjustment for proper fit, may be used for framed and frameless designs. Also, it can be made detachable for convertible bags, and for using your pack bag as hand luggage. Note the lift straps.

ability. This design is suitable for both framed and frameless packs, and it is ideal for a convertible pack bag, designed to be used either way. If you are attaching it to a bag make sure you use a slider at the lower attachment point; the sliders don't dig into your back like a tabler buckle will, and they still allow adjustment and removal of the straps.

The four-point attachment system for shoulder straps is found on quite a few of the best packs, usually framed, and it can also be used for semiframed designs. This style provides the greatest range of adjustments; a quick tug on the proper strap can shift weight to a different set of muscles for a while, providing relief on those long hikes.

With a frame, I prefer the four-point shoulder straps; they are easy to make and provide the ultimate in comfort for those heavy loads. For weekender-size frameless bags I use the three-point system; for my day packs I use the sewn-on style. When attaching shoulder straps to a bag or frame, make sure you take the vertical distance into account. Experiment to find the most comfortable fit.

Waist and Hip Belts. These can be used to take much of the load off those tired shoulders and transfer it to the strong pelvic structure. In addition, a belt holds the pack in the proper place, close to your back, and keeps it from flapping or swaying when you are moving quickly.

There are two types of waist belts—one piece and two piece. The original waist belt used on a frame pack was the Kelty two piece. At the time, the two-piece style was a genuine breakthrough in pack design, but it has its faults. Though there are some who still prefer it, the waist belt

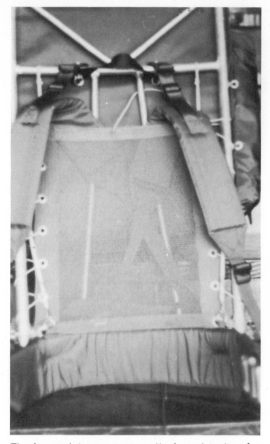

The four-point or crossover attachment system for upper shoulder straps; easier to make than the three point, wider range of adjustability, may be used for framed and semiframed designs. Some people find it the most comfortable, others prefer the simpler designs. It also can be made detachable. Note the lift straps.

most commonly found on quality packs today is of the one-piece design.

Width. For a belt intended merely to hold the pack in place and keep it from swaying, a piece of 1-inch webbing with a tabler buckle on one end can be slipped through a couple of accessory loops sewn on the back of the pack. This gives you a light, simple, detachable waist belt, which

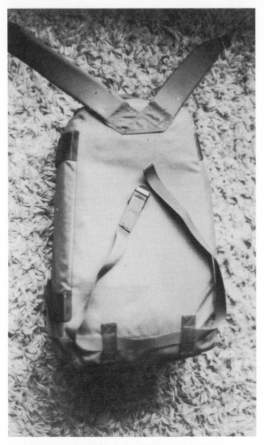

A simple detachable waist belt of webbing.

your breathing), you can use your waist size as the minimum length for your pack belt. The maximum length will depend on the bulk of the clothing between you and the belt. (If you are wearing a parka you will need quite a bit more belt.) Between the minimum and maximum, the buckle should hold the length you set securely and without slipping. A slipping buckle on a waist belt is a major nuisance with a heavy pack. In addition, make sure the buckle used is quick release; if you fall in a river you will wish it was.

Attachment. I prefer to make my belts detachable so that they may be used with convertible designs. If you do this, and use a handle and detachable shoulder straps, you can turn your soft pack or frame pack bag into a convenient piece of hand luggage. I find this feature useful, and it really isn't hard to add on. (See pages 82–83 and 89–91 for details on how to construct and attach waist and hip belts to both frameless and framed designs.)

Lower Shoulder Straps. These fit into the buckle on the end of the upper shoulder straps and attach to the bottom of the bag or frame. I use only 1-inch nylon webbing for my lower shoulder straps, of a type that works well with a tabler buckle (not all webbing will).

Attachment. For light-duty applications many manufacturers simply insert the end of the webbing into the back or side seam near the bottom of the bag. This is then sewn to the seam allowance with one to four rows of stitching. I find this marginally suitable, usable only with the lightest loads and careful handling. This is a common failure point on cheaper day

will be a useful addition to any day pack. For weekenders, or for larger day packs, this belt can be made of 2-inch webbing. The wider 2-inch web will accept some of the load, increasing comfort and capacity. For frame packs and weekenders with heavy loads, the belt should be about 5 inches wide and padded for extra comfort. (See pages 89–91 for details on how to make a padded hip belt, which may be sewn on to the back of a bag, attached with webbing to the frame, or made detachable.)

Length. Since a waist belt should be fairly snug (but not too tight or it cuts off

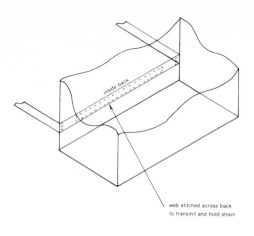

web stitched across back
to transmit and hold strain

A good way to attach lower shoulder straps; the web runs across the inside back of the pack. Any stress on these straps will be transferred to the large sewn seam across the back, instead of being concentrated in a small area.

packs, so there is room for improvements here.

For attaching lower shoulder straps to a frameless bag that will be carrying medium to heavy loads, the system shown will be much stronger. Details for installing such lower shoulder straps are given in Project 4-2. For attaching removable lower shoulder straps to convertible bags, the same trick of sewing the webbing all across the inside of the back can be used. Merely double over the web where it comes through the seam and add a tabler buckle or slider here. This allows the lower straps to be removed for when the bag will be used with a frame or as hand luggage. These web loops should be kept short, or they will flap around and catch on things.

For attaching the lower straps to a frame, the most commonly used system is the one shown. Folding over the end of the webbing under the grommet gives slightly better durability. If making your own be especially careful when installing the

grommets; this is another common failure point with frame packs (the grommets rip out here, too). Always install your lower shoulder straps as low on the frame or bag as possible; this will help the harness transmit the weight to you in an efficient manner. With wraparound frames the same point is usually used to attach the weight-carrying belt and the lower shoulder straps. Many people feel that this is why the wraparound designs pull backwards. You might experiment here by moving the lower shoulder strap attachment point back and see where it feels right for you.

Backbands. These are fabric, webbing, or mesh strips fitted tightly across the frame. They are intended to keep the hard items in the pack away from your back, and to allow air to circulate between the pack and your back, which is very important on a hot day with a heavy pack when you can rub your back raw. These

The usual method of attaching lower shoulder straps to a frame. Watch the grommets here.

backbands must be tight if they are to be effective, so install them that way and adjust periodically as the material stretches.

Since the main idea of a backband is to improve ventilation and comfort, make these bands wide, and make them out of heavy nylon mesh whenever you can; the mesh is usually available through mountain shops as replacement parts for many brands of frame. If you want to add the extra ounces, you can see if a full mesh panel laced across the frame feels right to you. This is the system I prefer. If you use a one-piece waist or hip belt of the wide padded type, you can usually forget about a lower backband altogether. The belt itself seems to do a good job of holding the frame in the proper place.

Bags

A bag designed for a frame pack is generally the largest type available. It will range from 2,000 to 4,000 cubic inches. The most common style, and the one best suited to general backpacking, is the three-quarter length. Leave the full-length bags to those involved with expeditions or really long trips. Get the bag to fit the frame that feels most comfortable to you, or buy it with the matching frame. If you buy the bag separately, make sure that it will fit and mount properly on your frame.

Outside pockets on a pack bag are a major convenience. Internal partitions help separate gear, but restrict the size of item you can stuff in. Both are very important to efficient and convenient loading. Top-loading designs are supposedly more reliable, but the rear-loading designs are much more convenient. Take your choice.

The most commonly used system of attaching the bag to the frame is the pin and grommet design. This involves two flaps inserted into the side seams to take the grommets. This can be done quite easily during construction, and you could also replace or add such a flap on your present bag without too much trouble. Again, if making your own, be careful of the grommet installation; grommets can rip out here also. The more grommets, the stronger the joint; three are a minimum for light loads, four or five are better for heavy loads. Watch the crossbar locations when planning grommet location (you don't want to drill into the crossbars).

A rear-loading frame pack bag design is shown on pages 111–116. I find the rear-loading design far superior for efficient, organized packing, for weathertight protection, and for any other number of good reasons. This is a personal choice; you may have different requirements. My designs specifically stress adaptability, but if you can't find something in this book to use, then you are on your own. If you know enough about backpacking to decide that none of my designs are exactly what you need, then you probably know enough to design your own pack without any help from me. Good luck.

MATERIALS, TOOLS, AND PROCEDURES
FOR PACKS

MATERIALS

Use the best materials you can get—packs must stand up to a lot of abuse. Fortunately the necessary materials are readily available (sometimes you may have to mail order), and the costs are very reasonable compared to the price of a pack you purchase already finished.

Fabrics

A pack is often subject to a lot of abuse on the trail—snagging on branches, carrying heavy loads, scraping on rocks, etc.—so the fabrics used to make a pack must be strong (tear strength, bursting strength) and tough (abrasion resistance). The strongest, toughest fiber in common use today is nylon. In addition, fabrics woven from nylon resist rot and mildew, which makes nylon fabric the best choice. In general, the heavier the fabric, the stronger and tougher it will be. In practice, it has been found that nylon fabric weighing between 7 to 11 ounces per square yard seems to have sufficient strength, without involving unnecessary extra weight. Ultralight (usually cheaper) packs are sometimes made from lighter fabric (right down to 1.9-ounce ripstop) but of course the durability will be decreased.

For all my packs, even the little belt pockets, I use heavy Cordura nylon. Cordura is made from fuzzy discontinuous nylon yarns, and it seems to stand up to abrasion better than ordinary nylon. Cordura nylon is the strongest, toughest, all-around best fabric available for packs. If you can't find it locally, look in the EMS or REI catalogs, or if you want a lot (50 yards or more) inquire from Howe & Bainbridge.

I prefer my packs waterproof, so I use the coated Cordura. This material has only one good side; watch out for that when laying out and sewing. (The coated side should end up on the inside.) If you waterproof all seams and use a zipper flap, your gear will stay reasonably dry even in a canoe.

Thread

If your machine will feed it, nylon thread is the strongest available. Use it, in the largest size that will feed, for ultimate strength. If you can't get the nylon thread to work, try Talon heavy-duty button and canvas thread (from Lightning Fasteners). This is a cotton wrapped/polyester core thread, available from some fabric shops in 70-yard spools. You will need two or three spools for a pack (see Chapter 3 for how to set up your machine to sew with these heavy threads and fabrics).

Webbing

I use quite a bit of webbing in my pack designs. Two-inch automobile seat-belt webbing is available everywhere, and it makes very good waist belts, shoulder straps, and accessory loops. The 1-inch webbing makes excellent accessory straps, loops, and harness straps. I always use nylon webbing; it seems to stand up better than anything else, it is easy to work with, it can usually be sewn by machine, it doesn't rot, and it is strong.

Zippers

I have never had any trouble with the YKK zippers (#10 Delrin), which I use for the main compartment with all my rear-loading designs. For smaller articles and tighter corners I like the YKK nylon coil in sizes 5 to 7. Get them with two sliders, opening from the middle, with closed ends. These are often called luggage-style zippers.

Velcro

Velcro is an excellent material for innovative designing. I use it in place of snaps for detachable pack pocket flaps, and in some places to hold occasional joints (e.g., a partition floor that can be opened up). I use quite a bit of the 1 inch, and occasionally some of the 2 inch. When sewing Velcro that will be exposed, sew the loop section to the outside; otherwise the hooks will snag on everything.

Buckles

I like the 1-inch tabler buckles for quick-release applications such as shoulder straps. They operate simply, smoothly, and they don't slip under the load. For the 2-inch waist belts you will have to scrounge around. The lightest, simplest belt buckle I have found is the Canadian Army plastic style. They are sometimes available in surplus stores for pennies.

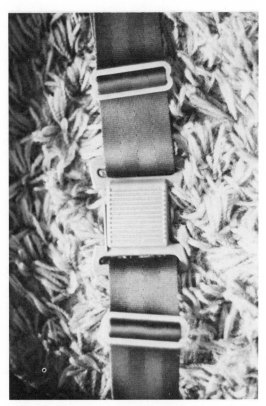

An Army surplus buckle of cast plastic; cheap, light, effective, and quick release.

Frames

For weekender frames there are a great variety of materials and designs that can be used effectively. The system I recommend consists of two simple 1¼ × ⅛-inch aluminum slats sewn into 2-inch web pockets on the back of the pack, and then bent to conform to the wearer's shape. These can be installed permanently, or made removable. If you want slightly more comfort and support, you can attach a third slat at the bottom to form a light, comfortable triangle slat frame.

For a frame pack frame the home builder has problems, unless he has access to high-quality aluminum tubing and welding. The welded aluminum tube frame is undoubtedly the desired frame for a heavily loaded pack, but it is beyond the capability of most home craftsmen. The tubing itself is not too expensive (I pay 60¢ a foot), but the welding costs plenty. If you decide to try one of these frames, get some 1-inch seamless aluminum tubing and have the welder try a few "T" joints. If he does a good job you're in business.

If a welded tube aluminum frame is out of the question, there are alternatives. Five-eights inch 6061-T6, .058 tubing and the inexpensive Jan Sport frame fittings can make up into a nice frame. If tube aluminum is not available, then you can make a pack frame from wood, either bolted or lashed together. These frames are okay for one season, and are light, cheap, and easy to make.

TOOLS

Since a pack is a relatively small item, it can be sewn by hand if necessary. Get a large needle and go. If a machine is available, the job will go faster and easier. Any home sewing machine in good condition should be able to handle the job, though you may have to turn it over by hand for sewing on webbing. Without a machine, an awl or a Speedy Stitcher makes those heavy-duty jobs much easier.

For frame packs you will need a few simple metal working tools such as a hacksaw, a file, and an electric drill. The aluminum tubing can be bent up in a number of ways, but if you can get hold of an electrical contractor's conduit bender for a few hours, you can do the job simply and neatly. These things cost only a few dollars to buy, but they are hard to find. For laying out the packs, a good carpenter's framing square is handy. You will also need a tape measure, a straightedge, and a soft pencil or chalk to mark with. If you will be making several packs, it might be worthwhile to cut out a pattern from cardboard. This will save considerable time on the layout.

PROCEDURES

Familiarize yourself with the various procedures in Chapter 3. Practice with the tools and scraps of materials until you feel your skill is adequate for the job. Set your machine up for the heavy materials that will be used. A good way to do all of these things is to try one of the small, simple belt pockets before you attempt the larger and more difficult packs.

OPTIONS, ACCESSORIES, AND MODIFICATIONS FOR PACKS

You will notice that I have carefully avoided giving out any detailed instructions on how to choose the right pack. I will leave this problem to you; there are far too many personal factors involved for an outsider to be of much real help. Instead of telling you what you need (how would I know?), I am going to offer you several features, options, accessories, and modifications that you can look over and then choose for yourself. These features can be added on to nearly any pack—the one you have now, the one you want to buy, and especially the one you want to make in the future.

I am putting this section before the projects for three reasons: First, if you intend to make one of the projects, the best place to plan for any additions or changes is before you start, not after. Consider these ideas carefully before you make your first pack.

Second, many of the items detailed here are required parts for any completed pack project (for example, a shoulder harness). To avoid needless repetition I do not include plans for shoulder straps with each set of pack plans, but rather give them once, in this section. The same goes for such items as waist belts, accessory straps, and so forth.

Third, many of these items are excellent practice. If you perfect your techniques on a smaller item, the larger items will go together much easier and much better.

An excellent place to look for ideas and features to copy is in your local mountain shops, or in any available backpacking catalogs; there are far more ideas there than I have room for in this one book. And remember, keep it simple. You should be trying for a practical, balanced, coordinated design, not the one pack that has everything. Do not try and stuff too many options or accessories onto one pack or you could end up with a monstrosity.

Accessory Loops

Most decent packs have some provision for strapping extra items onto the outside of the pack. These extras include such things as an ice axe, fishing rod, sleeping bag, and tent. Such accessory loops can provide a real improvement in versatility, usefulness, and capacity, and they are highly recommended for all packs—from the simplest day pack right up to an expedition pack.

Most of the commercially available accessory loops (on finished packs or as separate sew-on accessories) are simple leather squares with two slots cut out. These items have several disadvantages:

1. The quality varies; with cheap leather the slots will rip out.
2. Leather, in thicknesses strong enough to be durable, must be sewn on by a heavy-duty machine or with an awl.
3. They cost too much.

The simple, cheap, durable, easy to attach accessory loops have none of these disadvantages. Using the recommended dimensions, heavy-duty thread, and the stitch pattern recommended means these loops are on permanently, and they are plenty strong. For weight-supporting waist belts and some other heavy-duty applications, use the 2-inch web, and if you wish, you can double the fabric under the loop for extra strength.

These accessory loops can be used in many ways:

1. For ski straps
2. For detachable pack pockets
3. For detachable waist belts
4. For tent or sleeping bag attachment

Accessory Straps

For use with accessory loops, accessory straps provide a simple, convenient, and quick way to attach and remove items from the outside of the pack. With such straps there is no fumbling with knots and no time wasted. The best buckle to use for secure, nonslip, quick-release applications is the tabler style; no other design that I know of is as good, though there are some that are more complicated and more expensive.

Belts

The simple 1-inch web accessory strap makes an ideal waist belt for day packs. Make it detachable rather than sewing it on, since there will be many times such a waist belt will not be used, and the sewn-on belts will dangle down (annoying and potentially dangerous). As discussed earlier, a wide waist belt can help support any heavy pack with greater comfort. For weekenders and some convertible frame packs a simple, non-padded one-piece 2-inch web waist belt is a very desirable option. A surplus 2-inch web belt is ideal. This belt may be made detachable or sewn on, though I highly recommend making it detachable.

For maximum comfort with the heaviest loads a weight-supporting belt should be wider and it should be padded. If you approve of my system for detachable belts, you can make a padded belt that will fit in well. If not, you could easily sew one on, though again I highly recommend the detachable feature. The 2-inch web waist belt slips through the web loops on the belt and on the back of the pack.

For the ultimate in support I prefer the fit of a "conical" hip belt over a simple flat

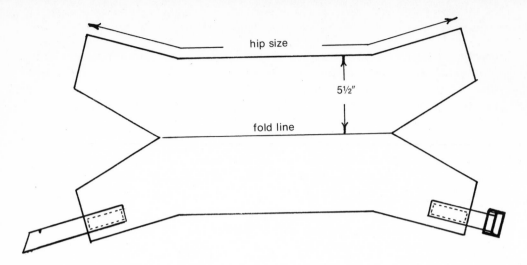

Cutout dimensions for conical hip belt.

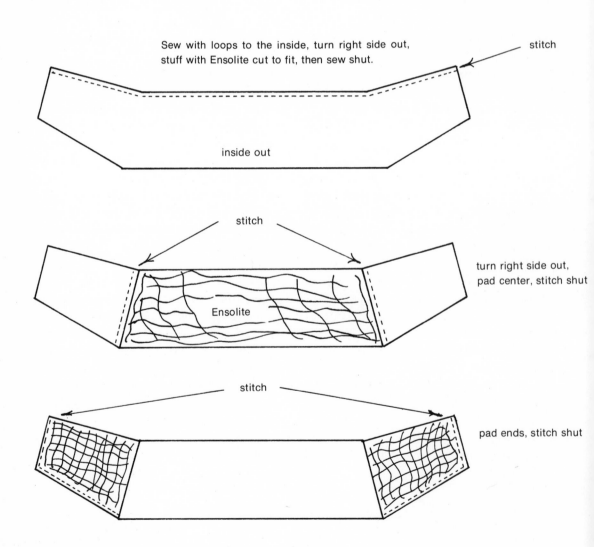

Sew with loops to the inside, turn right side out, stuff with Ensolite cut to fit, then sew shut.

stitch

inside out

stitch

Ensolite

turn right side out, pad center, stitch shut

stitch

pad ends, stitch shut

one. The conical-shaped belts distribute the weight more evenly and more effectively to your hips, which are not flat for most people. To get your belt to fit properly, some tailoring and fitting may be required. This belt is constructed in a very simple manner. You should use three pieces of Ensolite instead of one continuous piece to ensure a good fit at the sides. After stuffing the center compartment, sew it shut. These side seams help the fit. Then stuff and sew the two ends.

For attaching all such belts to a frame, almost any of the commonly used systems may be suitable; check out a few commercial packs for ideas. I like the grommet and pin system since it is easy to install, and provides quick but nonslip adjustment. These grommets may be placed in the web belt, in the web loops of the padded belt, or in both. If you are planning to use such a system, take note of pin placement in the frame and place the grommets and loops to suit.

This system works best for wraparound frames. For standard frames use whatever you like.

Floors

If you use the recommended heavy-duty Cordura, your pack bottom should last a long time. However, for lighter fabrics and heavy-duty applications, a double floor may be desirable. This double floor is sewn to the pack front, bottom, and back before construction, and no other extra work is involved. Sew all accessory loops, etc., to both layers for extra strength, and to prevent the fabric layers from working against each other.

If you are planning a partition, you will need an extra floor above the bottom one. Installing this partition floor must be done properly or else you will find yourself unable to turn the pack right side out or inside out, as the construction sequence may require. For an example of a pack with a partition floor, see Project 4-3 for complete details. Note that such a floor can be made detachable by using Velcro to hold it in place on three sides.

Handles

A simple but useful handle can be made from 2-inch webbing. Since such a handle will be supporting the entire weight of the pack, you should double the fabric under it and sew with heavy-duty thread and double stitching. A simple handle for light-duty applications (such as the ends of ditty bags) can be made from 1-inch webbing.

Partitions and Pockets

I usually make all of my exterior pockets detachable. (For details see pages 94–97.) Sewn-on pockets can be made to fit specific gear. They often have Velcro for the closure, which makes them simple, neat, and effective.

Partitions are simply internal pockets, so you can keep your gear in place inside your pack. Obviously, if you have a partition, you are going to need some way of getting gear in and out of it. This means an opening, usually secured by a zipper, in either the straight or arched designs. The arched design gives better access, but the straight design is easier to install. Both should have a flap over them to seal out rain and dust.

Shoulder Straps

Every pack will need some kind of shoulder straps. These can be as simple (2-inch web, sewn on) or as complicated (padded, detachable, fully adjustable) as you desire. They can be any one of the many designs currently available; check out the stores and catalogs for ideas. I give details for a few representative types, but there are many, many more.

The simplest shoulder straps to make and install are 2-inch seat-belt webbing with two tabler buckles attached to the ends. This is merely sewn on to the back of

Sew the fabric into a tube, good side to the inside, ½-inch seam allowance.

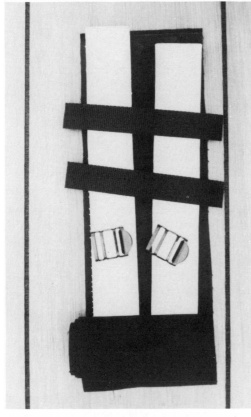

All that you need to make padded shoulder straps:
Ensolite—12 × 2 × ⅜ inches, for padding
Web—12 inches of 1-inch-wide web, for attaching buckles to straps
Buckles—two 1-inch tabler buckles
Fabric—5¾ × 34 inches, for tube

the pack. Use double or triple stitching, heavy-duty thread, and perhaps double the cloth under the stitching for extra strength. Padded shoulder straps require extra time and effort, but are well worth it for long hikes and heavy loads. My design for sewn-on padded straps is shown. First, sew a tube up from the fabric. Try the Ensolite for fit; it should be snug, but not too snug or you will have difficulty getting it in. Now turn the fabric tube right side out, to give you a finished seam. Slide the two pieces of Ensolite inside the tube. Fold the tube into a taper at one end and sew it shut. Force one piece of Ensolite tight against this closed end and sew across the tube where the Ensolite ends. Fold the

Fold and sew a taper at one end; 2½ inches is about right.

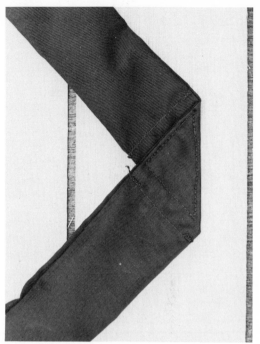

Fold the tube over at approximately a right angle, stitch Ensolite in place.

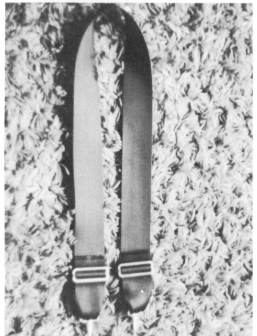

Taper other end, attach tabler buckles as shown.

tube over and stitch. Trim to length if necessary, then taper the other end. Sew on two tabler buckles to the tapered ends. Sew the finished padded shoulder straps to the back of the pack as detailed for web shoulder straps.

For duffel bags and fair-sized shoulder bags a 2-inch web strap with snaps on both ends will often come in handy. Install two "D" rings onto the item to be carried. Then such a shoulder strap can be snapped on and off your pack very easily and very quickly.

Lower shoulder straps can be installed in a number of ways, usually in the side seam. I prefer the method detailed in the Fresh Air Day Pack project.

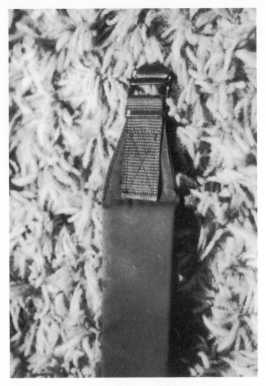

The shoulder straps shown will be easiest to make and attach to a frame pack. Make two, 12 to 14 inches long at the padded part, and be especially careful when setting the grommets.

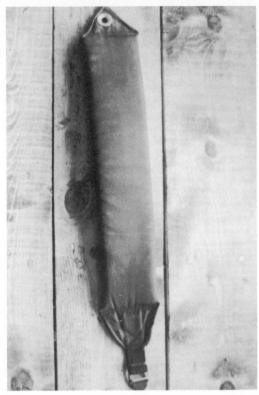

Two 2-inch sliders, two 1-inch snap hooks, and some 2-inch webbing make up into a useful shoulder strap.

PROJECT 4-1: POCKET FOR BELT (OR PACK)

Length—8 inches
Width—6 inches
Depth—3 inches
Weight—3 ounces
Capacity—Volume: 140 cubic inches
— Weight: less than 4 pounds

Design

This is an extremely useful item, and is a perfect project to practice on before undertaking one of the more complicated packs. The basic design and the construction techniques used are very similar to the much larger, more difficult packs. If you wish, you can make your belt pocket detachable and use it as a pack pocket, or you can use it strictly as a belt pack for short hikes or skiing. You can make several and use them as cases for such things as survival kits, first-aid kits, toilet kits, cameras, etc. This way you organize your gear into convenient little bundles that may be kept inside the pack, on your belt, or outside your pack, as the situation demands. Only the detachable pockets may be used as pack pockets, so this option is one that I recommend both for its usefulness and its convenience.

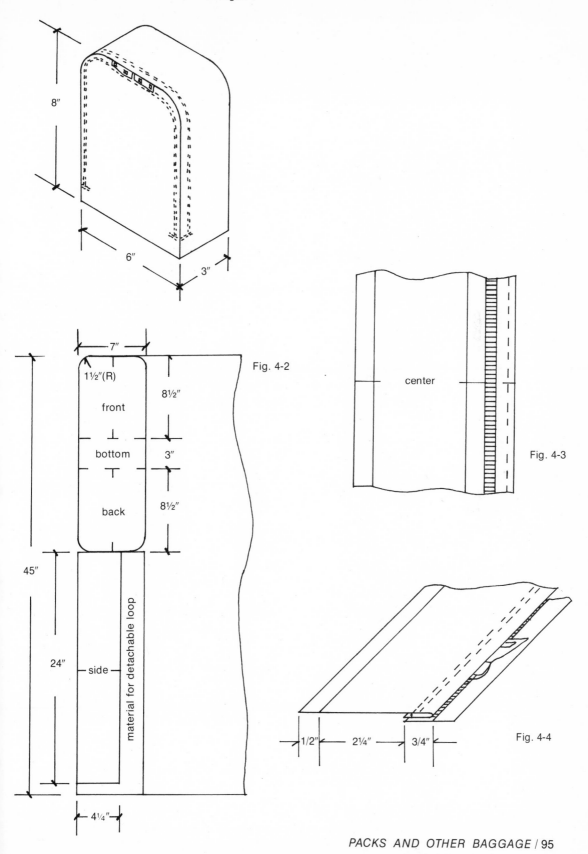

Fig. 4-1

8″

6″

3″

Fig. 4-2

7″

1½″(R)

front

8½″

bottom

3″

back

8½″

45″

material for detachable loop

24″

side

4¼″

Fig. 4-3

center

Fig. 4-4

1/2″   2¼″   3/4″

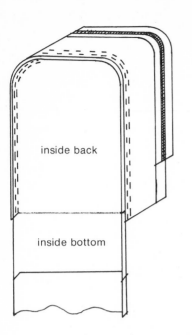

Fig. 4-5

inside back

inside bottom

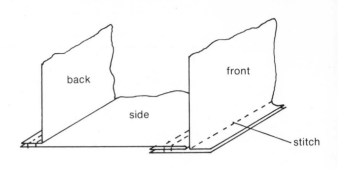

Fig. 4-6

back

front

side

stitch

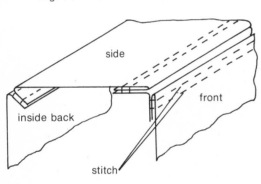

Fig. 4-7

side

inside back

front

stitch

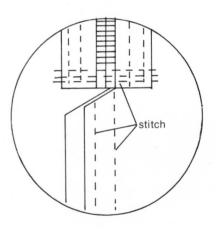

Fig. 4-8

stitch

Fig. 4-9

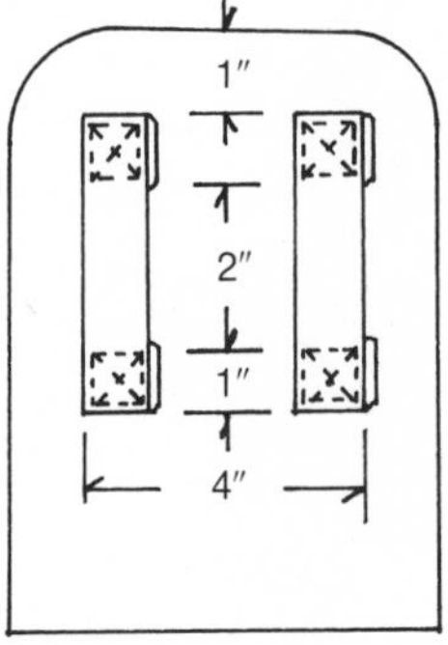

1"

2"

1"

4"

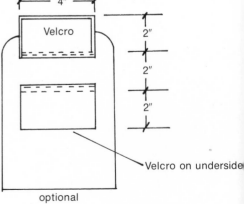

4"

Velcro

2"

2"

2"

Velcro on underside

optional

Fig. 4-10

Materials

Fabric. You can make this item out of any sturdy fabric because it doesn't carry much weight. However, if it is to be used as a pack pocket, I suggest you use the same material you will use for the pack. Cordura nylon is ideal: it's strong, tough, attractive, and easy to work with. You will need about 7 inches of 45-inch-wide material. If you make the web belt loops, you will need 12 inches of 1-inch-wide nylon webbing. If you choose to make the highly recommended optional detachable belt loops, you will need 4 inches of 2-inch-wide Velcro (both sides). You should be able to piece together a flap arrangement from the wastage.

You will also need an 18-inch zipper. I recommend a coil type (tight corners here), size #5 or #7. Either a single-slider type or one with two sliders can be used.

Construction

1. Lay out the pieces on the fabric. Fig. 4-2 gives a good layout for 45-inch-wide cloth, but you can piece it together from remnants if you want. Make alignment marks to help you when sewing.

2. Cut out all pieces and flame seal all fabric edges and webbing ends.

3. Mark the middle of the zipper's length and pin it to the edge of the side strip. Take care that it is centered and that both the good side of the fabric and the zipper pulls will end up on the outside when the zipper flap is completed. Sew the zipper on with one row of stitching, and be careful not to stitch too close to the teeth or the slider may bind. Fig. 4-3.

4. Fold over about ¾ inch of fabric to make a zipper flap. Pin and sew as in Fig. 4-4.

5. With the side and the back/bottom/front inside out, pin and sew the side to the back. Be especially careful around the curves. Fig. 4-5.

6. With the item inside out, pin and sew the exposed edge of the zipper tape to the front. Fig. 4-6.

7. Turn the item right side out, and pin and sew a finished zipper seam. Fig. 4-7.

8. With the item inside out, pin and sew the remaining portion of the front side seam under the zipper ends. Fig. 4-8. Sew shut the bottom side seams and reinforce the corners with extra stitching.

9. With the item right side out sew across the zipper ends at the bottoms. Use a tight zigzag or several rows of stitching (watch out for the zipper stops). Fig. 4-8.

10. Sew on web belt loops, as in Fig. 4-9, or if you wish to use the pocket as a pack pocket, sew on the detachable belt loop shown in Fig. 4-10. You should be able to piece together the flaps from the excess material. Use four pieces 4½ × 2¾ inches. Double them up rough side out, sew around three edges, and turn inside out to give you two flaps, 4 × 2½ inches, which have finished edges. Sew the Velcro to the flaps, and sew the flaps down securely with two rows of stitching.

11. Inspect for any rough spots, flame seal any exposed edges, and correct any stitching that is weak.

Length—17½ inches

Width—12 inches tapering to 8 inches at top

Depth—6 inches

Weight—14 ounces

Capacity—Volume: 1,000 cubic inches
        —Weight: less than 15 pounds

Design

This is a simple design that is easy for the beginner to sew. The back-bottom-front is one piece, which eliminates a potential weak spot along the bottom seam, and which also eases construction considerably. The seams along the front, back, and sides help the pack retain the tapered, rectangular shape even when overstuffed. Because of the tapered shape, the simple design, and the large zippered opening, you will find this pack comfortable, efficient, rugged, and easy to use. It will serve you well as a day bag for camping, or as a convenient and comfortable all-purpose tote bag for groceries or books. With the proper modifications, it can be adapted for specialized uses such as mountaineering or ski touring.

Following the given plans and dimensions will give you a versatile and comfortable pack, suitable for light loads and any size camper. It will conveniently carry enough gear for spartan overnighting. For longer trips and bulkier loads, the sleeping bag or some other bulky item may be carried outside the pack, nearly doubling its capacity (volume). When used for general hauling, day trips, or overnighting, it will be the best design for most people. This pack is probably the best first pack you can own. Later on, if you move up to a larger pack, you will still find it a useful accessory.

Recommended Options

The simple day pack design presented will adequately serve most people, but the basic design can be improved considerably with little effort. This particular design is especially suitable for modification or the addition of useful accessories. The most desirable options are padded shoulder straps, sleeping bag loops, and removable waist belt. See the section on "Options, Accessories, and Modifications" for a more detailed list of changes that you can easily make to this simple but versatile Fresh Air Day Pack.

Materials

Fabric. The recommended fabric is 8- to 10-ounce coated nylon Cordura. Material as light as 6 ounces may be used by doubling the bottom and reinforcing all points of stress, but unless you use sturdy materials you are really wasting your labor. Packs are subject to a lot of abuse; if you want your pack to last more than a few seasons, use the Cordura. Suitable fabrics are usually sold in 45-inch widths. A minimum of 21×45 inches is needed, but you might want to buy more than the minimum given (36×45 inches is about right) to allow for mistakes, or whatever options you will be adding.

Webbing. Web shoulder straps require 36 inches of 2-inch-wide webbing. Nylon seat-belt webbing is ideal, but if you wish, you can make the straps from a strip of fabric that is doubled over several times

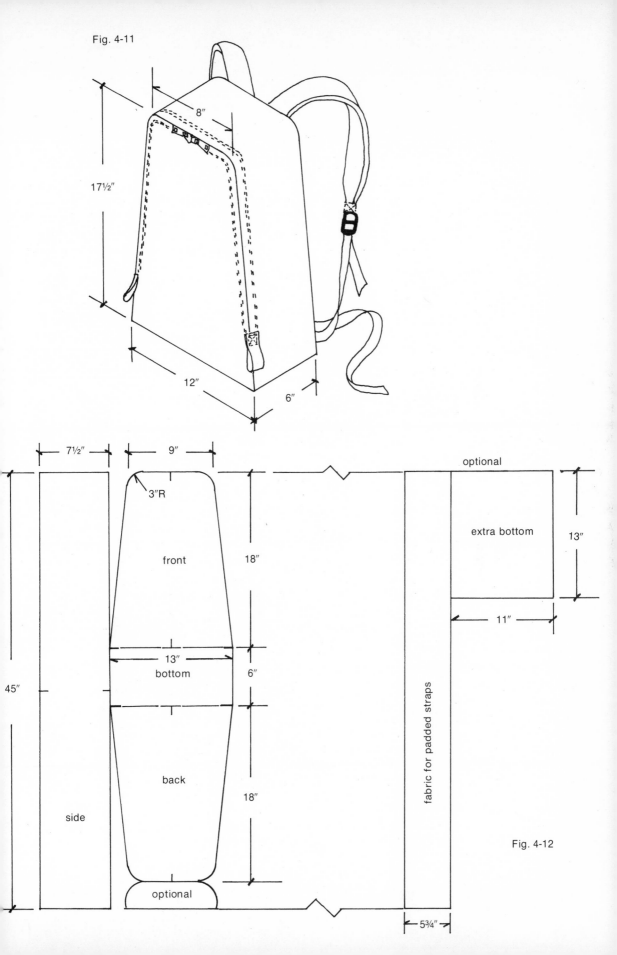

Fig. 4-11

8″

17½″

12″

6″

7½″   9″

3″R

front   18″

13″

bottom   6″

45″

back   18″

side

optional

optional

extra bottom   13″

11″

fabric for padded straps

5¾″

Fig. 4-12

Fig. 4-13

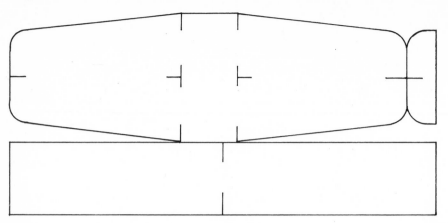

Fig. 4-14

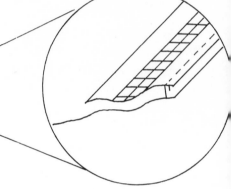

center

Fig. 4-15

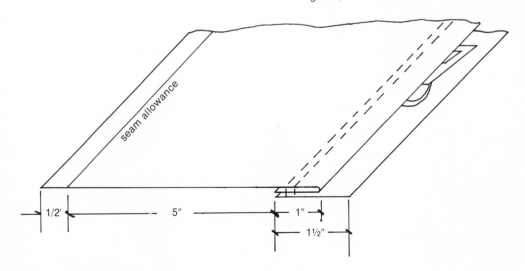

seam allowance

1/2'   5"   1"

1½"

Fig. 4-16

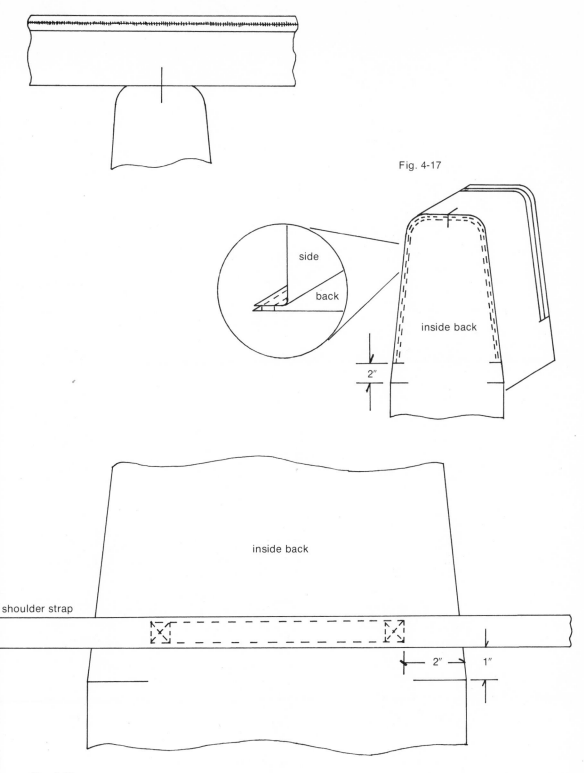

Fig. 4-17

side

back

inside back

2"

inside back

shoulder strap

2" 1"

Fig. 4-18

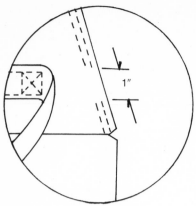

Fig. 4-19

1"

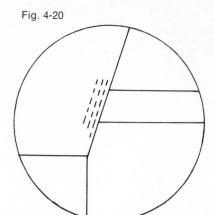

Fig. 4-20

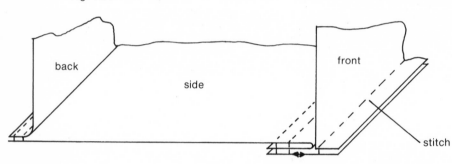

Fig. 4-21

back

side

front

stitch

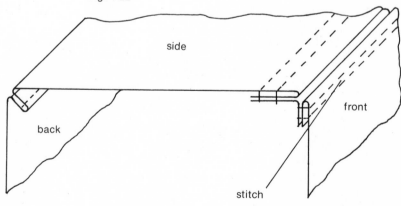

Fig. 4-22

side

back

front

stitch

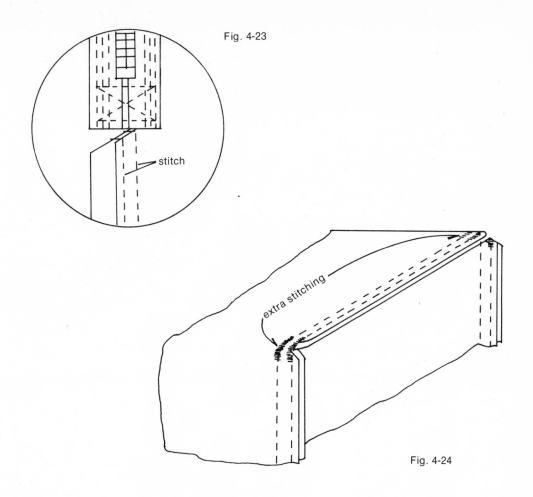

Fig. 4-23

stitch

extra stitching

Fig. 4-24

Fig. 4-25

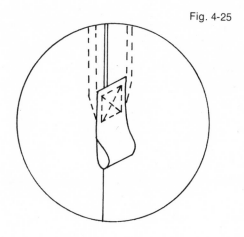

Fig. 4-26

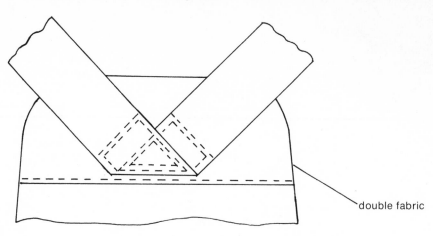

double fabric

Fig. 4-27

front edge

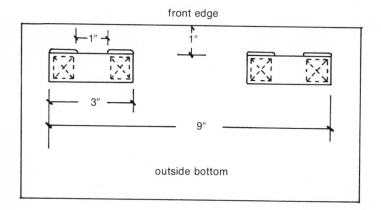

outside bottom

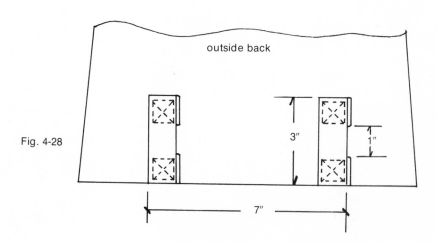

outside back

Fig. 4-28

and sewn. If you decide to make the recommended optional padded shoulder straps, you will need fabric and Ensolite instead of the 2-inch-wide web. You will also need 60 inches of 1-inch-wide nylon webbing for the lower shoulder straps, 60 inches of 1-inch webbing for the waist belt, and 36 inches of 1-inch webbing for the zipper pull tabs, sleeping bag loops, and to attach the buckles to the upper shoulder straps.

Hardware. Two buckles are needed for the shoulder straps and one for the waist belt. They should be of good quality, of the tabler or quick-release style. This design requires one 30- to 36-inch zipper. Get a #10 Delrin or nylon-coil zipper with two sliders, closed at both ends.

Options, Accessories, and Modifications. Each requires its own materials. Be sure to consider these accessories and modifications when calculating material amounts.

Construction

1. Study the section on "Options, Accessories and Modifications" and consider their suitability. If you are adding or modifying something, do so at the proper stage of construction rather than trying to change things later. Read Chapter 3 and make sure you understand the procedures and are familiar with the tools you will be using. Carefully read the following instructions, and make sure you clearly understand each stage of the construction before you begin.

2. Lay out the pieces on the fabric. See Chapter 3, "Procedures" for advice on layout. Try to minimize waste and be careful; mistakes here show up later. Make

alignment marks to aid in construction where shown in Fig. 4-13. Fig. 4-12 shows a good layout for this pack but there are others.

3. Cut out all pieces, collect all hardware, webbing, etc. Flame seal all fabric edges and webbing ends. (See Chapter 3, "Procedures.")

4. Sew on the optional shoulder strap reinforcing piece, and the two sleeping bag loops. Figs. 4-26 and 4-27.

5. Mark the middle of the zipper's length and pin it to the edge of the side strip. Take care that it is centered, and that the good side of the fabric and the zipper pulls will both be to the outside when the zipper flap is completed. Sew the zipper to the edge of the fabric with a single row of stitches. Be careful not to stitch too close to the zipper teeth or the stitching may bind the zipper slider. Fig. 4-14.

6. Fold over about 1 inch of fabric to make a zipper flap as shown in Fig. 4-15. Pin it and sew it down with two or three rows of stitching. Again, don't sew too close to the zipper teeth.

7. Turn your pieces inside out. Using your alignment marks, Fig. 4-16, pin the back to the side. Start pinning from the top and work your way down both sides until you are 2 inches from the bottom. Try to make the sides even at the bottom seams. Starting 2 inches from the bottom, sew up the back side seam. Use two or three rows of stitching and be especially careful to avoid wrinkles when sewing around the curves at the upper back/side corners. Fig. 4-17.

8. Sew the bottom shoulder straps to the inside of the back. Leave 2 inches at each side free from stitching or you will have trouble with the seam where it passes over the straps. Fig. 4-18. If you want the optional waist belt, sew the belt loops to

the outside of the back as shown in Fig. 4-28.

9. Leaving a 1-inch gap for the bottom shoulder straps to fit through the seam, finish the back side seams to the bottom back side corner. Fig. 4-19.

10. Insert the bottom shoulder straps through the gap in the back side seam. Close the gap by sewing three or four rows of stitches through the fabric and the webbing as in Fig. 4-20. If the webbing is pulled tight while sewing, the stress on these straps will be transferred to the strong seam extending across the back, rather than being concentrated at the back side seam.

11. With the pack inside out, pin the exposed edge of the zipper tape to the front of the pack as in Fig. 4-21. Make sure the zipper is installed properly, with the zipper pulls to the outside when the pack is right side out. Use the alignment marks on the zipper and the fabric to ensure that the zipper is centered along the front. Taking care not to sew into the zipper flap, sew the zipper tape to the front with a single row of stitches.

12. With the pack right side out, pin the fabric, folded over to the zipper tape. You may have to trim small wedge-shaped sections out of the tape-fabric around the top corners to allow the fabric to take this curve smoothly (see Chapter 3, "Procedures"). With the zipper open, sew the fabric to the zipper tape with two or three rows of stitching to give you a finished zipper seam. Fig. 4-22.

13. Cut the fabric under the two zipper ends as shown in Fig. 4-23. Pin and sew the remaining front side seam below the zipper ends to the bottom front side corner. Trim off the excess seam allowance and notch the corners as described in Chapter 3, "Procedures."

14. Pin the bottom side seam. Make sure the sides line up properly with the bottom. Sew the bottom side seam with two or three rows of stitching and reinforce the corners as shown in Fig. 4-24. Be careful here; the bottom seams and the corners are subject to a lot of stress. This is the most common area of failure.

15. Turn the pack right side out. You should now have a unit that is completely enclosed, except for small gaps just below the two zipper ends. With the zipper open, sew on the two web zipper pull tabs below the zipper ends as in Fig. 4-25. Try to close up any gaps in this area.

16. Make up whichever shoulder strap arrangement you prefer and attach it to the back of the pack. Fig. 4-26. Information on shoulder straps and shoulder strap attachment can be found on pages 80–82, 83–84, 92–93, and 94.

17. Carefully inspect the entire product. Make sure all cut edges are flame sealed, that all seams are straight with no weak spots, and correct any mistakes or rough spots. Test the pack by loading it and subjecting it to a few minutes of abuse. It is better to discover and correct any weak spots or mistakes now, rather than later on the trail.

PROJECT 4-3: FREEDOM WEEKENDER PACK

Length—24 inches (vary to suit your build)

Width—Bottom 14 inches, tapering to 10 inches at the top

Depth—7 inches

Weight—2 pounds, 12 ounces (without frame or extra pockets)

Capacity—Volume: 2,000 cubic inches
—Weight: less than 30 pounds

Design

A weekender pack is designed to carry fairly heavy loads, with a minimum of pack weight or bulk. This design is very similar to the day pack design given in Project 4-2, but it has been scaled up, and several important modifications have been made to improve handling with the increased loads. See the section on "Design Considerations for Packs," for a more extensive treatment of these modifications.

The given design is for a simple frameless weekender pack, suitable for general backpacking. It's extremely easy to make. If you want a pack for some specialized activity, then a more specialized, more sophisticated design could be used, or the design given could be modified further to make it more suitable. This design is very adaptable, and the additions recommended in the following list can improve it considerably. Take some time before starting this project to think about options, accessories, and modifications; with weekender packs, the accessories can make all the difference.

Recommended Options

1. Detachable pockets (these items add extra capacity and versatility far beyond the effort involved in including them); see Project 4-1.
2. Double floor.
3. Arched insert zipper for lower compartment (improves access to lower compartment).
4. Simple stay frame.

Materials

Fabric. The recommended fabric for this project is 8- to 10-ounce coated Cordura nylon. Lighter fabrics are not advisable here as weekender packs must be able to take a lot of abuse. You will need about 60 inches of 45-inch-wide fabric.

Hardware. You will need two 1-inch tabler buckles for the shoulder straps, and a 2-inch buckle for the waist/hip belt. You will also need a 30- to 36-inch double slider zipper for the back, and a 14-inch zipper for the bottom compartment access. I use a #10 Delrin zipper for the back, and a #5 Delrin zipper for the compartment. If using an arched compartment access opening, the nylon-coil zippers work better around curves.

Webbing. You will need about 96 inches of 1-inch-wide webbing for this pack. I have included a little extra to allow for accessory tie loops, etc. With this pack, the shoulder straps and waist/hip belt should definitely be padded. You will need sufficient Ensolite to stuff the shoulder straps and belt. Buy an Ensolite sleeping bag

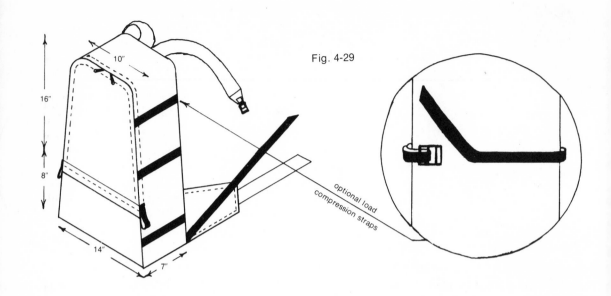

Fig. 4-29

optional load
compression straps

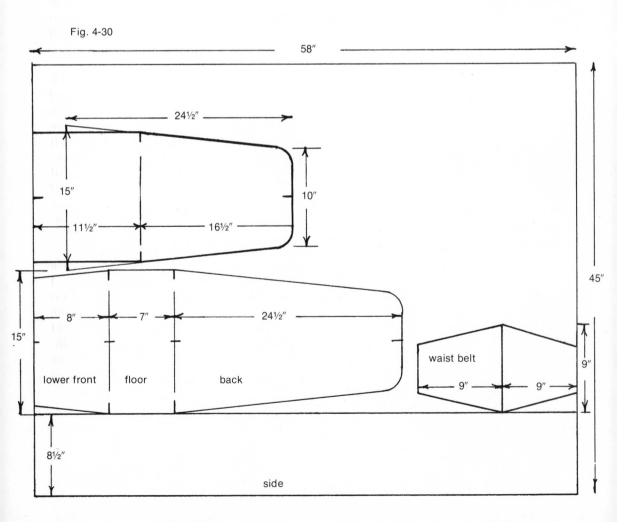

Fig. 4-30

58″

24½″

15″

10″

11½″

16½″

15″

8″   7″   24½″

lower front   floor   back

waist belt

9″   9″

45″

9″

8½″

side

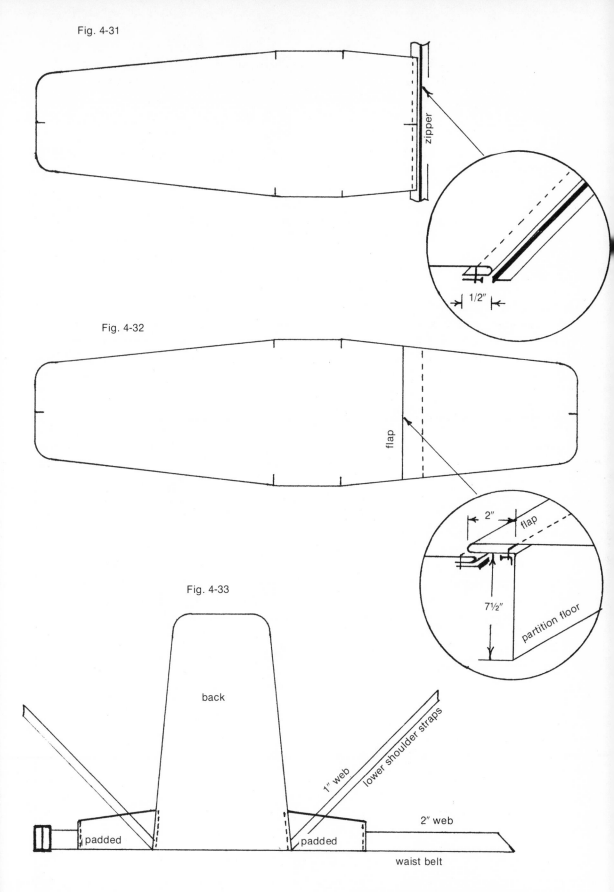

Fig. 4-31

zipper

1/2″

Fig. 4-32

flap

2″

flap

7½″

partition floor

Fig. 4-33

back

1″ web

lower shoulder straps

2″ web

padded

padded

waist belt

pad, and trim off the needed amounts from it (most such pads are too large anyhow). You will also need a length of 2-inch-wide seat-belt webbing to finish off your waist belt. The amount needed will vary with the belt design used.

Remember, options, accessories, and modifications will require extra materials; be sure to consider them when computing material amounts.

Construction

1. Definitely read up on design, options, and accessories before starting this project. If you are adding or changing something, try to work it into the construction sequence without disruption. Read Chapter 3, make sure you are familiar with the materials, tools, and procedures you will use, and read through these instructions to make sure you understand them completely before starting.

2. Since the design and fabrication of this pack are almost identical with those of the simpler day pack (Project 4-2), the day pack project is an excellent warm-up for this one. The main differences are: (a) the weekender pack has a simple compartment built in; (b) the weekender pack has a built-in, padded waist belt; (c) padded shoulder straps are standard with the weekender, and optional for the day pack.

3. Lay out the pieces on the fabric. There should be some extra fabric for pockets or a double floor if you are careful here. Make alignment marks to aid in construction. Fig. 4-30 shows a good layout.

4. Cut out all pieces, collect all hardware, webbing, etc. Flame seal the edges of the fabric, and the ends of the webbing.

5. Pin and sew the lower compartment access zipper to the edge of the back piece as shown. Fig. 4-31.

6. Pin and sew the other side of the lower compartment zipper to the front piece as shown. Fig. 4-32. You should have a 2-inch flap over the zipper, and the front and the back should match up evenly. Trim zipper ends to size, remove teeth for ⅝ inch from edges.

7. Turn back to Project 4-2, step 5. From here on identical construction procedures are used. Take care when sewing the side to the front that you do not sew into the upper compartment floor accidentally. Sew the compartment floor to the back with several rows of stitching only after all other construction is finished. Sewing in the compartment floor will prevent you from turning the pack inside out, so leave it until last. Fig. 4-33 shows how to attach the two-piece padded waist belt by sewing it in the back side seam. If using the two-piece padded belt shown, make sure you install the lower shoulder straps before stitching this area.

PROJECT 4-4: REAR-LOADING FRAME PACK BAG

Length—22 inches
Width—16 inches
Depth—8 inches
Weight—1 pound, 8 ounces (without frame or extra pockets)
Capacity—Volume: 2,800 cubic inches
—Weight: 40 pounds (or whatever you can carry)

Design

I favor rear-loading frame pack bags; if you prefer a top-loading design, you'll have to take a few minutes and work out a set of plans for one on your own.

The rear-loading design is remarkably convenient to use; that large flap folds down and out of the way for efficient loading and unloading. There is no struggling with layers of other gear on top of the desired item; whatever you want is readily accessible. I also find a zippered closure more weatherproof and more secure (no equipment dribbling out) than a flap.

The only valid criticism against the rear loader is that some designs feature several small compartments, which limits what and how you carry. This is no problem with a large single-compartment design, as given here. In fact, you could even add a lower compartment with removable or sewn-in floor to this design without encountering that particular problem.

The other major argument against rear loaders is based on speculations that they are less reliable than top loaders. In theory this may be true (and I, like anyone else, shudder at the thought of a zipper coming loose and leaking my gear all over the last day's trail), but in practice, in four years of making rear-loading bags for myself, and on a custom basis for others, I have never seen even one case of zipper failure. I am speaking now of #10 YKK Delrin zippers; these are the only ones I use here, and the only ones I have had experience with.

I trust these zippers completely, but if you have reservations, you can install straps across the back flap. Many commercial rear loaders now have these straps (I think more for psychological reasons than for security); however, such straps do come in very handy for adjusting your pack to fit larger or smaller than normal loads. If you are going to use these straps, make sure you use quick-release fittings that hold securely and won't slip. My favorite is the tabler-style buckles with 1-inch web. To add these "load-control straps" (that's what Jan Sport calls them), merely insert them into the rear side seam when sewing. Fig. 4-34.

You will notice that this pack is essentially a giant-size version of the detachable belt pack/pack pocket detailed in Project 4-1. The frame pack bag was purposely designed to be as simple as possible to construct, so no pockets are included. Of course, you could sew on pockets during construction, or you could make the pack to take detachable side, back, and top pockets. Fig. 4-35 shows an interesting method of attaching removable pockets that I also use on my packs.

Materials

Sixty inches of 45-inch-wide heavy (8- to 10-ounce) coated Cordura nylon is needed for this project. This will leave you plenty for pockets, straps, and other accessories. You will also need a 44- to

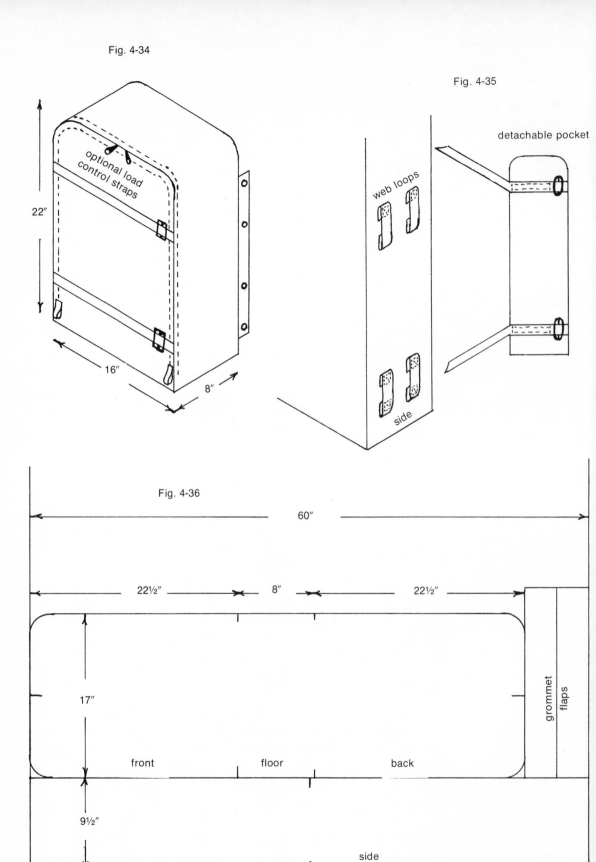

Fig. 4-34

Fig. 4-35

optional load
control straps

22″

16″

8″

web loops

detachable pocket

side

Fig. 4-36

60″

22½″

8″

22½″

17″

grommet

flaps

9½″

front

floor

back

side

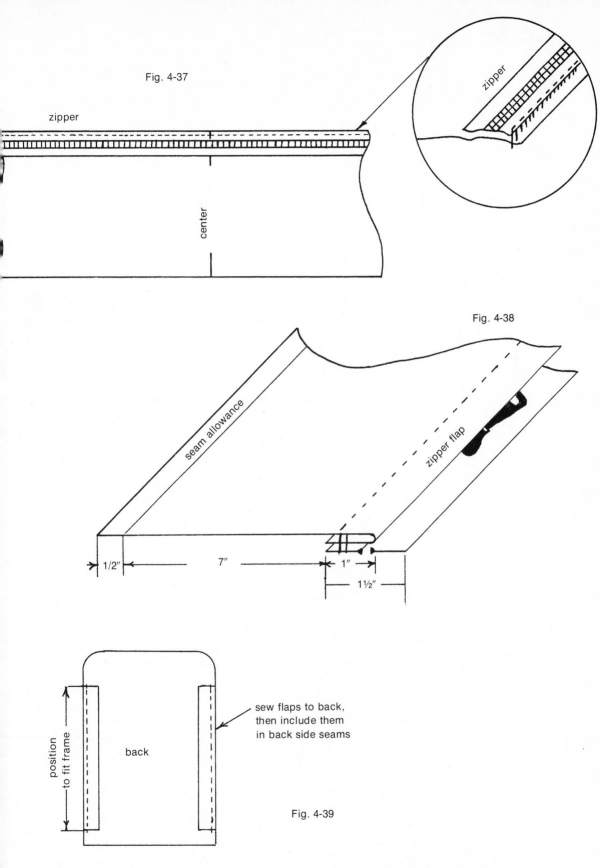

Fig. 4-37

zipper

center

zipper

Fig. 4-38

seam allowance

zipper flap

1/2″   7″   1″

1½″

position
to fit frame

back

sew flaps to back,
then include them
in back side seams

Fig. 4-39

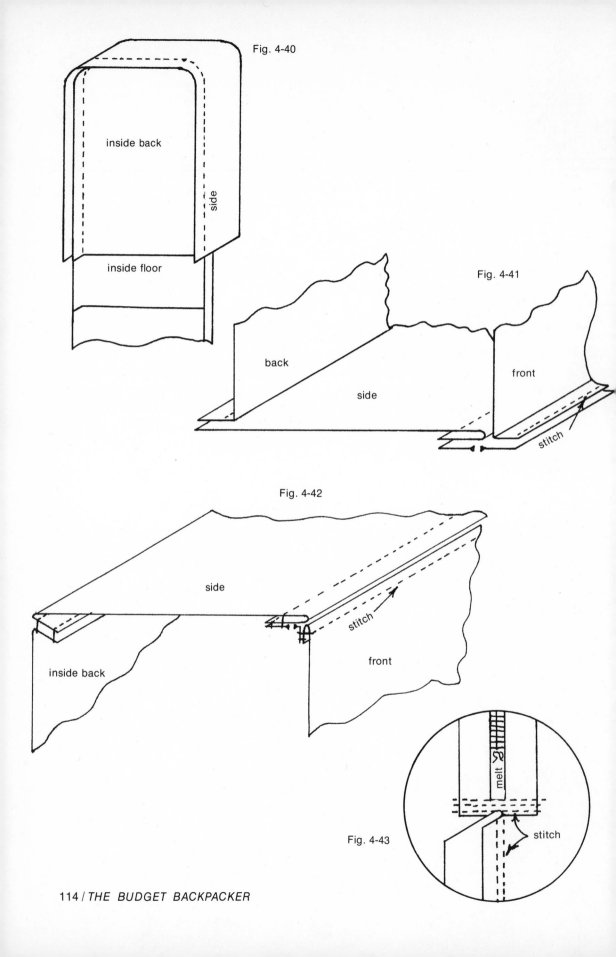

Fig. 4-40

inside back

side

inside floor

Fig. 4-41

back

side

front

stitch

Fig. 4-42

side

stitch

inside back

front

melt

stitch

Fig. 4-43

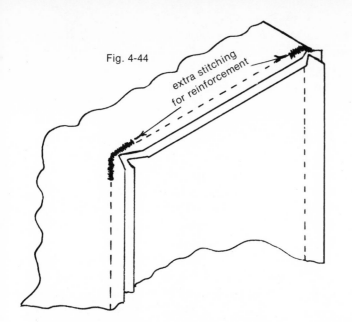

Fig. 4-44

extra stitching for reinforcement

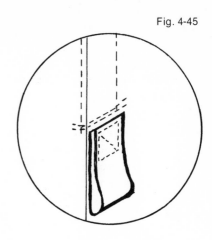

Fig. 4-45

48-inch #10 Delrin zipper with two sliders, and about a dozen grommets. If you don't want to bother with setting grommets, your local tarp repair will do it for a few dollars.

Construction

1. This is a very easy project; even a beginner should be able to turn out a good pack with little trouble. Read Chapter 3 on the materials, tools, and procedures you will be using, and practice with them. The best way to practice would be to make a belt pack/pack pocket (see Project 4-1 for detailed instructions).

2. Lay out the pieces on the fabric; Fig. 4-36 gives one way of doing it. Make alignment marks to aid you in putting your pack together.

3. Cut out all pieces, flame seal all fabric edges.

4. Mark the middle of the zipper's length, center it on the edge of the side piece, pin, sew with a single row of stitches. Take care that the good side of the fabric and the zipper pulls will both end up on the outside when the zipper flap is completed, and make sure you don't sew too close to the zipper teeth or the stitching might bind the slider. Fig. 4-37.

5. Fold over 1 inch of fabric to give you a zipper flap, pin, sew with two rows of stitches. Fig. 4-38.

6. Fig. 4-39 shows the grommet flaps used to attach the bag to the frame. These flaps may have to be modified (shortened or shifted) to fit different frames. The main things to consider here are grommet placement (determined by the holes and pins in the frame) and where you want the pack to ride on the frame. To make the flaps, fold a strip of cloth lengthwise, rough side out, and sew across the ends. Turn right side out for finished edges on flap, sew in place. Fig. 4-39.

7. Turn your pieces inside out. Using your alignment marks, center the side and the back at the top, pin, and sew. Try to make the sides even at the bottom seams, and take care when sewing around the curves at the upper corners. Fig. 4-40.

8. With the pack inside out, pin the exposed edge of the zipper tape to the front

of the pack as shown, Fig. 4-41. Make sure the zipper is installed properly, with the zipper pulls to the outside when the pack is right side out. Taking care not to sew into the zipper flap, sew the zipper tape to the front with a single row of stitches.

9. With the pack right side out, fold the fabric at the front, and pin to the zipper tape. You may have to trim small wedge-shaped portions out of the tape/fabric around the corners to make them smooth. With the zipper open, sew the fabric to the zipper tape with two rows of stitches. This gives you a finished zipper seam. Fig. 4-42.

10. Cut the fabric under the zipper ends as shown in Fig. 4-43. Pin and sew the remaining front side seam under the zipper ends to the bottom front side corner.

Notch the corners (for details, see Chapter 3, "Procedures").

11. Pin the bottom side seams. Make sure the sides line up properly with the bottom. Sew the bottom side seams with two rows of stitches, and reinforce the corners with extra stitching. Fig. 4-44.

12. Finish the pack by sewing zipper pull tabs of web or leather over the small gaps just below the zipper ends. Fig. 4-45.

13. Install grommets (see step 6) to match location of holes and pins in frame.

14. Inspect the finished pack for loose or crooked stitching, and any cut edges that were not properly flame sealed. Correct any mistakes, load the pack up, attach to frame, and shake it around for a few seconds to make sure the grommets and stitching won't fail.

PROJECT 4-5: FRAMES; TRIANGULAR STAY, FLEXIBLE TUBE, WRAPAROUND

Design

The advantages of having a frame are many, and are discussed thoroughly in the section on "Design Considerations for Packs." Here are plans for four different types of frames, one of which should be adaptable to your needs.

Triangular Stay Frame

This type of frame is one of the lightest, most compact designs around, and it is very easy to make at home. I find this frame ideal for weekender packs, but you might also use it on a rectangular frame pack bag to make it convertible. Fig. 4-46 gives the details. The entire frame is removable, to convert the bag to a frameless

design, or the frame could be permanently attached.

Flexible Tube Frame

The use of Jan Sport fittings and ⅝-inch O.D. aluminum alloy tubing makes the construction of a flexible tubular frame fairly easy. The only major problems encountered will be in trying to bend the tubing smoothly and accurately. If you use an electrician's conduit bender, you will achieve acceptable results without any trouble, but it is possible to bend up a frame without one. Fig. 4-47 shows one possibility; this particular one to fit a rectangular bag.

Wraparound Frame

The flexible tubular frame discussed above could be easily modified to give you

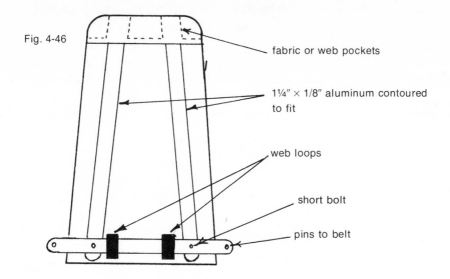

Fig. 4-46

fabric or web pockets

1¼″ × 1/8″ aluminum contoured to fit

web loops

short bolt

pins to belt

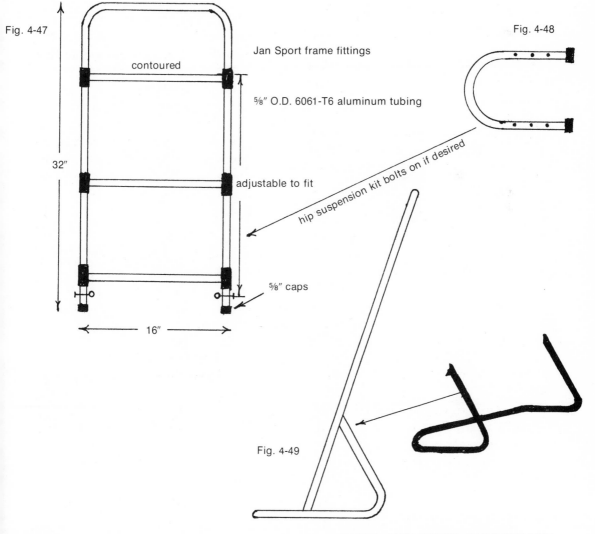

Fig. 4-47

contoured

32″

adjustable to fit

⅝″ caps

16″

Jan Sport frame fittings

⅝″ O.D. 6061-T6 aluminum tubing

hip suspension kit bolts on if desired

Fig. 4-48

Fig. 4-49

a nice wraparound hip carry frame. Jan Sport sells a kit (Hip Suspension kit) that will convert such frames quickly and easily. It may be installed permanently, or removed when not needed. Fig. 4-48.

Tubular Wraparound Frame

If you want a solid, welded tubular wraparound frame, one similar to the design shown in Fig. 4-49 might be suitable.

PROJECT 4-6: DITTY BAGS/STUFF SACKS

Length—18 inches
Diameter—10 inches
Capacity—These bags are generally made with some specific article in mind; they should be fitted accordingly. This one is for a three-season sleeping bag.

Design

In the smaller sizes, ditty bags can be made as flat "envelopes"—one side folded, sew across the bottom and up the other side, with a simple drawstring closure for the open end. These bags are great for small items or for anything flat. Fig. 4-51.

In the larger sizes, and for bulkier items, an insert bottom should be used. With a round bottom the ditty bag becomes the perfect stuff sack for carrying and protecting your down gear. For trail use make them small, to compress the down for efficient use of pack space, and make them waterproof. For lengthy storage of down gear, make them large (to keep the loft) and always make them breathable. The addition of a simple 1-inch web grab handle to one end, and a weatherproof interior flap to the other, greatly improves the usefulness of any stuff sack. Fig. 4-50.

When computing dimensions it might be helpful to keep these facts in mind:

Diameter—the desired finished diameter plus 1 inch for seam allowance gives you the diameter to use for cutting out.

Circumference—the desired finished diameter times pi (3.14) plus 1 inch for seam allowance gives you the length to use for the outside of the circle.

Length—the desired finished length will be much less than the cut-out length because of draw hem seam allowance (1¼ inches), bottom seam allowance (½ inch), and the extra cloth needed for the closure.

Using a rectangular insert bottom instead of the round one, and then adding a few simple straps, turns the larger stuff sack into a superlight day pack. This design could be identical to a simple day pack, and could easily double as a climbing or side trip pack when not in use for carrying your sleeping bag. If you like this idea, remember to use slightly heavier material for your combination stuff sack pack; and when using it as a pack, always keep the loads light. Fig. 4-52.

Materials

For stuff sacks and ditty bags to be used on the trail, the ideal material is coated, waterproof ripstop nylon. This material is light, tough, and strong. For larger stuff sacks that can expect abuse (a sleeping bag sack lashed below the bag on a frame pack), tougher, heavier coated taffeta can be used. For a combination stuff sack/pack, the lightest fabric you can use with some degree of reliability is 3- to 4-ounce coated nylon. I have seen, and owned, such superlight sack/packs made from 1.9-

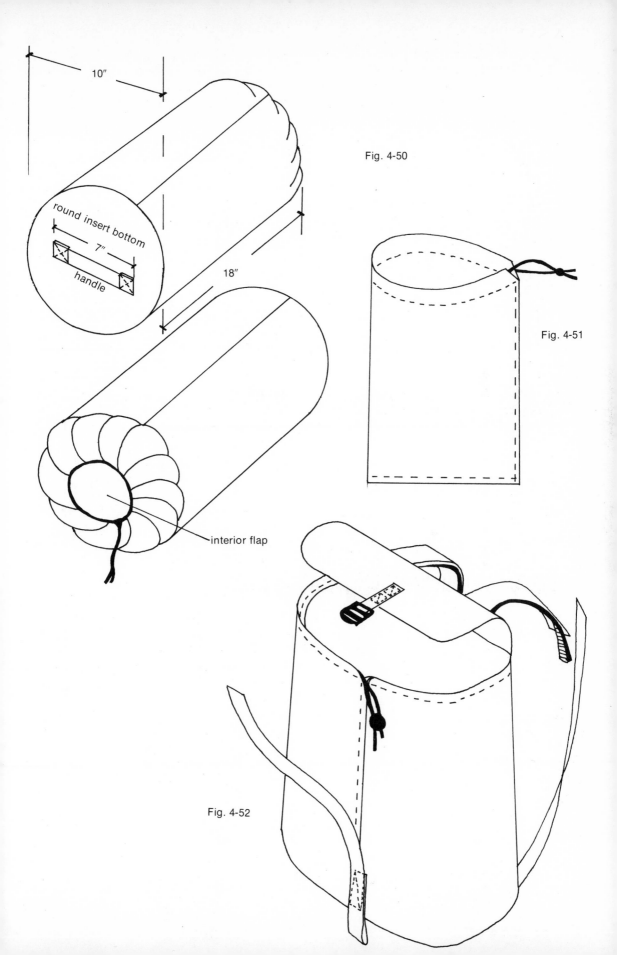

10"

round insert bottom

7"

handle

18"

Fig. 4-50

Fig. 4-51

interior flap

Fig. 4-52

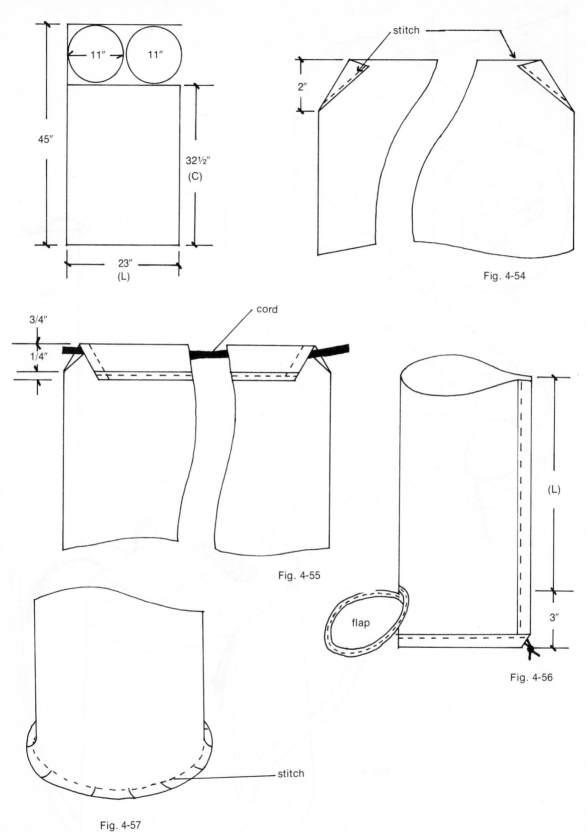

Fig. 4-53

11"   11"

45"

32½"
(C)

23"
(L)

stitch

2"

Fig. 4-54

3/4"

1/4"

cord

Fig. 4-55

(L)

flap

3"

Fig. 4-56

stitch

Fig. 4-57

ounce ripstop, but these are too easily destroyed. If you don't mind the weight, a stuff sack/pack can be made of any tough, heavy material, but then it would really be more of a rucksack than a stuff sack.

Construction

1. Lay out the pieces on the fabric. The pattern given is for a stuff sack with a round insert bottom; you could omit the bottom, or use a rectangular insert bottom if you desired. Fig. 4-53.

2. Cut out all pieces, flame seal all edges and webbing ends.

3. Fold over the fabric as shown to give a finished draw hem. Insert draw cord in hem. Figs. 4-54 and 4-55.

4. Fold over ½ inch around the edge of one of the circles to give it a finished edge.

This will serve as an interior flap. Pin and sew around the edge. Now sew the finished interior flap to the inside, 3 inches from the end with the draw hem. About 1 inch of double stitching placed opposite from where the cords tie will be right.

5. With the sack inside out, sew the side seam together. You should now have a tube with the interior flap and drawstring at one end. Fig. 4-56.

6. Sew a 1-inch grab handle to the outside of the remaining circle. This will be the insert bottom. With the handle to the inside, and the tube inside out, pin and sew around the circumference of the circle. Try to make the seams work out evenly here; it may require slight trimming or repinning. Fig. 4-57.

7. Inspect, then turn right side out. Tie a knot in draw cords, or use a cord clamp.

PROJECT 4-7: DUFFEL BAGS/HANDLEBAR BAG

Length—21 inches
Diameter—10 inches
Capacity—Volume: 1,550 cubic inches
　　　　—Weight: whatever you can carry with one arm

Design

While this type of luggage is not strictly for backpackers, you could use it for shipping your gear to the trail. These bags will also come in handy for lugging gear around town, or for loading onto your own vehicle (truck, dune buggy, horse, whatever). I would like to caution you that if any lengthy walking is involved, duffel bags and any other form of hand luggage are a pain to carry. Walking with luggage should always mean "backpacking," so if

you can think up some way to carry your duffel bag on your back, things will be easier. A snap-on single shoulder strap of 2-inch web is a big help for heavy loads and long hauls, or you could even use two shoulder straps to rig up some kind of duffel bag/backpack. As a last resort, when your arms wear out, try slipping them into the two handle loops and carrying the duffel like a pack; it still won't be easy, but it will at least be an improvement. See pages 80–82 for details on a 2-inch web shoulder strap suitable for duffel bags.

Materials

Fabric. Duffel bags should be able to stand up to a lot of abuse (baggage handlers) and a lot of abrasion (bouncing around in your car trunk), so I recommend heavy, coated Cordura nylon. You will need 22 inches of 45-inch-wide fabric if

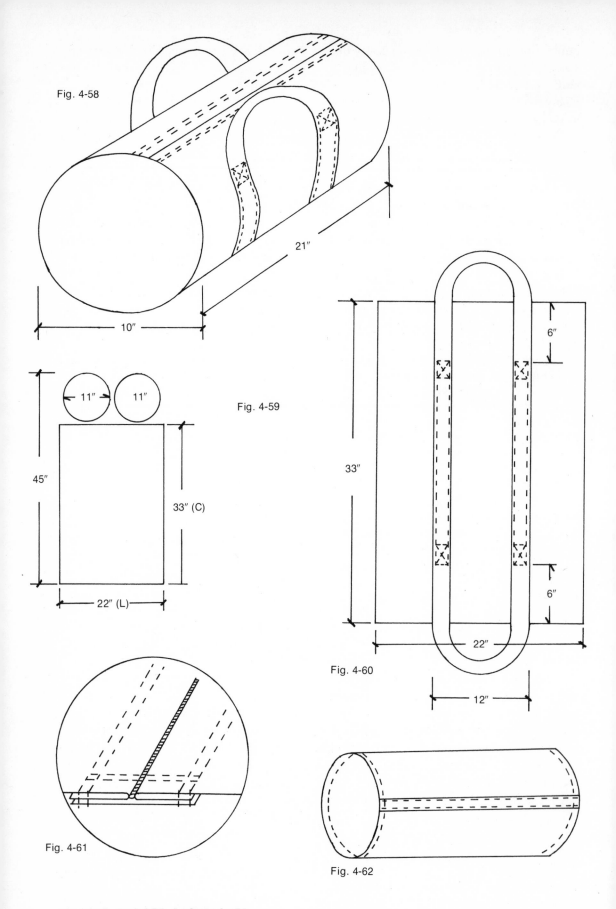

Fig. 4-58

21″

10″

11″ 11″

45″

33″ (C)

22″ (L)

Fig. 4-59

6″

33″

6″

22″

12″

Fig. 4-60

Fig. 4-61

Fig. 4-62

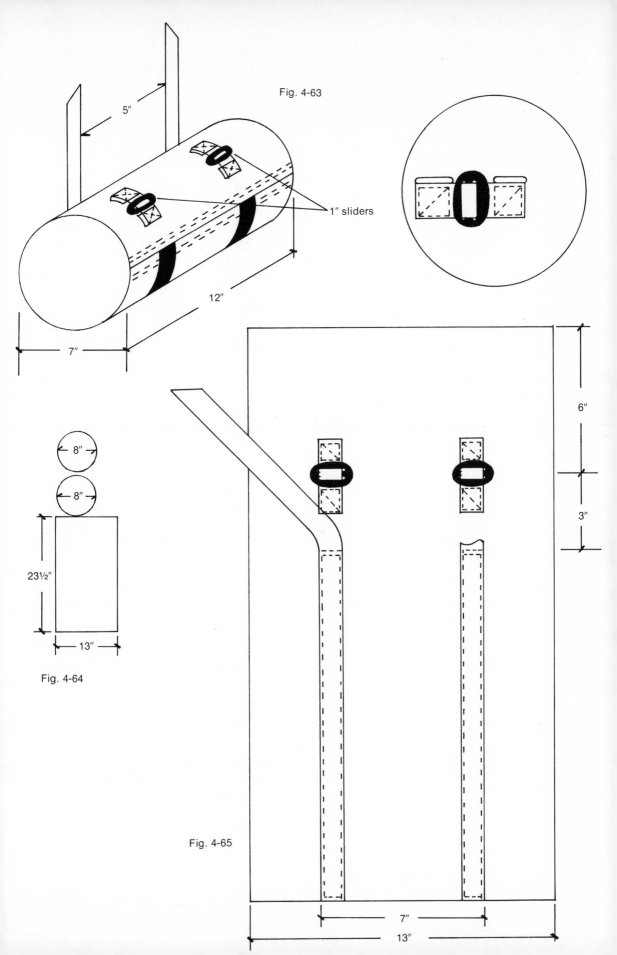

Fig. 4-63

1" sliders

5"

12"

7"

8"

8"

23½"

13"

Fig. 4-64

6"

3"

Fig. 4-65

7"

13"

you use the given dimensions. In addition, you will need about 100 inches of 2-inch-wide nylon seat-belt webbing for the handles. Make them long enough to slip over your shoulders; you may never need to do so, but if you need to and can't you will be sorry. You will also need a 21-inch zipper; a large nylon coil or Delrin #10 should be used for strength and durability.

Construction

1. Lay out the pieces on the fabric. The dimensions given are for a bag with finished diameter of 10 inches, finished length 21 inches. To change dimensions is easy; just remember to allow 1½ inches extra around the circumference for the double zipper flaps, and ½ inch extra for seam allowance everywhere else. Fig. 4-59. (See Project 4-6.)

2. Cut out all pieces, flame seal all edges and webbing ends.

3. Sew the webbing to the side as shown. Fig. 4-60.

4. Sew one side of the zipper tape to one edge of the side along the length. Take care that both the zipper pulls and the good side of the fabric will be to the outside when the zipper flap is completed. Fold over about ¾ inch of fabric and sew it down with a double row of stitches to give you a half-width finished zipper flap. Repeat step 4 with the other half of the zipper tape. Fig. 4-61.

5. With the bag inside out, pin and sew one end of the tube to the circumference of one of the ends. Try to make the seams work out evenly here; it may require slight trimming or repinning. Repeat step 5 with the other end. Fig. 4-62.

6. Inspect, then turn right side out.

A smaller duffel bag, with slight modifications, also makes an ideal handlebar bag for a bicycle or motorcycle. If you are making it to fit a ten speed, with dropped handlebars, make sure the bag will fit between them, and that it does not interfere with your brakes. These bags usually cannot be used with touring brakes.

Motorcyclists will appreciate a handlebar bag for storing tools, lunches, etc. These bags work best with motorcross-type bars (with a reinforcing crossbar). Make sure the bag does not interfere with your steering, and make sure it is attached to both the upper and lower parts of the handlebars. Otherwise the bag may rotate or bounce around, beating the hell out of your instruments, or possibly ripping off.

HANDLEBAR BAG

Length—12 inches
Diameter—7 inches
Capacity—Volume: 260 cubic inches
—Weight: keep it light or it may affect your steering

Materials

You will need 13 inches of 45-inch-wide fabric. I recommend waterproof nylon Cordura. You will also need a 12-inch zipper, two buckles (1-inch sliders or 1-inch tablers), and 60 inches of 1-inch nylon webbing.

Construction

1. Lay out the pieces on the fabric as shown in Fig. 4-64.

2. Cut out all pieces, flame seal all webbing ends and fabric edges.

3. Sew the webbing to the side as shown. Fig. 4-65. Finish as in steps 4, 5, and 6 on duffel bags.

Project 4-8: Sports Bag/Bicycle Panniers

Length—16 inches
Width—8 inches
Depth—10 inches
Capacity—Volume: 1,200 cubic inches
—Weight: whatever you can carry with one arm

Design

A simple, straightforward, easy to make item that will come in handy for carrying almost anything you could want. Obviously, it is not designed for backpacking, but I am sure you could find a good use for one if you made it. This size is just about right for a minisuitcase, overnight bag, flight bag, or sports bag. If you want to, you could easily change the dimensions; don't go too much smaller or it will become too restrictive in capacity, but also don't enlarge the dimensions too much or it will become too bulky and unwieldy for you to carry.

You will notice the split full-length seam I use for the zipper; you could use an inserted zipper here, but I feel this type of seam is much neater. It gives the article a finished look, and the double zipper flaps do provide some weather protection. See Fig. 4-68.

The plans are for a very simple bag, but you could easily modify it (outside or internal pockets, accessory tie loops, etc.) to be more suitable for whatever activity you have in mind. Take a look in the luggage section of any large store for some good ideas.

Materials

Fabric. You can make this bag out of any tough, sturdy fabric. Since this item will certainly be subject to a lot of abrasion, I suggest you use Cordura nylon throughout, or at least for a double floor. You can patch the bag together from remnants or else use about 28×36 inches of fabric to make up the bag without extra seams.

Webbing. You will need about 96 inches of 2-inch-wide nylon seat-belt webbing for the handles. You will also need 12 inches of 1-inch-wide nylon webbing for the zipper pull tabs.

Hardware. The recommended zipper is a #7 to #10 nylon-coil type, 20 to 24 inches in length. You may use a zipper with one or two sliders. Two 1-inch D rings are not absolutely necessary, but they do provide a convenient place to snap on an optional shoulder strap, which will be quite helpful with heavy loads carried for longer distances. The cost and effort involved in adding such D rings is minimal.

Construction

1. Lay out the pieces on the fabric. Fig. 4-67 gives the dimensions. Note that you will need two side pieces if you follow the given design for a split full-length seam for the zipper. If you use an insert zipper seam, make one side 9×36 inches.

2. Cut out all pieces and flame seal all fabric edges and web ends.

3. Mark the middle of the zipper's length, pin it to the edge of one of the side strips, and sew it on. Take care that it is centered, and that both the good side of the fabric and the zipper pulls will be to

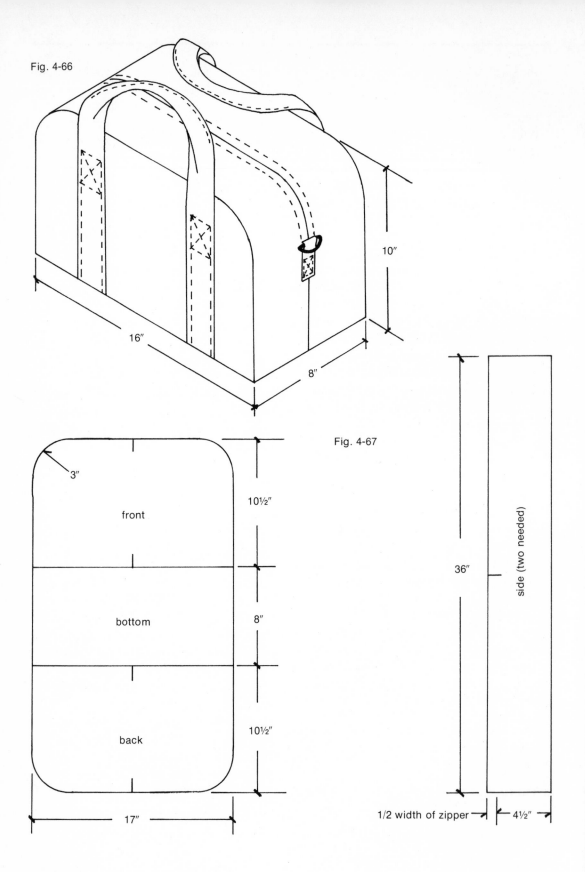

Fig. 4-66

10"

16"

8"

Fig. 4-67

3"

front

10½"

bottom

8"

back

10½"

17"

36"

side (two needed)

1/2 width of zipper

4½"

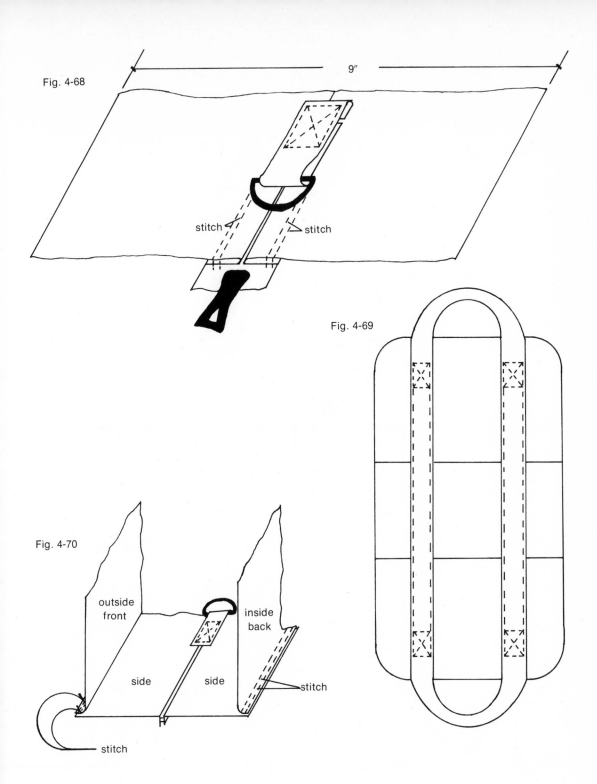

Fig. 4-68

9"

stitch

stitch

Fig. 4-69

Fig. 4-70

outside
front

inside
back

side

side

stitch

stitch

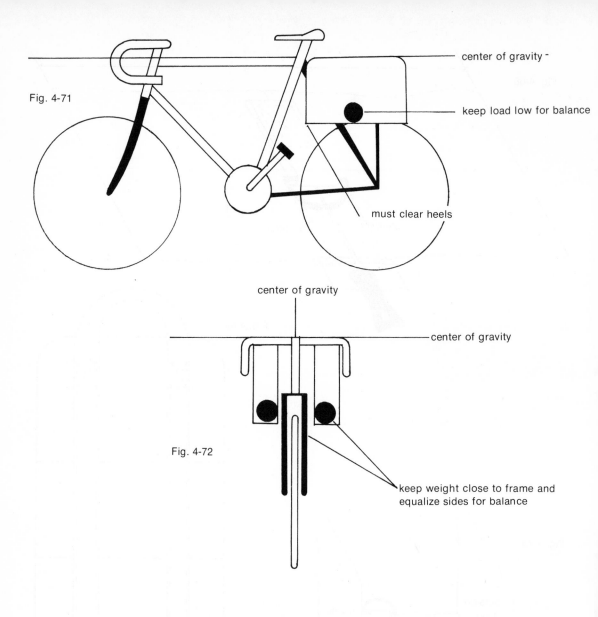

Fig. 4-71

center of gravity

keep load low for balance

must clear heels

center of gravity

center of gravity

Fig. 4-72

keep weight close to frame and
equalize sides for balance

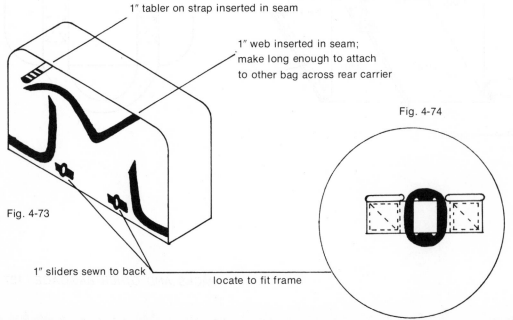

1" tabler on strap inserted in seam

1" web inserted in seam;
make long enough to attach
to other bag across rear carrier

Fig. 4-74

Fig. 4-73

1" sliders sewn to back

locate to fit frame

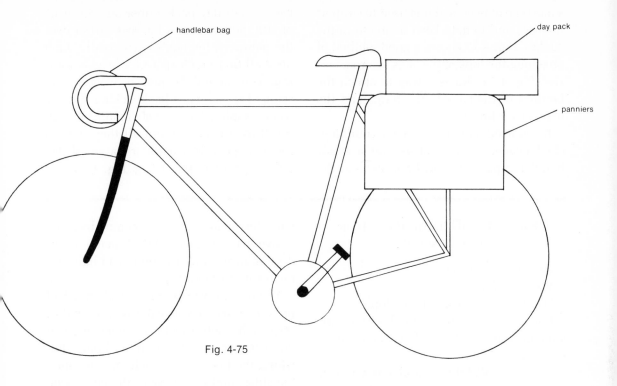

handlebar bag

day pack

panniers

Fig. 4-75

the outside when the zipper flap is completed. Fold over about ¾ inch (or one-half the width of the zipper) to make a zipper flap, and then sew it down with two rows of stitching. Repeat step 3 with the other side strip, to give you the seams shown in Fig. 4-68.

4. Sew the sides together below the zipper ends, then sew on the two web zipper pulls, with or without D rings. Fig. 4-68.

5. Sew on the 2-inch webbing as shown in Fig. 4-69. If you wish you can double the webbing over and sew it together for slightly more comfortable handles. Note Fig. 4-66.

6. With the bag inside out, center the side to the back with your alignment marks, pin, and sew with two rows of stitching. Be careful not to sew into the

web handles. Repeat step 6 with the front side seam. Fig. 4-70.

7. Pin and sew the bottom side seams, reinforce the corners with extra stitching.

8. Inspect all seams and edges, open zipper and turn bag right side out.

The design given for a sports bag can be easily modified to turn the bag into one-half a set of bicycle panniers. Since these panniers must be fitted to each size of bike, no dimensions will be given. When constructing such bags the critical point is the lower front corner, which must clear the heels when pedaling. Also keep in mind that the load should be carried as low as possible, and kept as close to the frame as possible for proper balance. Figs. 4-71 and 4-72.

There are many ways to attach such bags to the rear of the bike; see some commercial designs for ideas. Usually some type of rear carrier is used to support the bags and to help keep them out of the spokes. Fig. 4-73 shows a good method of attaching the tops of the bags to a rear carrier. Fig. 4-74 shows a way to attach the bottoms of the bags to the frame and the rear carrier brace.

If you need more capacity for your bicycle luggage, see Project 4-7 for a small handlebar pack that will supplement the panniers. If you still need more capacity, use a small day pack, either on your back or strapped on top of the rear carrier over the panniers. Remember, you really don't need all that much space for bicycle touring; you should be just as weight conscious here as when backpacking. I know some people who spent six months hosteling through Europe and all they needed for their gear was panniers, a small day pack, and a handlebar bag. Fig. 4-75.

PROJECT 4-9: DULUTH PACK (FOR EMERGENCIES)

Length—18 inches
Width—16 inches
Depth—Sewn as a flat envelope
Capacity—Volume: as much as you can stuff in; the big flap will cover a lot of overflow.
        —Weight: as much as you can carry. These are the famous (infamous?) packs used by the early fur trappers to open up the continent. The voyageurs carried some really amazing loads in them.

Design

In my opinion the Duluth pack has seen its day; there are newer, more efficient packs that will work just as well as canoe packs and that won't be such an abomination on long portages. However, there are still many people, some of them experienced outdoorsmen, who swear by the Duluth. To each his own.

The design of the Duluth is so simple that it is the best and easiest pack to rig up in an emergency, with a minimum of tools and work. You can make one out of nearly anything handy—an old tarp, a ruined tent, the remains of your sleeping bag, etc. I have even seen one Duluth made out of deer skin, used by the hunter to haul out his meat after butchering.

The plans given are for a nicely finished pack, just in case you actually want to do a respectable job. But for emergencies you don't have to get fancy; don't bother finishing the flap edges, stitch outside along the sides, and forget about the fancy web and buckle flap closures—a piece of rope threaded through a hole will do the job.

Materials

For a nice job use heavy Cordura nylon or heavy canvas. The Cordura will last longer, but the canvas will breathe and help ventilate your back. These packs can be made in any reasonable size—some of them are immense—but keep them as small as is practical unless you have a strong back. The dimensions given are for a fairly small pack, but one that should be comfortable if not loaded with anvils. If you follow them you will need 18×45 inches of fabric. You will also need some 1-inch-wide web, some 2-inch-wide web (or folded fabric), and two 1-inch tabler buckles.

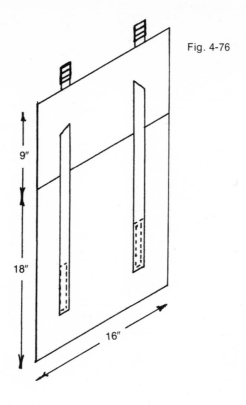

Fig. 4-76

9″

18″

16″

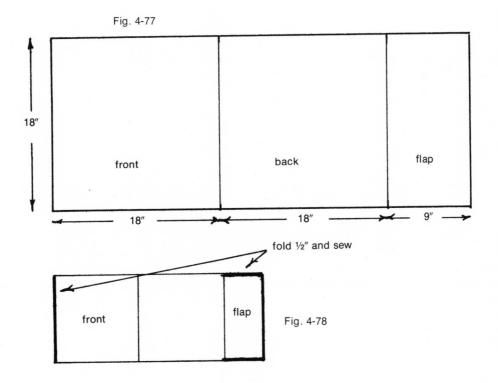

Fig. 4-77

18″

front

back

flap

18″

18″

9″

fold ½″ and sew

front

flap

Fig. 4-78

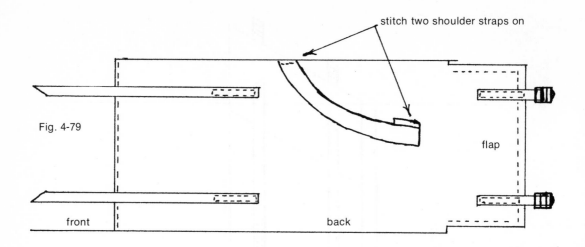

stitch two shoulder straps on

Fig. 4-79

flap

front   back

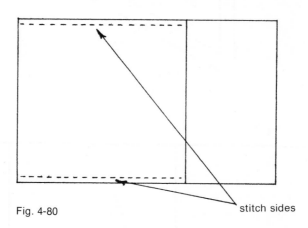

Fig. 4-80

stitch sides

Construction

1. Lay out the pieces on the fabric.

2. Fold over ½ inch of material along the flap edge and the front edge to give finished edges. Fig. 4-78.

3. Sew on the webbing as shown. Fig. 4-79.

4. With the pack inside out, double stitch along the two sides with a 1-inch seam allowance. Make these seams strong. Triple stitch where the lower shoulder straps pass through the seams. Fig. 4-80.

5. Turn right side out and inspect. If using canvas do not try to flame seal. If using nylon, flame seal the edges to prevent raveling if desired.

PROJECT 4-10: BOXES AND BAGGIES

There are many other useful items that will come in handy on a camping or backpacking trip. Plastic boxes, plastic bags, and rigid wall boxes can be used to store and transport many things.

I use rectangular air-tight plastic containers (available at most stores in the cookware section) to keep my food in on backpacking trips. These containers are waterproof, insectproof, and seal in flavor and freshness. They also solve one of the most annoying problems with a soft pack: as the food gets eaten the pack gets lighter and the volume decreases, making for a sloppy pack. These containers keep the same volume empty or full, which allows for efficient packing and consistency.

Many car campers and canoeists like to carry a strong, rigid wall grub box, made of plywood or fiberglass, to provide convenient storage and handling of their food. These could be made up at home, but are available commercially from many companies. One of the nicest grub boxes I have seen is the Rec-Pac, from L. L. Bean. This pack is light, waterproof, and it can be comfortably carried on the back just like a pack. Take a look in the Bean catalog for a good view of how you could attach a pack harness to a grub box.

Another good idea is the small, medium, and large sizes of Ziploc sandwich bags. I use them to store such things as maps (folded to the right part, viewed right through the Baggie in the rain), items of clothing (spare socks), and to organize loose articles in the pack (toiletries, miscellaneous).

Then there are the backpacker's best friend, the large, light plastic garbage bags. Some backpackers actually use them to collect garbage (theirs and whatever they find), and they are also handy for storing dirty, smelly laundry, filthy pots and pans, and any other items you want to keep isolated. They are also perfect for making absolutely sure your gear stays dry inside a pack.

5

Clothing

Dressing to suit the weather needs little or no explanation—when it's cold you naturally add extra layers of clothing, and when it's warm you take some off. This rather simple principle is the main basis for choosing outdoors clothing. From this we can elaborate, selecting garments that are compact, light, and durable until we come up with a versatile, coordinated wardrobe, suitable for backpacking under any and all conditions. Such a wardrobe is very important to comfortable and enjoyable backpacking, or to any outdoors activity.

If you are at home and the weather changes, there's no problem; all you have to do is reach into your closet and change into the appropriate outfit to suit the conditions. If you are camping or backpacking, however, you can't do that; a camper or backpacker can't very well carry his whole closet along with him. Accordingly, a lot of time and thought should go into selecting the right clothing for your wilderness excursions. Here are some points to consider when choosing your wardrobe.

Versatility

Every item of clothing should be as versatile as possible. Items that serve multiple purposes are best; they eliminate altogether the weight and bulk of those other items they replace. For example, instead of carrying long underwear, pajamas, a spare shirt, and an extra pair of pants, carry a sweatsuit, which will serve perfectly well as any or all of these items.

The Layer System

Coordinate your clothing so that you can add or take off layers as conditions dictate. This method adds considerably to the comfort, flexibility, and adaptability of your wardrobe. For colder weather a shirt, a down vest, a light down jacket, and a shell parka make up into a flexible, coordinated system that is a much better choice than a single heavy parka. Surprisingly, in terms of weight and warmth, the layer system can be almost as efficient as heavier, more specialized clothing. Keep this principle in mind for all your clothing, even socks.

Durability

Such activities as backpacking, camping, and climbing are extremely hard on clothing. Get clothing that is extra rugged, to stand up to the extra abuse. Easy care items that are field washable (no dry cleaners in the bush) are recommended. For those interested in their appearance, permanent press clothing usually holds up a little better after some time in the bush. Don't get overly concerned with how you look; strength and suitability should always take precedence over style.

Fit

For outdoors activities get clothing that fits loose, so that it doesn't hinder your full range of movements. Pants that are too tight can restrict leg movements when climbing, and shirts that are too short pull out when you bend over. Clothing that is too tight may also restrict circulation or cause chafing, so too large is better than too small. This is especially true if the item is to be used with extra layers of clothing underneath. Remember to keep the layer principle in mind when fitting; choose items that can be worn together without too much bulk or constriction.

Weight and Bulk

Since you will have to carry your wardrobe along with you, weight is a prime concern. Each item should be as light as possible, but don't sacrifice durability or suitability. Your whole wardrobe has to fit inside your pack. For summer camping this may not be a problem, but for cold-weather camping you may have an in-teresting time stuffing it all in. Down remains unsurpassed at providing optimum warmth with minimum bulk, so it is one of the best insulations for cold-weather clothing.

For cold-weather camping you would be wearing most of your insulated gear, but if conditions change, or if you are very active, you may have to shed your warmer clothing, and you should have room in your pack for it. Lashing insulated clothing to the outside of a pack should be a last resort, unless it is protected from snagging and dampness by a sturdy, waterproof stuff sack.

Conditions

Obviously you don't need an insulated expedition parka on a trip into Death Valley, but carrying a lightweight down vest or jacket is good insurance for all backpacking trips. Such items are ideal for keeping off the cold night air or extending the warmth rating of your sleeping bag, and remember, conditions can change. Quite a few people die from exposure each year; if you plan for cold weather it is no problem, but if you don't it can kill you. Plan your wardrobe for the conditions you expect, then throw in a little extra (down jacket, nylon windbreaker, gloves, balaclava) just in case.

Clothing List

As you can see, choosing the proper wardrobe for backpacking is not a simple matter. In fact, I've been at it for years and each trip seems to have something new added, something modified, or something discarded. Here is a list of what I feel the well-dressed backpacker should have in his closet. You probably won't need all of these items for any single trip, but this list provides you with a guideline of what you may find useful. For each trip spend a little time choosing the proper clothing, as dictated by conditions and personal tastes.

General Clothing

Mountain Parka—breathable, water-repellent shell; large to fit over parka

Windbreaker—breathable nylon shell; may replace mountain parka

Shirt—wool for warmth and comfort in all weather conditions, flannel for warmer weather

Pants—tough, water repellent, large for freedom of movement

Sweatsuit—cotton or polyester, with hood

Socks—thick wool and thin wool

Underwear—cotton, not too tight

Net Underwear—for extreme cold, and for improved ventilation when warm

Swimsuit—light nylon or cutoffs (double as hiking shorts)

Headwear—very important for cold-weather protection of neck and head and for protection from hot sun; I like a balaclava for winter, a crusher for summer

Gloves—lightweight, liners for mitts, wool good here, too

Belt—wide, leather or web, sturdy construction, buckle not uncomfortable with pack waist belt

Boots—heavy boots for rough conditions, medium boots for general backpacking, lightweight camp shoes for comfort and lounging

Rain Gear

Poncho—for rain garment and many other uses

Cagoule—a cross between a poncho and a rain jacket; used primarily by mountain climbers

Rain Jacket—breathable or coated; breathable doubles as windbreaker

Rain Chaps—especially for walking through wet bush after the rain

Cold-Weather Clothing

Insulated Parka—large, to fit over vest and other layers

Insulated Vest—useful by itself, or as liner for parka

Insulated Bivouac Pants—for extreme conditions, or as liner for sleeping bag

Mitts—insulated liners and shell are preferred

Mukluks—insulated liners and shell here, too

Keep in mind that this list is for clothing suitable for general camping and backpacking. Other activities may call for more specialized clothing. Cross-country skiing, bicycling, mountain climbing, and kayaking, for example, all have their own individual requirements for clothing, and specialized clothing has been designed to suit these specialized activities.

Here is more specific information for your backpacking wardrobe.

General Clothing

Included under general clothing are all the items necessary to fill out your backpacking wardrobe. Most of them are not specialized. Actually, the clothes you already have in your closet can be used in most cases. (See Chapter 8, "Scrounging," for advice on how to complete your wardrobe without going bankrupt.) Of course, if you can afford them, any of the mail-order or local shops specializing in backpacking and camping equipment have enough clothes to satisfy anyone. When buying clothing for backpacking, make sure you look for quality. Avoid any clothing designed to cash in on the surplus look or the outdoors look; a lot of this so-called outdoors clothing is flimsy, cheap, and just not suitable.

Mountain Parka

This seems to be the in item among backpackers, mountaineers, and outdoorsmen. These parkas have become so popular because they are just about perfect for their intended use.

A mountain parka is a lightweight, noninsulated garment that is designed to be worn as a shell over insulated clothing or as a breathable rain/wind/cold garment on its own. This is the best way, I think, to describe the true mountain parka, though there are those who are making parkas that are insulated or nonbreathable and giving them this name. The insulated mountain parkas serve no useful purpose that a shell and down jacket wouldn't, and are nowhere near as versatile, which is the main advantage of such rigs. They are not even much lighter. Waterproof mountain parkas sacrifice all of their usefulness in colder weather, and gain little, if anything, in improved weather protection (excess condensation with nonbreathable garments may more than eliminate any extra waterproofing abilities). Their only advantage is that they have the illustrious "mountain parka" look to them, so they appeal to those people who need an insulated or waterproof garment and who like the style.

A true mountain parka will be made of tightly woven cotton, or of a cotton and synthetic blend. This fabric will resist wind penetration and will be adequately water resistant, while still remaining breathable, to provide a single garment that is light, warm, comfortable, and dry. I also like ripstop nylon for ultralight parka shells for certain applications. This material sacrifices a slight amount of weather resistance, but gives minimum weight and bulk. However, the best mountain parkas will be made out of a cotton and synthetic "intimate" blend, weighing 2.5 to 6 ounces per square yard. This fabric combines durability, lightness, and weather resistance better than anything else on the market today.

Good quality mountain parkas are made with two layers of cloth—the outer layer is made from a blended fabric and the lining is usually of lightweight nylon. Two layers of fabric resist penetration by wind and water much better than a single layer. The best mountain parkas are made with two layers of blended fabric; a slightly heavier way to go, but probably worth it. This lining may extend throughout the entire garment, or it may be concentrated only in the areas of most usefulness (shoulders, hood, sleeves to the elbows, body only to the waist).

My mountain parka has four outside pockets. There seems to be a competition on to see who can include the most pockets in one garment, with some manufacturers getting a little ridiculous here. Large cargo pockets are sometimes handy, but check out their placement to see if you can even use them while backpacking. The shoulder straps on a pack will cover the breast pockets on many of these parkas, greatly restricting their usefulness, while the waist belt fits over the lower front pockets, just about rendering them useless, too. Quite a few of these parkas feature an extra large pocket in the back, for use as a makeshift pack they say, but again I question the practicality of this feature. If you stuff in anything hard or sharp and strap on a pack, your back is going to object strenuously to the arrangement. I

A mountain parka—a lightweight, breathable garment combining warmth and weather protection.

sizes and numbers to suit your own taste.

If these two items are combined, you end up with a versatile, coordinated system, designed to go together with a minimum of bulk or constriction. If making the mountain parka to fit over a down parka, be sure there is enough extra fabric in the shell to accommodate the extra thickness; otherwise the shell may restrict the loft of the down, actually lowering the warmth of your garments rather than increasing it.

Windbreaker

A windbreaker serves much the same purpose as a mountain parka. Tightly woven, lightweight ripstop nylon or nylon taffeta can be used with the mountain parka pattern to make an ultralight wind/rain shell for mountaineering, winter camping, or backpacking. In these applications every ounce of weight and cubic inch of volume should be carefully trimmed. A ripstop or taffeta windbreaker can serve adequately as a mountain parka, with only a fraction of the weight or bulk. Make sure you use only breathable fabrics for cold-weather garments; otherwise condensation problems will arise. Gore-Tex is a new fabric that is ideal for a lightweight wind/rain shell.

Shirt

Wool is the standard for backpackers; the warmth, water repellency, and comfort of a wool shirt will rarely be equaled by any other material. To be most effective these shirts should be tightly woven and fairly heavy. I take my wool shirt on every backpacking trip. It serves as a shirt in the winter, and as a light, warm, water-repellent jacket in the summer. Even in

suppose it could serve as a stash for a down jacket or sweater, but why not just carry them in your pack? Personally if I need to carry a bunch of small items, I prefer my day pack rather than having a multitude of garment pockets on my mountain parka.

Project 5-3 is a nice, simple mountain parka. This design utilizes inset sleeves, which aren't quite as neat as raglan sleeves, but adequate. Note that it is the same pattern as the one for the shell of the insulated parka in Project 5-5. I designed both these parkas for use with detachable hoods. You will also find no provisions for extra pockets, which may be added in the hottest weather it still comes in handy; the nights can be very chilly at the higher altitudes, where the thinner air doesn't retain as much heat as in the lowlands.

Where a lighter shirt is desired, or if you can't wear wool due to allergies, a cotton flannel shirt serves fairly well. Cotton is not as warm as wool when wet (in fact, it is downright cold), but cotton will wick moisture away from the skin, making it more suitable for very hot weather. If choosing a shirt for warm weather, don't make the mistake of picking one that is too thin. A hot sun can give you a sunburn right through a thin shirt; as you can imagine, sunburned shoulders and a pack do not go well together.

Pants

Most people I see on the trail are wearing blue jeans. Denim is tough, strong, and wears and looks well, but it does have a habit of freezing your legs when wet. Wool pants are preferred by many, for their warmth and water repellency, but wool won't wear as well as the tougher fibers. Patches can be sewn over the areas of high wear (knees, rear) to considerably lengthen the life of wool pants or any other pants.

I find the Canadian and U.S. surplus combat pants to be strong and very well made. While I usually wear jeans, if I had to choose only one pair of pants to last me a long time on a tough trip, I would take my combat pants. Incidentally, combat pants are available in two weights—the winter-weight combats are just about three times as heavy and sturdy, and already come with reinforced patches at the knees and the rear. These patches also have a liner that is waterproof, making sit-ting or kneeling in the snow not as uncomfortable as it usually is.

Don't overload those gigantic pockets on the thighs. If those pockets are heavily loaded, they cause a very tiring effect, making you put extra effort into every step you take.

Sweatsuit

I discovered the benefits of a sweatsuit several years ago and now rarely go camping without one. Mine has a hooded top, with a zippered front, and pants with elastic at the waist and ankles. A sweatsuit is one of the most versatile items of clothing you can carry, serving well as lounging outfit, pajamas, long underwear, spare shirt and pants, and as a windbreaker or jacket.

Socks

Wool socks are the only way to go. At first I didn't believe this, being used to the thin synthetic dress socks, but after trying wool socks for hiking and backpacking, I switched over to wool for all my wear. I thought that wool socks would be too warm for summer wear, but I find my feet stay dryer and more comfortable in wool than in anything else, even when it's sweltering. Wool also cushions the step, relieving my tired feet somewhat and pampering them a little.

I generally fit all my new boots with one pair of thick wool socks. Then when they are broken in I go to two pairs—one thick, one thin—and adjust up and down from there as conditions dictate. Don't try to gain extra warmth by adding extra socks unless your boot has enough room inside to accommodate them; if you cramp your feet with socks that are too thick for the space, you do more harm, by cutting off circulation, than you do good, by adding thickness.

Underwear

For summer, I wear cotton shorts and undershirts. Cotton absorbs excess perspiration, and wicks it away to the outside where it evaporates. This helps keep you cool and comfortable. Undershirts may be the T-shirt type, with short sleeves, or the tank-top style, with no sleeves. For backpacking, make sure the shoulders on the tank-top-style shirts lie flat; if they are thick or ridged the pack straps will emboss their design onto your shoulders. Add to this a sunburn, from a tank top that gives no protection, and you get a real mess. The short sleeved T-shirts also absorb perspiration from the armpits. This means that you wash such undershirts more frequently, but the outer shirt less. If the outer shirt is wool, which may have to be dry-cleaned or carefully hand washed, this can be a real blessing.

Net Underwear

Many people don't know that net underwear is very useful for keeping you cool when it is too hot. If worn under a tight layer of clothing (your sweatsuit), net underwear functions as a trap for air, dividing the space up into hundreds of little pockets of dead air that do an excellent job of insulating. If worn under a loose shirt, the net underwear allows air to contact and circulate around your skin, carrying off excess perspiration and keeping you cool.

Net underwear is available in cotton, cotton/wool blend, nylon, and nylon blends. Get whatever you feel most comfortable with.

Swimsuit

When I am concerned with the weight of my pack, I carry a lightweight pair of nylon swim trunks that double nicely as underwear. If I can afford a few extra ounces I carry a pair of cutoff jeans, for use as swimwear or hiking shorts. In the summer, shorts are usually the most comfortable way to go, but bring along a pair of pants for evening and for trips through scratchy brush.

Headwear

The importance of the head as a control for body comfort has already been mentioned. For protection from the sun, a hat with a wide brim and a high crown is best. For backpacking, unfortunately, the cowboy-style hats that otherwise would be most suitable usually hit the back of the pack. This can be annoying and can actually give you one hell of a headache from straining your neck forward all the time. My solution involves a lower pack, a narrower brim, trimming the brim, or folding it up out of the way à la Zane Grey.

For winter, when the neck may be exposed too much for comfort even in a hat or toque, I prefer the balaclava, which may be rolled up or down to suit conditions. Mine is dark orlon; dark colors absorb more heat than light colors—something to consider with hats.

Gloves

Important as part of a mitt/glove combination system, gloves also are useful wherever tactile impressions and manipulation are critical. Ski gloves are perhaps the best for providing warmth without too much bulk, though wool glove liners inside leather work gloves make a cheaper, sturdier rig. The knit wool gloves insulate just like the net underwear does, by breaking up the air into pockets and immobilizing it, and the leather provides wind protection, and wear and water resistance. Some golf or driving gloves, designed for maximum ventilation, also work well as very thin liners.

Belt

A belt is not just to hold your pants up; in an emergency or around camp it can serve any number of other useful purposes. Get a belt that is wide (for comfort), strong (say you needed to tie your pack up in a tree), and find one with a sturdy, simple buckle. I prefer belts made of 1-inch nylon webbing, with a tabler buckle, just like a sleeping bag strap. They are strong, light, easy to adjust, stay in adjustment, and don't have any holes to stretch or tear out. They also coordinate nicely with your backpacking gear, replacing broken pack straps and other items as if they were meant for it. Whatever you use for a belt, make sure the buckle won't dig in when worn under a tightly cinched pack waist or hip belt.

Boots

I use a pair of Vasque boots for rough country, light Dunham "Waffle Stompers" for general backpacking and daily street wear, and Wallabee crepe-soled moccasins for lounging, canoeing, and light hiking. Mountain climbers will need heavier boots, and winter mountaineers will need even more. Since anything other than mukluks are out of the question for the do-it-yourselfer (and it's much more feasible to purchase even the mukluks), you should restrict your efforts to keeping your boots in good shape, and possibly to minor repairs.

RAIN GEAR

Rain gear is designed to do one thing—to keep you dry and comfortable when the rest of the world is wet. Because most rain gear is made of nonbreathable, waterproof materials, adequate ventilation must be designed in or sweat will condense on the inside of the clothing. This condensation is particularly troublesome if the clothing fits tightly, and if the wearer is exerting himself at some strenuous activity. Too much condensation can make you just as wet and miserable as the rain.

To balance adequate wind and rain protection with adequate ventilation, some compromises must be made. A large, loose, flappy poncho provides the best ventilation, but wind and blown rain can find its way in through the large gaps. A tight waterproof jacket and pants provide the best weather protection, but condensation is a major problem with such suits. Some of the most satisfactory compromises are to fold your poncho and wear it. Remember to fit waterproof suits large for extra ventilation, and make the cuffs large and loose to promote air circulation; make your waterproof garments with vents (monsoon style), or make your rain garments from breathable, water-repellent fabrics or from Gore-Tex.

Poncho

I prefer a poncho for my main rain garment for the simple reason that it does the best job of keeping me dry and comfortable, and it also doubles as a ground sheet, a tarp, or as a nice, lightweight bivouac or shelter. I like a large poncho (about

58×108 inches) with a section at the back that folds up when not used over a pack. This type of poncho is known as a pack poncho. See Project 5-2 for detailed instructions on how to make your own pack poncho.

Cagoule

The cagoule is a cross between a poncho and a rain jacket. It is used primarily by mountain climbers, who want the protection and ventilation of a poncho, but who can't have a large, flappy garment that might catch the wind and sail them off a cliff. If a poncho is worn properly it will do everything that the cagoule will and will still retain the extra versatility and adaptability of the poncho.

Rain Jacket and Pants

A lightweight rain jacket is often chosen instead of, or as a supplement for, a poncho. The rain jacket weighs much less than the poncho, and provides somewhat better rain protection; however, you can't use a rain jacket as a shelter, tarp, or ground sheet. If you also need one of these, the poncho may be a better choice. On the other hand, if the poncho is in use as a shelter, tarp, or ground sheet, then you are deprived of your rain garment. For this reason I carry both; the jacket is light and compact enough that I never even notice it until I need it.

If you choose a rain jacket made from Gore-Tex, or from light, breathable nylon (preferably Zepel or Scotchgard treated to improve its water repellency), then this garment can also double as an effective windbreaker or shell. Only breathable garments should be worn in cold weather, so if considering using your rain jacket as a shell, be sure it is breathable; otherwise condensation problems will occur. Condensation problems will also occur with tight waterproof rain jackets worn when engaged in strenuous activities. For these two reasons I prefer my rain jackets to be loose fitting and breathable, but I also have a nice waterproof rain jacket for special situations.

Rain pants are often included with a rain jacket to make a lightweight rain suit that provides complete protection. Waterproof pants will be especially useful when walking through wet brush or grass after a rain. Unfortunately, I have never found any waterproof pants that didn't cause condensation problems. If you are getting a pair of these pants, be sure to get them large, with loose-fitting cuffs for maximum ventilation.

Rain Chaps

Because of the condensation problems involved with rain pants, I prefer to use rain chaps instead. These chaps are individual pant legs that tie up to your belt at the hips. They do essentially the same job as the rain pants, but because they are open at the top there are fewer problems with sweating and condensation. When used with a poncho they provide the best wet-weather system yet devised. See Project 5-1 for instructions on how to make your own rain chaps.

COLD-WEATHER CLOTHING

Dressing for the cold involves some unique and interesting problems that require considerable ingenuity to solve. An understanding of how the body works will be a great help in understanding and solving the problems facing us here. (See the insulation section in Chapter 3 for information on how insulation works.)

Everyone knows that when we are hot or when we work hard, we sweat more than normal. When in a cold environment everything possible must be done to minimize sweating and the heat loss that goes with it. This is the number-one rule of cold-weather survival. Aside from the major heat loss involved in excess sweating, sweat can freeze into clothing, permeate clothing insulation, and wet skin is much more susceptible to freezing than is dry skin.

Sweating is best controlled by adjusting your activity level (slowing down) or by flexibility of insulation. Flexibility is provided through ventilation (open your jacket zipper, open up your cuffs) and through the layer system (add layers of clothing when cold, take off clothing when warm). Ventilation is somewhat more convenient and works faster than the layer system, so it is the preferred control for minor adjustments. This is why your parka should be made with a zippered front, rather than made in the nonzippered, pullover style.

All cold-weather parkas should have provisions for a hood; the head and neck region is one of the major radiators of heat. External control is provided here by wearing or taking off a hood or balaclava. This is one of the best ways available to control and adjust your body heat and sweating.

Another major source of heat loss is the arteries carrying blood to the hands; they pass very close to the surface just inside the wrists. Opening or closing your cuffs can provide considerable control; this is why parkas should have cuffs that are adjustable. For maximum efficiency in extremely cold conditions, knit cuffs

provide better insulation, but no flexibility. The femoral arteries (just inside your thighs) are another major source of heat loss, and insulated pants that cover this area help considerably. Insulated pants are usually too warm if worn with other insulated clothing and they often promote excess sweating. For this reason they are usually reserved for extreme cold, or for such sedentary activities as ice fishing.

The layer system of dressing provides for major, semipermanent adjustments in your warmth level. Trial and error here will soon show you how to dress for whatever conditions you find yourself in. This will differ with each person (different metabolic rates, level of fitness, when you ate, what you ate, etc.).

The main trick with the layer system is to use several thin layers to provide flexibility and versatility, without too much weight. Dead air is still the best insulator known to man, and several layers of thin clothing work well as an insulator by trapping several layers of air and immobilizing it. Light fabrics (1.9-ounce ripstop) are best for this purpose as they billow out and provide thickness without weight. Two layers of ripstop nylon provide considerable warmth, far beyond what you would expect. Of course, if these two layers of ripstop are separated by stuffing them with down, then you get a large increase in warmth with only a small increase in weight and bulk. This is why down vests and jackets are among the most popular items sold for outdoors use.

Tight fabrics, such as ripstop nylon, taffeta, 65/35 mountain cloth, etc., provide further warmth by minimizing wind chill and air movement close to the body. However, if the fabric is woven too tight or coated to make it waterproof, then you can run into condensation problems as moisture-laden air has difficulty getting out. Condensation is more of a problem in enclosed spaces than in large ones (clothing fabric must be somewhat more breathable than tents or sleeping bags), so keep this factor in mind when choosing fabrics and designing clothing.

Insulated Parka

Insulated parkas are available in many different styles, made with several different types of construction, and insulated with several different materials. Add in the fact that there are literally hundreds of manufacturers making them, all making their own individual versions, each version with the features that they feel are most desirable, and a bit of clarification is in order.

The length, thickness, and purpose is one way of sorting out parkas into some semblance of organization. The longest, thickest, warmest, most sophisticated, and most expensive parkas are generally known as expedition parkas. They usually weigh between 2½ to 4 pounds; they are cut oversize at the sleeves, shoulders, and girth to enable wearing extra clothing underneath; the front and back together have a loft of 4 to 6 inches; and they are extra long, fingertip length or longer, to provide extra warmth to the lower body. They may have sophisticated, specialized features such as knit cuffs, built-in hoods, extra capacity pockets inside and out, no sewn-through seams, and an extra-large overlapping zipper flap at the front. Many of them are made with an outer layer of breathable 65/35 mountain cloth, for water repellency and increased durability and resistance to snagging and abrasion.

Not quite as heavy, thick, or warm as the expedition parkas, the regular insulated parka is generally the best choice for the average backpacker. These are usually 3 to 4 inches thick, they are palm or fingertip length, and they are not as sophisticated in design or detailing. Most of them have detachable hoods.

The insulated jackets are cut wrist length, with detachable hoods (sometimes optional) and are generally lighter, cheaper, and thinner (2½ to 3½ inches) than the parkas. For the active backpacker and climber interested in adequate warmth with minimum weight and bulk, they are a good choice.

Insulated sweaters differ from the jackets in several important respects— they are shorter, lighter, thinner, and most of them come without a zipper flap and without a hood. Sweaters are most useful as lightweight garments for cool summer nights, or for use as liners in a combination expedition parka system.

These different styles of insulated parkas are available in several different constructions. The best expedition parkas are made with a minimum of sewn-through seams, for a minimum of thin cold spots. The double-quilted construction is quite popular for insulated clothing (least sophisticated, easiest to make, slightly heavier), but slant-box baffled and "V"-baffled clothing are becoming more popular as more manufacturers learn how to use these constructions properly in garments. For the do-it-yourselfer the simpler double-quilted construction will be more than adequate and much easier to sew.

If the two layers are made as separate items, you have the combination system of construction, which provides all the warmth of the double-quilted construction, with the sophistication, versatility, and adaptability not generally available in an expedition parka. There are a few commercial firms that offer such combination expedition parkas, but the cost of

An insulated parka may be combined with an insulated vest to give you a warm, sophisticated, combination expedition parka.

tion. Occasionally you will find such items with an extra layer of fabric added to the outside. This extra layer of fabric is not quilted, to provide maximum warmth and thickness, and can be another layer of the usual ripstop or else a layer of 65/35 water-repellent cloth. The 65/35 cloth is heavier and much sturdier than ripstop, making it ideal for use in areas where wear and snagging are a problem. A separate shell mountain parka (65/35 cloth or ripstop) serves the same purpose as the extra layer of fabric, and provides more versatility. Keep in mind that it is also much easier to clean, repair, or replace a separate shell than a sewn-on one.

Down and feather mixtures in various proportions remain as the most popular filler for insulated garments. They provide minimum weight and bulk, but they are unsuitable for wet conditions, and they are expensive. There are many synthetic and natural fibers being used as insulation in clothing, but for high-quality, lightweight equipment, the only fibers now acceptable are Fiberfill II and PolarGuard. (See the insulation section in Chapter 3 for a rundown on these materials and for their suitability in garments.) I feel that fibers offer a significant advantage over down, when used in insulated garments. Clothing is much more susceptible to moisture, especially sweat, and condensation is more of a problem here.

such outfits is generally much higher than for an ordinary expedition parka of normal construction. This is because you have two finished items, with twice as much work and detailing. Of course, to the do-it-yourselfer this extra work is not a severe handicap. This is the system I prefer, and the one I recommend to do-it-yourselfers interested in obtaining a versatile, superior parka (and you get a "free" vest or sweater thrown in). See Project 5-5 for construction details for such a parka.

Regular parkas, jackets, and sweaters are rarely made with anything but the simple sewn-through (quilted) construc-

Insulated Vest

This has to be one of the most popular items ever invented. In terms of practical warmth, light weight, and minimum bulk, a good example of this garment can't be beat. But not all insulated vests are the same. Some are thicker, some are longer, and some have such extra features as zippered flap with snaps, baffled seams, provisions for hood, insulated hand-warmer pockets, etc. You can make your vest as simple or as sophisticated as you want; you can make it out of down or PolarGuard or Fiberfill II, or you can make it out of sturdy 65/35 water-repellent cloth instead of the usual nylon ripstop. Take your choice.

Because a vest has no sleeves, most people think that their arms will get cold. In actual fact, the body sends extra warmth into the extremities whenever the torso is adequately protected. If your torso is kept warm, your arms and hands stay fairly warm even in some surprisingly cold conditions. A vest was chosen for a parka liner because of this fact, and because an extra layer of insulation at the armpits and elbows seems to contribute more to bulkiness and constriction than it does to warmth. The best vests made are actually sleeveless jackets. (See Project 5-4 for construction details for a vest with optional sleeves.)

Insulated bivouac pants—for severe conditions, or for use as a bivouac bag or sleeping bag liner.

Insulated Bivouac Pants

Very few backpackers will ever need a pair of insulated pants. If you do need such pants, then get them with zippers down the insides of the legs. These "bivouac" pants are much easier to put on in cold conditions; you don't even have to take off your skis or snowshoes; just wrap the pants around you like a blanket and zip up. In addition, the legs can be joined together to make a bivouac bag, suitable for emergencies or for use as a liner for a sleeping bag, to extend its warmth. Some pants have zippers up the outsides of the legs; they retain the easy entrance feature but will not make up into a bivouac bag.

Mitts

For serious winter use mitts are much preferred over gloves. While gloves offer more dexterity, they isolate the fingers from each other, making for colder fingers. The solution to this dilemma is to put the layer principle to work here, too. A good coordinated system involves leather mitten shells, orlon mitten liners, and orlon knitted gloves. These items are all cheap (the whole setup costs less than $6), are readily available, and work just about as well as anything else.

If you have extra money or time to spend, expedition mitts (shells with down- or wool-insulated liners) are available commercially, or you could make them at home. Prices on commercial mitts are not out of line for the amount of finicky work involved. If you do decide to make or buy expedition mitts, get shells with long, large cuffs that fit over the sleeves and seal with a drawstring. Short cuffs and elastic hems are not as suitable here. Fibers work better than down at resisting compression and dampness for this application; 65/35 water-repellent cloth makes good mitten shells. I added a set of 65/35 fabric gauntlet cuffs to a pair of cheap leather mitts for an excellent mitten shell, at about one-tenth the work and price of a commercial pair.

Mukluks

Mukluks are widely regarded as the warmest, lightest, best footwear available for severe winter conditions. Mukluks were invented by the Eskimos, who ought to know what they are doing when it comes to cold-weather gear. Today mukluks are available with shells of leather, Cordura, vinyl, and plastic; with liners of foam, Fiberfill, felt, or sheepskin; and with soles that include leather, Cordura, crepe, and even Vibram rubber.

Mukluks are warm and comfortable because they use the layer principle. They consist of an outer shell (with or without extra thick, tough sole) and an inner liner that may be removed for drying or versatility. Mukluks are available in a dazzling array of materials and designs, with prices to suit every budget. The specialists who make this equipment can probably do a much better job than you can; therefore the do-it-yourselfer has no real reasons for making his own.

MATERIALS, TOOLS, AND PROCEDURES FOR CLOTHING

MATERIALS

With clothing, selecting and using the right materials is very important. The proper balance between breathability/wind protection, weight/durability, and water resistance/condensation can be critical here, and is a major factor in clothing comfort and suitability.

The materials that go into outdoors clothing are fairly specialized, so they are not commonly available through your local sewing shops or fabric centers. The mail-order backpacking stores and the kit manufacturers carry the needed components, and dealing with them has advantages; they are knowledgeable and take considerable time and trouble to pretest and select materials that are most suitable for outdoors use. From their selection choose the proper materials to suit your application.

Fabrics

For use in down-insulated clothing, a fabric is needed that is light, tough, and downproof. Ripstop nylon is very light, strong for its weight, and if tightly woven and properly treated (Kendown, Zepel) can be downproof, wind resistant, and water repellent. This makes it ideal for lightweight down-insulated clothing and for other applications where light weight is the main consideration.

For down-insulated clothing used where snagging or abrasion may be a problem, a heavier outer fabric may be preferred. For heavy-wear applications, nylon taffeta is tougher than ripstop, and is also a tighter weave, making taffeta more resistant to down, wind, and water, without extra treatments. The two fabrics are comparable in price, so the choice between them is close (lightness versus extra durability and weather resistance).

For down-insulated clothing subject to extreme abuse (expedition garments, mountain climbing), a blended cotton/synthetic fabric makes up into a very tough, very weather-resistant, very heavy outer layer. If choosing a blended fabric for use in down-insulated clothing, get one that is tight (downproof) and fairly light in weight, to avoid compressing the down any more than necessary.

For use in fiber-insulated clothing, a lighter fabric with a looser weave (lower thread count) is acceptable, and may even be preferred. Fibers will not migrate through loose fabrics and will not spill through a rip, as will down, so for this application lighter, looser fabrics will do. A lighter fabric will also make up in part for fiber's inherent inefficiency as an insulation, as compared to down. This can result in finished garments that compare favorably in weight/loft ratio with down-insulated ones. As with lightweight down garments, an extra shell garment may be worn to provide extra protection from wear and the weather.

For use in these outer shell garments, ripstop, taffeta, and blended cloth all have their points. For the ultimate in light weight and compactness choose wind- and water-repellent ripstop; for a good compromise between lightness and durability, with better weather resistance, choose nylon taffeta; for the ultimate in durability, with the most comfortable wet-weather characteristics, choose blended cloth. The most popular arrangement is a combination—an outer layer of blended cloth lined with ripstop.

Any breathable shell garment can be considerably improved by using extra layers of fabric (adding a lining or a yoke to the shoulders, for example). They can also be further improved by the addition of special weather-repellent treatments, applied to the fabric at the factory (Zepel), at home (Scotchgard), or by your dry cleaners, but don't use the dry-cleaning treatments with insulated clothing—they reduce the loft by coating the insulation.

For use in rain clothing, there will be some call for nonbreathable, coated fabrics. Nonbreathable fabrics should not be used for clothing to be worn in cold weather—sweat freezes inside the garments—and are definitely not as suitable for clothing designed for active use. I recommend coated fabrics only for ponchos, rain chaps, and perhaps for loose-fitting rain jackets. Such rain jackets will be ideal for really wet conditions where you aren't working hard (boating, spectator sports, duck hunting). Either coated taffeta or coated ripstop can be used (weight versus durability again).

As you can see, with such an array of compromises, alternatives, and options, choosing the right fabrics for clothing can be confusing. To help you make the right choice, carefully read Chapter 3, "Fabrics," and watch and copy what the better manufacturers are using.

Insulations

The materials used to insulate your garments can have a very great effect on their suitability and your comfort and safety. The alternatives right now are down, or one of the synthetic fibers (Fiberfill II or PolarGuard). (See Chapter 3, "Insulations," for a rundown on these materials.)

For use in clothing, down offers marginal weight reduction over the fibers. The fibers can use a lighter fabric (they don't spill out of rips like down and more efficient construction (no baffling or interior layers of quilting). In clothing, this nearly cancels out down's weight advantage. Fiber-insulated garments are on the market today that compare favorably with down garments, if weight and warmth are the only criteria. However, down still retains the advantage where compressibility is a factor. For certain applications down may be the best choice.

The really significant differences between down and the fibers show up when choosing insulated clothing for wet conditions; both Fiberfill II and PolarGuard are far superior to down in wet conditions. Even if relatively dry conditions are expected, the fibers lose little or no loft due to sweat buildup under prolonged wear (and down does), the fibers are easy to dry out (down is not), they dry quickly (down does not), and they also are more suitable for active wear (more sweat). All in all, some very impressive reasons for choosing the fibers for insulated clothing.

For the do-it-yourselfer, fibers are a hassle to work with, but so is down. The techniques involved in construction with these materials are quite different, but good equipment can be made from any of these materials with patience and attention to detail. Choosing between Fiberfill II and PolarGuard is difficult; Fiberfill II comes prequilted to ripstop nylon, which is convenient, but which limits your fabric choices and complicates layout, cutting, and sewing. PolarGuard comes without backing, so twice as much fabric must be budgeted for. PolarGuard has longer fibers and resists lumping better, and is said to loft better after repeated washings. None

of these are critical, however. Incidentally, when comparing prices between Polar-Guard, Fiberfill II, and down, the fibers win by a long shot.

Hardware

Zippers are a major component of most large garments. Every time you want to take off clothing, adjust ventilation, or put on more clothing, that zipper will get used. A poor zipper can ruin an otherwise perfect garment; use good zippers.

I like #5 and #10 Delrin zippers for clothing. Zippers in clothing rarely have tight curves, but if they do you might substitute a #5 nylon coil. Get them with two sliders, for adjustment of ventilation; get them in the proper type, separating for jacket fronts; and if planning on making garments reversible, get them with double tabs on one slider.

The only other items used here are drawstring ties (cord clamps) and Velcro tabs. One-inch Velcro is available by the foot, cut into 2-inch sections for a tab. Black zippers and black Velcro go with every color fabric; other colors may not.

TOOLS

You will need the standard tools for making clothing—a sewing machine, measuring tape and carpenter's square, and layout tools—large flat space, straightedge, triangles, and patterns. Patterns are easily made by scaling up the diagrams given with each project; they are drawn to scale. Make your patterns full size, and cut them out of cardboard to make layout on the fabric much simpler and more accurate. Cheap fabric may be sewn together and used for trial fittings, or old, worn-out garments that fit properly can be taken apart and used for patterns.

PROCEDURES

With proper fitting patterns, making clothing can be simple, quick, and can result in garments that are functional and attractive. Without such patterns, designing and making clothing can be exasperating, it can take many extra hours of trial and error for fitting, and can result in clothing that is too small, much too large, or poorly tailored. While style is not a major consideration for outdoors clothing, there is no reason why you have to look like you are wearing a tent.

Tailoring is the process whereby a good sewer can modify a standard pattern or garment until it looks right for the person wearing it. This is more art and instinct than science, so little concrete advice can be given here. With outdoors clothing, a large, bulky fit is important for function (ventilation, the layer system, freedom of movement), so don't get too involved in tailoring these garments.

When you look at the project patterns you will see that they have been designed with extra room and with a square cut for ease of layout and construction. Leave them this way for best results. Both men and women can use these patterns effectively as they are, though if your body is much slimmer or stouter than average, then some adjustments may be advisable.

Note that all these garments were originally made to fit me. I fit the "average male" dimensions fairly closely (5 feet, 9 inches, 160 pounds, chest 38 inches, waist 30 inches, sleeve 32 inches, neck 15½ inches, pant length 31 inches). If you come at all close to these dimensions, use the medium patterns as given for a fairly decent fit. Where relevant, dimensions are given for both small and large patterns that may help somewhat in sizing, though some fitting is to be expected. Remember, with this clothing a loose fit is always a better alternative than a too tight fit.

If the item is to be worn as part of a coordinated layer system, then this must be taken into account when designing and fitting. For example, the large mountain parka fits over a medium insulated parka; the medium insulated parka fits well over a medium vest or light medium down jacket; the medium vest is large enough to be worn by me over a wool shirt and bulky underwear.

The critical areas in fitting such systems are the armpits (extend the lower part slightly if necessary); the sleeves (they are designed full but for an insulated liner trim them for a tighter fit, or make the liner as a sleeveless vest); the body (increase girth until insulation is not restricted by outer layers); and the neck (two insulated collars take up a lot of room, leave one out or stuff lightly).

OPTIONS, ACCESSORIES, AND MODIFICATIONS FOR CLOTHING

All of this clothing could be modified by small detail changes that could add considerably to the comfort, appearance, and usefulness of your clothing. My designs use what I feel are the best arrangements, but if your opinion differs, here are some ideas. Many more ideas are available from the commercial manufacturers of such gear. Browse through the stores and catalogs, and examine the best gear for innovative, original, and useful ideas that you could incorporate into your do-it-yourself clothing.

Collars

We have already discussed the head, neck, and throat as sensitive and critical areas in heat conservation and comfort control. A properly designed, well-fitting collar is very important for efficient insulation and ventilation in these vital areas, and therefore very important to your comfort. My favorite collar is simple to make (a high tube, 3 to 4 inches); fits fairly loosely (snug enough to keep out winds, but will not constrict if worn over thick clothing); it has an overlapping flap at the front to protect the sensitive throat area; and it doesn't have snaps to attach a hood (metal snaps conduct cold to the skin; use Velcro or set snaps in separate flap).

Cuffs

Like the collar, the cuffs of your garments are very important for ventilation and heat conservation. They must open wide enough to fit over bulky mitts or mukluks and to provide ventilation out the wrists and ankles in warmer weather. As you move, your motions will pump air in and out of these openings, making for a very efficient ventilation system. Conversely, these cuffs must shut tight when the weather turns colder; otherwise a significant amount of heat will be lost. I dislike cuffs that use elastics or tightly knit sections; while they may be efficient in cold weather, they will prevent ventilation if the weather improves. I also dislike snaps; they conduct cold, are awkward to work with mitts on, often rip out, and aren't fully adjustable.

Drawstrings

Drawstrings come in handy at the cuffs, at the waist of jackets, and at the waist of pants. I much prefer a 1-inch web belt, held by wide, sturdy belt loops, to a drawstring for a pair of pants, but for lightweight applications the drawstring may be preferred. The belt won't dig in, as will a drawstring, and will have many other uses as well.

Flaps

Flaps over zippers, for weather protection, and over pockets, for security, are

A tunnel flap; a variation of the standard design.

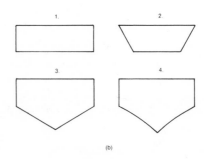

Flaps can be any shape; the first two are easier to make, the last two somewhat more attractive.

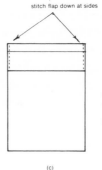

Another style; no Velcro tabs needed to seal, but slightly harder to get into.

very good ideas for outdoors clothing. Pocket flaps can be made as shown. I prefer Velcro tabs (1 to 2 inches) for these applications; they are easier to use than snaps, they are lighter, they don't transmit cold, they are easier to install without special tools, and they are sturdier and last longer without failing.

Hoods

A hood is almost a necessity in foul weather; it provides rain protection, wind protection, and if insulated it provides considerable warmth to the sensitive and important head, throat, and neck region. There are many different types of hoods that could be suitable.

For use in insulated garments, I much prefer the detachable-type hood. This may be attached to the collar with sewn-on Velcro tabs, or attached to a separate flap around the collar. For best efficiency, there should be a drawstring around the face, and a large front that comes up enough to cover the chin and perhaps the mouth.

For mountain parkas, rain jackets, and even ponchos, your hood could again be removable. This is one feature that I feel has definite merit. A built-in hood on an insulated parka, rain jacket, mountain parka, or poncho can be a real nuisance at times; it is hot, obstructs vision, and dangles at back most of the time anyway. Of course, a hood is important, so I am not advocating hoodless outdoors clothing—only that the hood be made a detachable option, for use only as required.

A detachable hood could be made from waterproof fabric, for a rain jacket or poncho, from nylon or blended cloth, for a mountain parka, or it could be made insulated, for an insulated parka, or as an addition to your hoodless sleeping bag for

A good hood design—covers the chin, throat, and mouth, and seals up tight with a drawstring. This one was made from the plans shown.

extra warmth. All of these hoods could be mixed and matched, adding versatility to your garments. Incidentally, sweat shirts, wool shirts and jackets, and other garments are available with built-in hoods that add considerably to their warmth and practicality. Whenever choosing a shirt or jacket of this type, one with a hood is preferable.

All of my projects are designed without hoods. I strongly recommend these detachable hoods as very useful accessories. If you want a built-in hood, just attach the hood where the collar normally goes, and leave out the collar entirely.

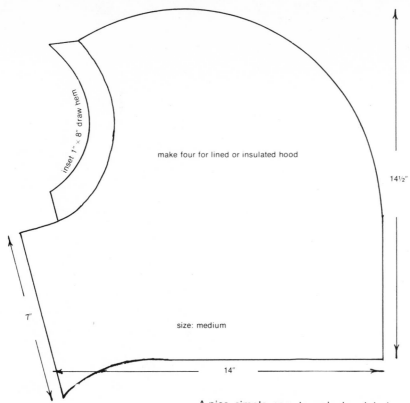

inset 1" × 8" draw hem

make four for lined or insulated hood

14½"

size: medium

7"

14"

A nice, simple, easy-to-make hood design; as given it is detachable, but it may be sewn on in place of a collar if you want a built-in hood instead. If insulating, stuff lightly with down and quilt.

Pockets

Pockets are an option that is highly influenced by personal tastes and preferences. For some activities pockets may be useful, but for backpacking, where your gear is more efficiently carried elsewhere, these pockets serve little or no useful function. In addition, the straps and fit of a backpack often severely restrict the use of some of these pockets. If making your garments for backpacking, I recommend that you restrict yourself to four patch pockets each for jackets and for pants. Locate these pockets so that they interfere as little as possible with your pack straps.

Patch pockets are the easiest to install, the easiest to use, and the best looking.

There are several variations available. The top-loading handwarmer pockets, which are an integral part of the front patch pockets, are comfortable and very useful for storage as well. The built-in flap is easy to make, and is less trouble to locate and attach properly.

Pockets can be used to store items in; merely turn inside out, stuff items into pocket, and close with flap. This is a convenient feature, and it saves the weight and inconvenience of carrying a stuff sack. Also, the items stuff up into a rectangular shape that may fit more efficiently into your pack, rather than the inefficient tubular shape common to most stuff sacks.

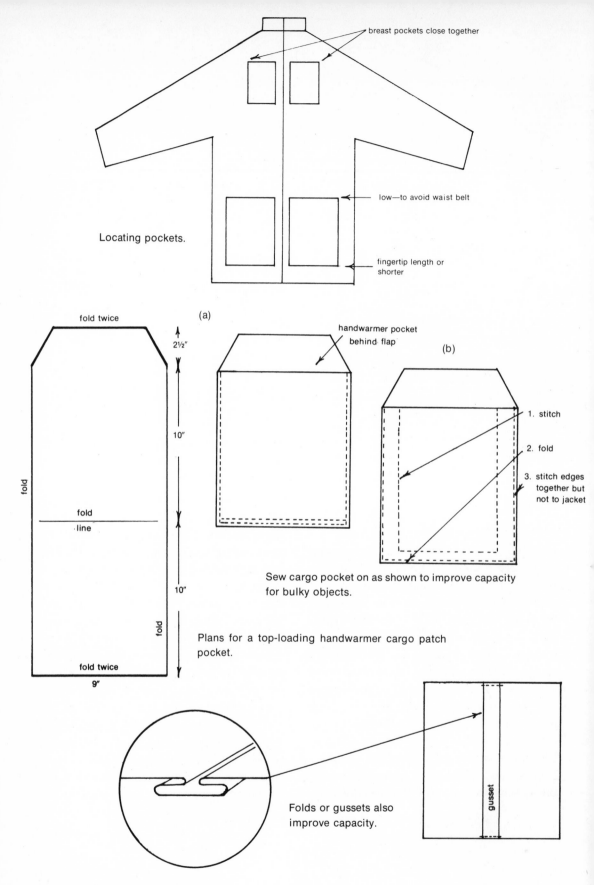

breast pockets close together

Locating pockets.

low—to avoid waist belt

fingertip length or shorter

(a)

fold twice

2½"

10"

fold

fold line

10"

fold

fold

fold twice

9"

handwarmer pocket behind flap

(b)

1. stitch

2. fold

3. stitch edges together but not to jacket

Sew cargo pocket on as shown to improve capacity for bulky objects.

Plans for a top-loading handwarmer cargo patch pocket.

Folds or gussets also improve capacity.

gusset

One-inch web belt loops may be sewn to the inside of the pocket, for attachment to your belt, or for convenient attachment to the outside of your pack.

Yoke/Patches

Wherever extra strength, weather protection, or abrasion resistance is needed, extra layers of material should be sewn on. These extra layers look best if sewn on before the item goes together, but if necessary they can be added after construction or whenever wear or tearing occurs. For jackets an extra yoke and reinforced cuffs and sleeves are nice. For pants, reinforced knees are almost a necessity, and a reinforced rear is sometimes worthwhile, too. For climbing gear, abrasion patches made of thin, strong leather will look attractive, and will take most of the wear encountered from ropes and rappeling. (Nylon fabric will melt if exposed to too much heat, and rappeling down a rope can melt nylon fabrics and cause them to stick to your skin.)

Normally, a patch is made with the same fabric that went into the rest of the garment, though contrasting colors and textures can add a stylish look. I make almost all my patches from blended cloth, which is attractive, wears well, and provides good weather protection. Two layers of any fabric is several times more effective, in terms of strength, wind resistance, and water resistance, than a single layer of the same fabric. For this reason breathable garments should be lined, or at least given a yoke and double sleeves. A yoke pattern is included with the mountain parka (Project 5-3). This yoke can be used to give extra durability and attractiveness to vests, insulated parkas, and other items. It will fit in well with the other projects. Cuffs and hems should also receive an extra layer of abrasion-resistant fabric, to take the heavier wear associated with these areas. If a draw hem is used, the drawstring tube should be made of a heavier material (Cordura or blended cloth, for example).

Project 5-1: Rain Chaps

Size—large enough to fit over pants and boots

Weight—approximately 5 ounces

Design

Rain chaps are easier to make than rain pants (almost anyone should be able to make a pair of these in less than an hour); they are lighter than rain pants, they provide more than adequate protection, and, if properly fitted (large), they give less of a condensation problem.

Chaps consist of two independent pant legs that are attached to your belt by some kind of a loop. Make sure your chaps will slide over your largest boots easily, and that they are large enough to fit over your most bulky wet-weather outfit without constricting the thighs or knees. Because they have no seat or crotch, rain chaps can't cause constriction. Make them long enough to adequately cover your boot tops, but don't make them too long or you will be stepping on them and wearing them out before their time. Make the attachment points sturdy, to avoid ripping out the loops if you ever do snag these things, and make those loops easy to operate (you shouldn't have to undo your belt to take them off).

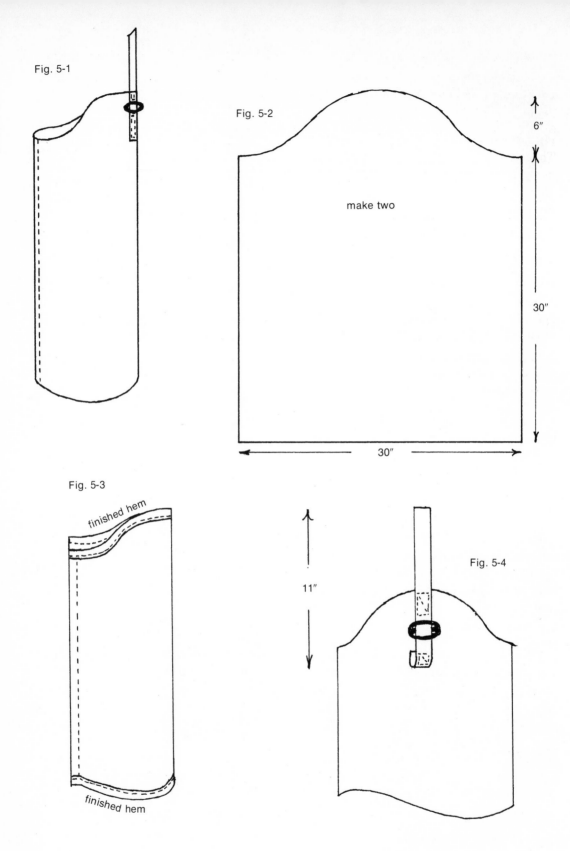

Fig. 5-1

Fig. 5-2

make two

6″

30″

30″

Fig. 5-3

finished hem

finished hem

11″

Fig. 5-4

Materials

Your rain chaps can be made out of the lightest polymer-coated ripstop. For longer life and heavier use, however, make them out of urethane-coated taffeta. The amount of fabric needed will depend on the size you make these items. I needed about 1 yard of fabric 60 inches wide for my rain chaps.

Construction

1. Lay out the rain chaps on the fabric. Fig. 5-2. Cut out two of these. Because you are using coated materials that shouldn't fray, you don't have to finish the fabric edges, though you could use folded/ finished seams for a more finished appearance.

2. Fold over the fabric once or twice along the top and bottom edges to give you finished hems. With the fabric inside out, sew along the edge of the fabric with a 1-inch seam allowance to give you a tube. Try on for fit. If satisfactory, fold over and sew this seam down to give you a finished edge here also.

3. Sew on the web belt tie loops as shown. Repeat steps 1 to 3 for the other rain chaps.

4. Inspect for missed stitches, puckered seams, holes, etc. If desired you can coat the seams with flexible waterproofing, but this is not really necessary.

PROJECT 5-2: PONCHO

Size—53×82 inches (regular) or 58×108 inches (pack poncho)

Weight—6 ounces to 20 ounces (depends on size and fabric used)

Design

This is another item that is easy to make; you should be able to turn out a decent one in a couple of hours. This one is excellent practice for the more complicated projects (tents, clothing), and if you make it you will have one of the most useful, versatile items of camping gear available today.

If you are going to use the poncho with a pack, or if you plan on using it as a shelter, make the poncho the size and shape shown. If you want a smaller poncho, the best way to make it is from a single piece of 55-inch-wide fabric, cut to suitable length. Make the poncho long enough to fit about to the knees. The longer poncho has the hood offset from the middle, and the excess fabric at the back is folded up when not in use.

The design given is for a poncho without a hood. If a hood is desired, use the pattern given on page 153. This can be sewn on or detachable, or you could invest in a cheap rain hat.

For extra versatility, your poncho can be used as a shelter. See Chapter 6 for more information and ideas on the use of ponchos as shelters.

This poncho is made with web pullouts at the corners and sides. I used web here because it is easier to install than grommets, and because web pullouts are usually stronger for such applications. You could install grommets or snaps along the hem of your poncho if desired, but this adds unnecessary weight and cost to this project.

Fig. 5-5

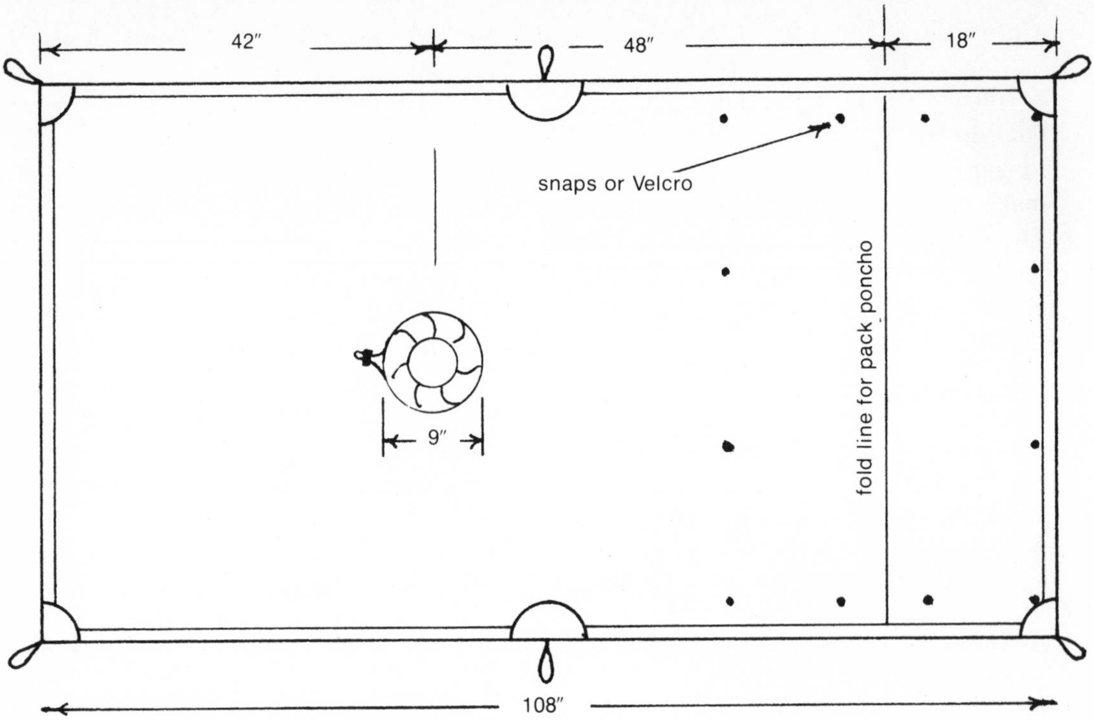

42"   48"   18"

snaps or Velcro

fold line for pack poncho

9"

108"

Fig. 5-6

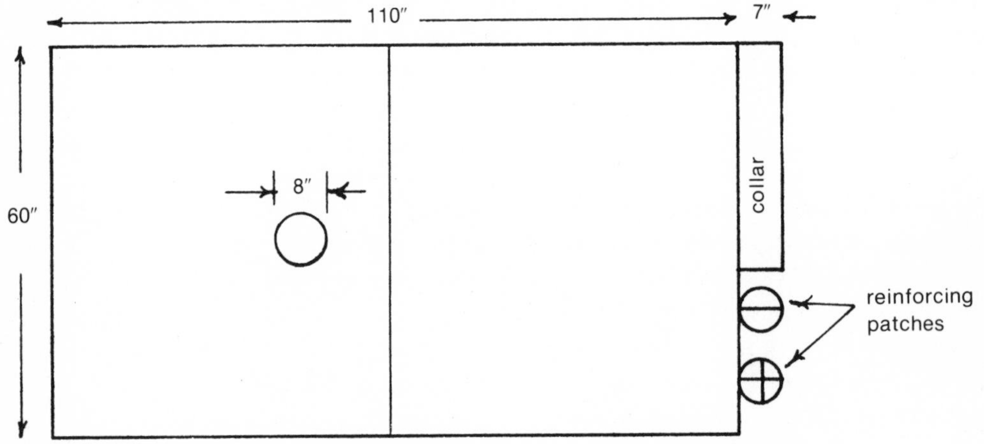

110"   7"

60"

8"

collar

reinforcing patches

Fig. 5-7

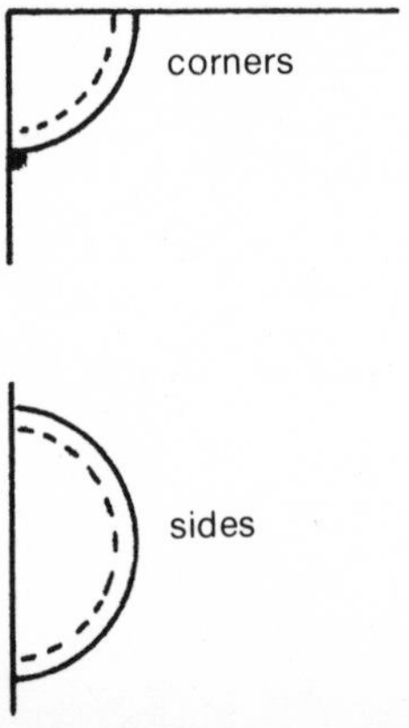

corners

sides

Fig. 5-8

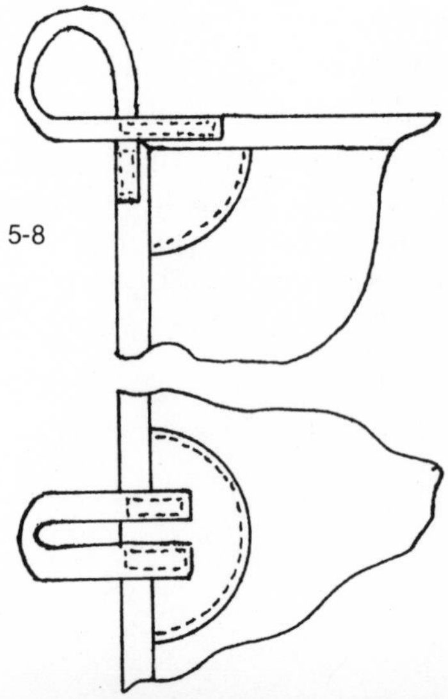

Fig. 5-9

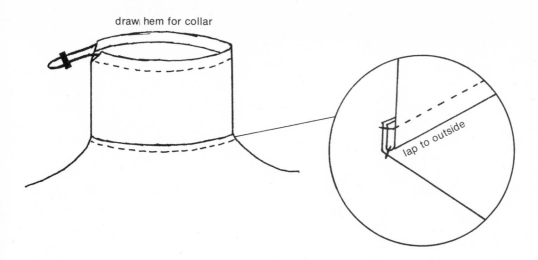

draw hem for collar

lap to outside

Materials

You will need 118×60 inches of fabric for a pack poncho. This can be one piece of 60-inch fabric, or pieced together from 55-inch fabric. See Fig. 5-6. Use coated taffeta (2- to 3-ounce weight), as lightweight ripstop ponchos snag and tear rather easily. You will also need about 48 inches of ½-inch or ¾-inch-wide nylon web, and a few 1×2-inch Velcro tabs (if the back folds up).

Construction

1. Sew on the pullout reinforcing patches as shown in Fig. 5-7. Fold and stitch the edges of the poncho twice to give you finished edges. Sew on the web loops as shown in Fig. 5-8.

2. Install the collar, which is a simple tube with a drawstring hem at one end. Sew the collar to the poncho with 1-inch seam allowance. Fold over the fabric once or twice to give you finished edges. This can be a lap-felled seam, with the lap installed to shed water like a shingle.

3. If making a pack poncho, which should fold up at the back when not used with a pack, install Velcro tabs or snaps to hold the folded fabric up.

4. Inspect all seams; coat with flexible waterproofing if desired.

PROJECT 5-3: MOUNTAIN PARKA

Size—Large; to fit over bulky clothing

Weight—single layer with yoke: 1 pound, 6 ounces

—with light nylon lining: 1 pound, 10 ounces

—with two layers throughout: 2 pounds, 4 ounces

Design

This design is for a simple mountain parka that may be made by a beginner. This parka is fitted with a detachable hood, for ease of construction and versatility. See pages 152 and 153 for plans for a detachable hood, which could be sewn on.

Lining your mountain parka will contribute a great deal of extra warmth and weather protection, at the expense of some extra weight. The cheapest mountain parkas are made with a single layer of blended fabric. They are light, but not as weatherproof or attractive as the others. The addition of the yoke, shown in the plans, will help such a single-layer garment considerably, as the shoulders and hood are the areas of highest rain penetration.

Lining your parka with nylon is a good way to get extra utility and protection, with very little extra weight. This is one of the most popular arrangements for mountain parkas. Lining throughout with a second layer of blended fabric is the ultimate for warmth and weather protection, but adds a significant amount of weight. Lining your mountain parka will involve just about twice the work, so consider that when deciding.

My mountain parkas are made with only four pockets, in the arrangement shown in Fig. 5-10. Extra pockets could be added in, but I feel this is a waste of time for backpackers, who should be using their packs to carry things in.

Materials

As previously mentioned, mountain parkas should be made from blended cotton/synthetic fabrics. Some of the best mountain parkas available are made from very tightly woven cotton, but such fabrics are difficult to find. Some lightweight wind shells are styled like mountain parkas, but are made from nylon taffeta or ripstop. These are very light and provide good service, but are not as warm or durable as mountain parkas that are made from blended fabrics.

When choosing a blended fabric for a mountain parka, choose one that is tight (better wind and water resistance), fairly heavy (better abrasion resistance), and get fabric that is made with "intimate-blended" construction, rather than the "woven" construction (see Chapter 3 for details).

You will need a 26-inch separating zipper for this item. Get one with two sliders, so that you can open it from the bottom for ventilation and freedom of movement. I prefer #5 Delrin zippers here, but many manufacturers use a #10. You will also need about 40 inches of 1-inch-wide Velcro (both hooks and loops) for pocket closures, wrist adjusters, and hood attachment.

The amount of fabric you will need depends on the size of the parka, and whether or not you line it. For a lined, medium jacket (full lining in body and double sleeves), I needed 17 feet of material 45 inches wide. See Fig. 5-11 for layout.

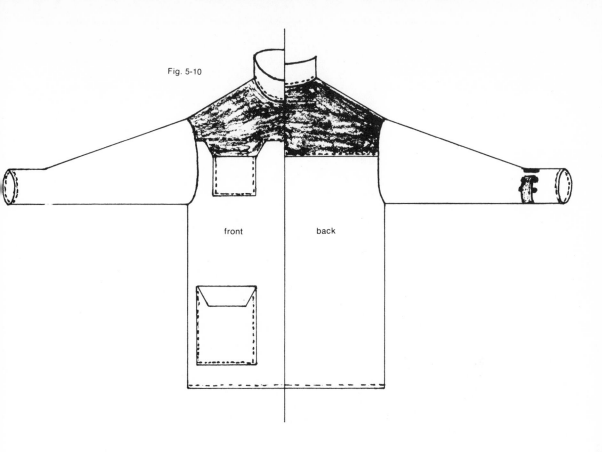

Fig. 5-10

front   back

Construction

1. Read through Chapter 5 for information on design, materials, procedures, and options or modifications. If you plan to make any modifications, or to include any options, make sure you allow for this in gathering materials and in construction. Carefully read through the following instructions, and make sure you understand them completely before starting.

2. This project is relatively simple, but fitting, sizing, and tailoring it to suit you may complicate it considerably. The fabrics used here are expensive, so to practice procedures and for trial fittings, you might want to construct a mock-up from cheaper fabrics (an old bed sheet, for example). Even if you are experienced at

sewing, this will help considerably. As an alternative, take your dimensions off an old noninsulated parka shell or jacket that fits you properly. Transfer patterns to the expensive fabric only when you are satisfied with the fit.

Remember that too large is better than too small. If fitting the parka to go over an insulated vest or light insulated jacket, don't worry, it should be large enough as given. If fitting to go over an insulated parka, you will probably have to go up one size (large mountain parka fits over medium insulated parka). To assist you with fitting, Fig. 5-11 includes a chart of dimensions to use. These dimensions are not to be taken as final; it is quite likely that some fitting and tailoring will still have to be done.

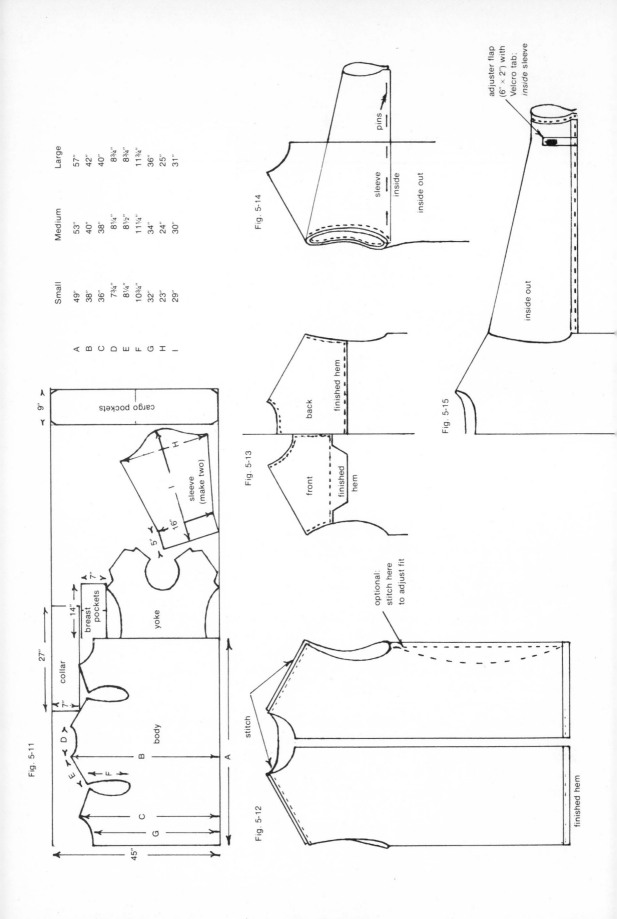

	Small	Medium	Large
A	49"	53"	57"
B	38"	40"	42"
C	36"	38"	40"
D	7¾"	8¼"	8¾"
E	8¼"	8½"	8¾"
F	10¾"	11¼"	11¾"
G	32"	34"	36"
H	23"	24"	25"
I	29"	30"	31"

Fig. 5-11

Fig. 5-12

Fig. 5-13

Fig. 5-14

Fig. 5-15

cargo pockets

breast pockets

collar

yoke

body

sleeve (make two)

stitch

optional: stitch here to adjust fit

finished hem

front

back

finished hem

finished hem

sleeve
inside
inside out

pins

inside out

adjuster flap (6" × 2") with Velcro tab; inside sleeve

Fig. 5-16

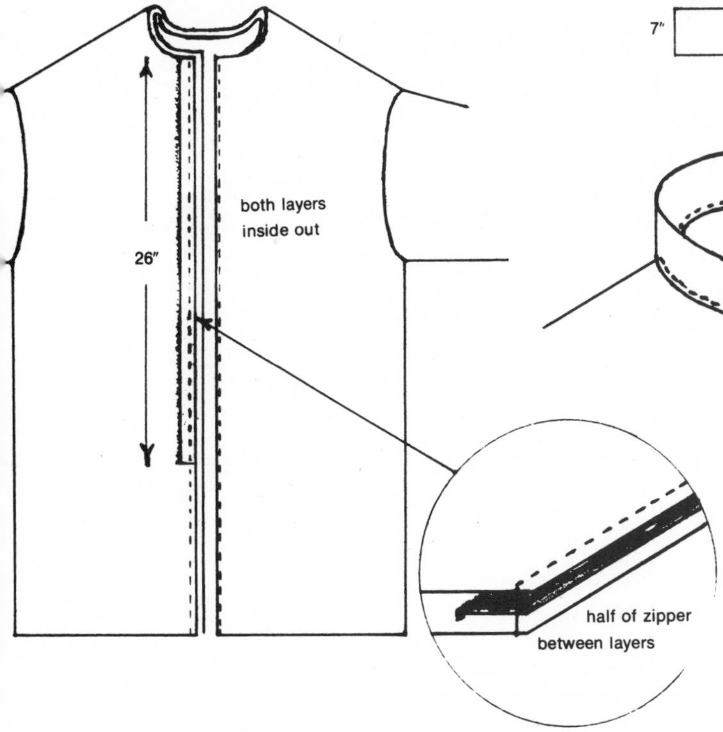

both layers
inside out

26″

half of zipper
between layers

27″

7″ collar

Fig. 5-18

3″

trim

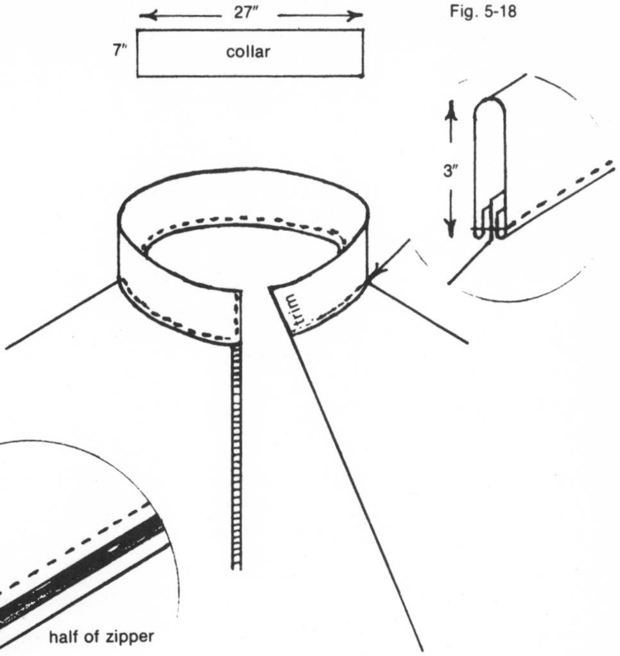

Fig. 5-17

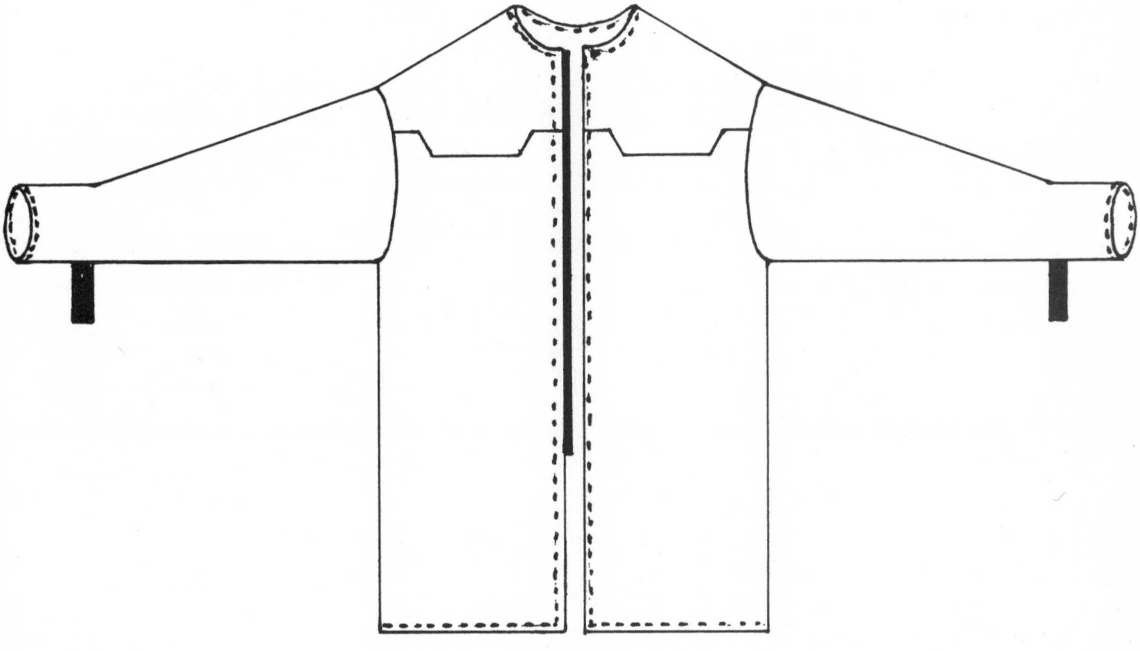

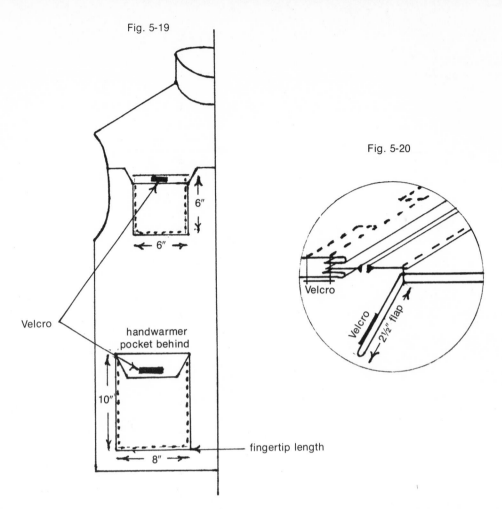

Fig. 5-19

Fig. 5-20

6″

← 6″ →

Velcro

handwarmer
pocket behind

10″

8″

fingertip length

Velcro

Velcro

2½″ flap

Dimensions for the sleeves are given. This includes a considerable amount of extra fabric at the shoulders to allow for enlargement of the armholes if necessary, and the sleeves are cut long (when arms are extended straight to the front, the sleeves should not pull back off the wrists). Trim as needed after trial fittings.

3. After finding a satisfactory pattern, lay out the parka as shown in Fig. 5-11. Cut out the pieces, collect all hardware. Because this fabric will not melt like nylon, do not try to flame seal the edges. To finish seams, fold, serge, or turn them to the inside.

4. With parka inside out, sew the shoulders. Fig. 5-12. Use 1-inch seam al-lowance (fold twice) here if no lining or yoke will be used. Otherwise use ½-inch seam allowance. Try on for fit. If too long, trim at bottom. Fold and stitch along bottom hem. If much too large in girth, adjust by sewing along sides. This will change your shoulders (trim outsides) and your armhole (enlarge).

5. With parka right side out, and with shoulder seam allowance to outside, sew on yoke around neck, around armholes, and once across back. Make double folded, finished seams for the front flaps, and fold seam across the back before stitching down yoke. Fig. 5-13.

6. With parka inside out, pin on sleeves and try for fit. Enlarge armholes or trim

upper sleeve to suit. Sew sleeve into arm-hole with 1-inch seam allowance. Fig. 5-14.

7. Pin sleeves into a tube and try for fit; trim to suit. Make up a flap, install flap and Velcro adjustment patches on end of sleeve. Sew sleeve seam. Finish end of sleeve by folding once and stitching around wrist opening (or fold twice if no lining is used). Fig. 5-15.

8. If making a lined parka, repeat steps 4, 6, and 7. Leave out the adjusting flap for the sleeves, but still fold around the wrist opening and stitch.

9. Fit one parka inside the other. The easiest way to do so is shown in Fig. 5-16. Include one-half zipper in one front seam (right side for men, left for women). Make sure the jackets will end up with finished seams everywhere for both inside and outside.

10. Turn right side out. Finish at wrists, bottom, and around neck by stitching the two layers together. Stitch down the front on both sides to finish here. Fig. 5-17. The yoke and the wrist flaps go on the outside.

11. Add the simple tube collar. Start at one end, pin around neck opening, tuck in overlap at other end, sew down. Fig. 5-18.

12. Sew on the pockets. Fig. 5-19. Double fold and stitch at the pocket tops and the front pocket flaps to avoid fraying. Locate those front handwarmer pockets to be comfortable when your hands are in them. Sew them on evenly and correctly or else the thing that will be most noticeable about your parka will be crooked pockets.

13. Sew across the yoke as shown in Fig. 5-20.

14. Sew other half of zipper and Velcro tabs to parka front. The width of the flap may provide adjustment to tighten parka slightly. I used a 2½-inch flap. When sewing on this half of the zipper, use pins to line up the yoke, bottom, and pockets evenly. Otherwise, any differences here will be very noticeable.

15. Inspect parka for faulty seams and fit. Correct as needed.

PROJECT 5-4: DOWN VEST

Size—jacket length, fitted over wool shirt

Weight—13 ounces

Weight of fill—5-ounce down

Loft—2½ inches (both sides; sewn-through construction)

Design

This vest is designed as part of a combination expedition parka. Vests make good parka liners because they provide extra warmth and, being sleeveless, they add no extra bulk at the armholes or sleeves. This vest is actually styled as a jacket (sleeves optional). The high tube collar, long cut, drawstring, zippered flap with extra Velcro closures, and the optional handwarmer pockets are all suitable for the best jackets. You could even make provision for adding a hood to your vest, if you really wanted to go the complete route.

On the other hand, you could leave out the zipper, you could make it shorter (but not too short), you could change the collar (a knit collar is not as bulky for a vest used as a liner), and you could leave out the pockets (vests used as liners have little use for pockets, especially insulated handwarmer pockets). This would give you the simplest, lightest, and least bulky vest available—ideal for use as a liner, or for stashing away in some small, out of the way place in your pack for "just in case."

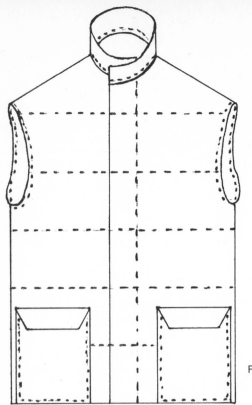

	Small	Medium	Large
A	44″	48″	52″
B	34″	36″	38″
C	32″	34″	36″
D	6¾″	7¼″	7¾″
E	8″	8¼″	8½″
F	10″	10½″	11″
G	28″	30″	32″

Fig. 5-21

Fig. 5-22

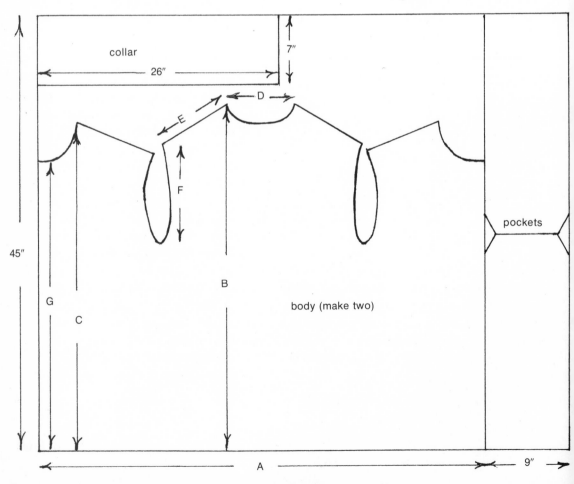

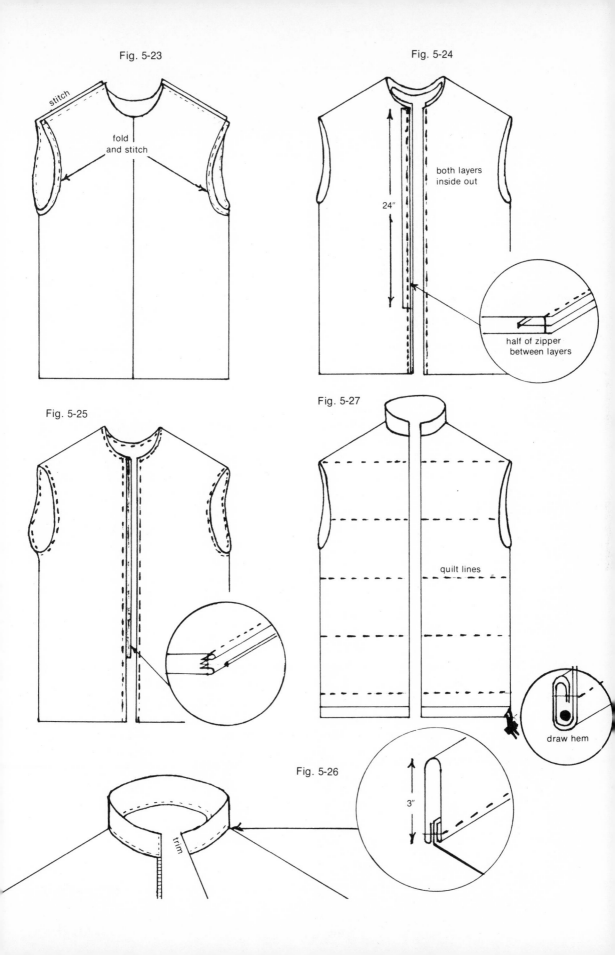

Fig. 5-23

stitch

fold
and stitch

Fig. 5-24

both layers
inside out

24"

half of zipper
between layers

Fig. 5-25

Fig. 5-27

quilt lines

draw hem

Fig. 5-26

trim

3"

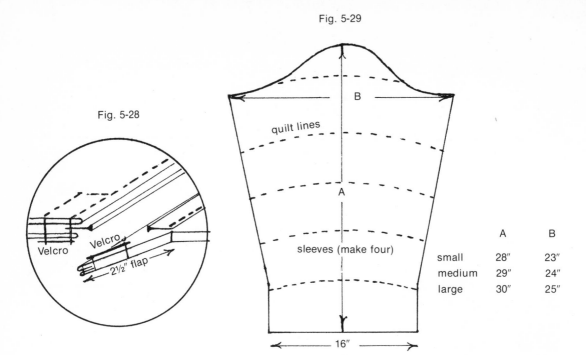

Fig. 5-29

Fig. 5-28

quilt lines

B

A

sleeves (make four)

Velcro

Velcro

2½" flap

	A	B
small	28"	23"
medium	29"	24"
large	30"	25"

16"

This vest is cut square, for ease of construction and to fit as many people as possible. Tapered or fitted vests are easily made, but I see little reason for doing so. The drawstring at the bottom seals off this location nicely, and if the vest is to be used with insulated pants, or if worn by a woman, the extra room at the hips will be needed.

Materials

I make all my vests from lightweight ripstop nylon. If making a vest for use without a shell, I would consider using blended fabric for the outer. I prefer to carry a windbreaker or parka shell for extra protection and weather resistance, and where minimum bulk and weight are the goal, ripstop is best. You will need approximately 3 yards of 45-inch-wide ripstop for a vest.

To insulate my vest, I used 5 ounces of good quality down. You could go as high as 6 ounces for a vest this size, but no higher or you will be wasting down.

If you decide on the optional insulated handwarmer pockets, ½ ounce of down will be about right. If you want a zipper, a 24-inch #5 Delrin (one slider or two) will do. You will need about 14 inches of 1-inch Velcro for flap tabs and pocket closures, and more if attaching a hood. You will also need about 60 inches of nylon cord and a cord clamp for the drawstring.

Construction

1. Read Chapter 5 for information on clothing design and options. Decide on how you want to make this item (the choices are many), and provide for any options or modifications in the materials and construction.

2. This is an extremely simple project, suitable for beginners. Fitting such an item should be fairly simple, but Fig. 5-21 includes a chart of dimensions to help

you. The only critical areas here are girth (wrap a tape around you while wearing what you expect to have on under the vest, then add about 10 inches); armholes (try the vest for fit before stuffing); and the neck (it should be large enough that it won't constrict with a thick wool shirt on, but tight enough to seal out drafts). Length is easily adjusted, but do this after insulating. The insulation will puff out the fabric and draw up the hem a surprising amount. Leave extra here for this.

3. After arriving at suitable dimensions, lay out the pieces on the fabric. Cut out all pieces, collect all hardware. If using the recommended fabric, flame seal all cut edges. If using blended fabric for the outer shell, serge or fold all seams.

4. Sew the shoulder seams and fold and sew around the armholes. Use ½-inch seam allowance. Fig. 5-23.

5. Repeat step 4 with the other shell. With the two shells inside out, sew them together at the fronts. If including a zipper, insert half as shown. Fig. 5-24.

6. Turn right side out, pin and sew armholes, neck, and finish at the front by restitching here also. Fig. 5-25. Double stitching at all these points is a good idea for strength and to prevent down leakage.

7. Add your collar. If you start by pinning the end and traveling around the neck, you can trim and tuck the surplus at the other end for a neat fit. Sew one end and all around the neck opening, but leave the other end open for stuffing. Stuff with down (not too much needed here) and sew shut. Fig. 5-26.

8. Stuff vest with down from the bottom (stitch most of the way shut first),

finish off seam at bottom, pat down out evenly, then sew in quilt lines to hold down in place. Fig. 5-27. Try to make those quilt lines work out evenly at the front, and if extra protection at the shoulders is desired, pat extra down into this section before sewing. Spacing can be anywhere from 4 to 8 inches.

An alternative method is to compute down volumes for each compartment, then sew the quilt lines and fill from the front (leave the flap side open).

9. Add drawstring hem and pockets if desired. Fig. 5-27. Those handwarmer pockets can be made with an extra layer of fabric at the back, and could be insulated. Locate them to suit a comfortable hand position.

10. Add the other half of the zipper, and the Velcro flap tabs. Fig. 5-28. Take care when sewing on this part that the stitch lines, pockets, top, and bottom all line up properly. I use a 2½-inch flap, and pin carefully so that there is no shifting when I start sewing.

11. Inspect stitching; look for loose stitches, or down leakage. Sewing and ripping seams in down-insulated gear leaves needle holes that may leak down persistently, so it's most important that you do it right the first time.

12. Fig. 5-29 shows the optional sleeve pattern. To make a sleeve sew two pieces together around the edges (leave open at cuff). Turn right side out, fill with down, sew cuff shut. Quilt as shown. Attach to vest armholes, sew sleeve side seams. See Project 5-3, for how to install sleeves and finish cuff.

PROJECT 5-5: FIBER-INSULATED PARKA

Size—large, to fit over insulated vest
Weight—3 pounds
Loft—3 inches (both sides; sewn through with shell)

Design

There are a lot of different ways to make an insulated parka, and your ideal design might differ considerably from mine. This parka is made to be worn with an insulated vest (Project 5-4) as a combination expedition parka. This arrangement provides the ultimate in warmth, versatility, and sophistication, with little sacrifice in lightness. Notice that this design is for a very large, long, loose parka; leave it that way for best results. This parka can also be worn without the vest in warmer weather or if active. This is one feature that few expedition parkas have.

I used Fiberfill II for insulation in this item because of its superiority as a wet-weather insulation. Expedition parkas are usually very bulky, no matter what insulation is used, so there is little reason to use down here, and lots of good reasons for using fiber.

This project is made for a detachable hood, but a hood could be built in if desired. It also may be made with a yoke, which will add considerably to the warmth and water repellency of the parka. I put four exterior patch pockets on my parka, just like the noninsulated mountain parka, and find that this is the best arrangement for me. I dislike interior pockets for cold-weather gear, but those large exterior cargo pockets, with insulated hand-warmer pockets behind, are very desirable and useful. I also included a drawstring at the bottom of my parka, for closing off this area if bivouacing (with the insulated bivouac pants, Project 5-6).

Materials

I needed about 96 inches of Fiberfill II prequilted to ripstop for this item. If making it with PolarGuard, include an extra 96 inches of fabric to take the place of the prequilted ripstop lining used with the Fiberfill.

You will need about 120 inches of 45-inch-wide material for the exterior shell. I used ripstop for my outer shell, with a yoke and sleeves of heavier blended fabric. You might want to use blended fabric throughout if you don't mind the weight. Fitting a mountain parka to go over one of these monsters is not really practical, so here is where a layer of blended cloth for the outside can be put to best use.

You will need a 26-inch #10 zipper for this garment. A #5 will also work, and will save a fraction of an ounce. Get Delrin zippers, with two sliders, to open from the bottom for ventilation. You will also need about 40 inches of Velcro (hooks and loops) for pocket closures, wrist adjusters, flap tabs, and hood attachment, and 60 inches of nylon cord and a cord clamp for a drawstring.

Construction

1. Read through Chapter 5 for information on design, materials, procedures, options, and modifications. If planning any changes from the given plans, be sure to allow for them in the materials and in construction. Carefully read through the following instructions, and make sure you

Fig. 5-30

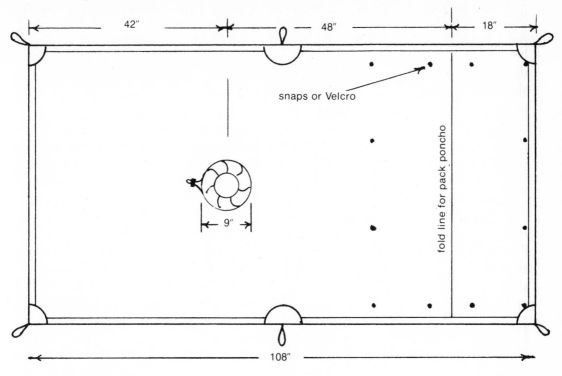

42"

48"

18"

snaps or Velcro

fold line for pack poncho

9"

108"

Fig. 5-31

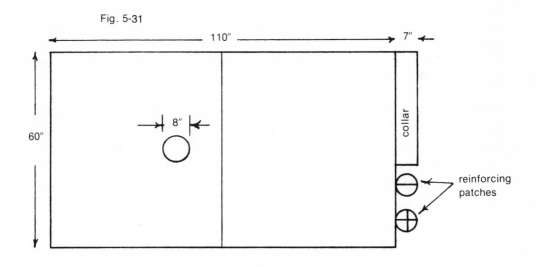

110"

7"

60"

8"

collar

reinforcing patches

understand them completely before starting.

2. Making the mountain parka (Project 5-3) is a very good warm-up to making this insulated parka. In fact, the insulated parka and the mountain parka are basically identical, but instead of making the liner of thin fabric, you make the liner of thick insulation prequilted to fabric. Construction is the same, except for the extra hassles of working with insulation, and design is modified only slightly (the outer shell is made slightly oversize to fit over the insulation).

3. Sizing and fitting this item can get complicated; the basic idea is to estimate size, then fit up an inner insulated garment to suit. Using this as a pattern, make your outer shell slightly larger. The given patterns have extra material in the appropriate locations to allow for fitting at sleeves, armholes, neck, and length. Girth should be estimated by wrapping a layer of prequilted ripstop/insulation around you loosely, overlapping about 3 inches for a flap.

4. After estimating your size requirements, lay out the parka inner shell (body and sleeves) on the prequilted ripstop/insulation. Fig. 5-31. Work on the ripstop side, but be careful of making marks that may show up in the finished garment. Stitch around these pieces with a seam allowance ½ inch smaller than your marks. Cut out the pieces, using your layout marks for cutting. If you fail to sew the edges before cutting, you are in for a lot of extra grief. Flame seal the ripstop (careful here, Fiberfill II will burn) and flame seal the outer (nylon) or serge (blended fabric).

5. With the two layers of ripstop touching each other, pin and sew the shoulders. Fig. 5-12. Try on for fit at armholes, neck, and girth. Adjust if necessary.

6. Pin the sleeves into the shoulders. This is done most easily with the sleeves placed to the inside of the garment. Fig. 5-14. Try for fit; enlarge armholes if necessary. Sew the sleeves to the armholes. Make sure the fabric of the sleeves and the fabric of the body line up to the same side.

7. Pin sleeves into a tube and try for fit; trim length to suit, fit to wrist (leave loose for ventilation). With sleeve insulation to the outside, sew the sleeve together. Fold about 1 inch of sleeve back at the wrists, pin and sew around the wrist opening. Fig. 5-15.

8. With the insulated liner completed, make up a fabric shell outer to fit. This shell should be slightly larger at the armholes and wrists and in girth to accommodate the extra bulk of the insulation. From here on, the insulated parka and the mountain parka go together in the same way. (See Project 5-3.) The only differences are in the collar (use only one layer of fiber insulation here or your collar will be too thick) and the pockets (the handwarmer pockets should be insulated). If you have a small amount of down, this is better for insulating the collar (stuff in one end of the tube collar).

PROJECT 5-6: BIVOUAC PANTS

Size—to fit; high at waist, full cut for freedom of movement

Weight—1 pound, 8 ounces (depends on insulation and size)

Loft—3 inches (both sides; sewn through with shell)

Design

Bivouac pants differ from regular insulated pants in that they have zippers on the inside seams of the pant legs. This enables you to join the legs together to make into a bivouac bag suitable for emergency sleeping or for extending the warmth of your sleeping bag. I feel that all insulated pants should have this feature. In addition, putting zippers on the inside of the pant legs can allow them to go on and off over skis, snowshoes, and boots; just wrap the pants around you like a blanket and do up. This easy entrance and exit feature is also available in pants with zippers running down the outside of the legs, but these pants will not have the bivouac feature.

Very few people will ever really need the warmth of insulated pants; net underwear, a sweatsuit, a pair of thick pants, and a windproof lightweight shell will usually suffice. I have used this layer system in frigid Canadian winters, and rarely have I felt a need for insulated pants. But for those of you who want them, here they are.

Materials

Because of their superior wet-weather characteristics, I favor fiber insulation for bivouac pants. Because they may be subjected to a lot of wear and abrasion, I like blended cotton/synthetic fabric for the outer layer. You will need about 60 inches of prequilted Fiberfill II/ripstop. You will also need 60×45 inches of light ripstop fabric for the lining. This design calls for two zippers (28 inches, separating, #5 Delrin, two sliders) and for three or four Velcro tabs (1×2 inches) to seal the fly. I recommend using a belt (1-inch web) instead of a drawstring (nylon cord and cord clamp), though draw hems at the cuffs are recommended (60 inches of nylon cord).

Construction

1. Read through this chapter for information on materials, procedures, and design considerations that will affect your project. Carefully read through these instructions, and make sure you understand them completely before starting.

2. Lay out the inner shell on prequilted Fiberfill II/ripstop. Sew around the layout lines about ½ inch inside, then cut out the inner. By sewing before you cut out you will keep the layers of fabric, backing, and fibers in their proper places while handling. Fig. 5-33.

3. Lay out the outer shell on the fabric. Cut out, serge (blended cloth), or flame seal (nylon) all the edges on both layers. Fiberfill II will burn, so be careful.

4. With the inner and outer shells inside out, and with the zipper halves included in the seams, stitch around the outside of one leg. Leave the cuff open, to allow you to turn the leg right side out. Fig. 5-34.

5. Turn the leg right side out, try for fit. If satisfactory, stitch around the edge again to finish. This time close off the cuff. Fig. 5-35.

6. Repeat steps 2 to 5 for the other leg;

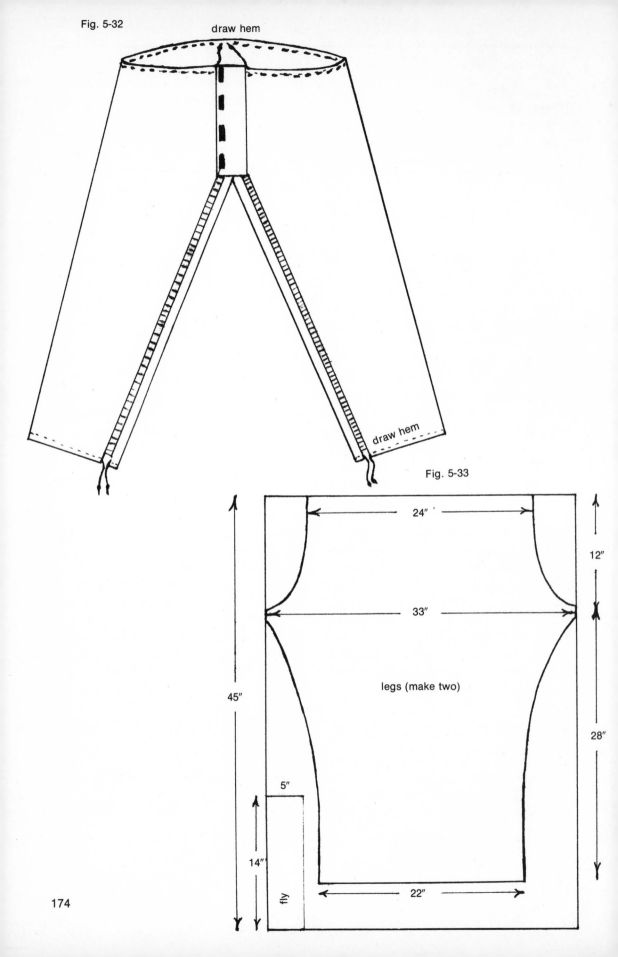

Fig. 5-32

draw hem

Fig. 5-33

draw hem

24″

12″

33″

legs (make two)

45″

28″

5″

14″

fly

22″

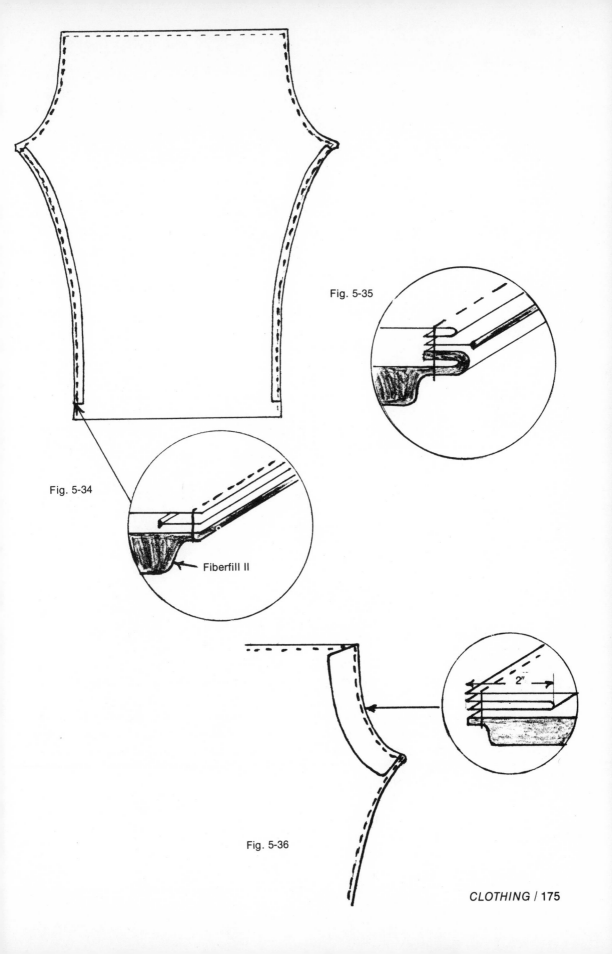

Fig. 5-35

Fig. 5-34

Fiberfill II

2"

Fig. 5-36

Fig. 5-37

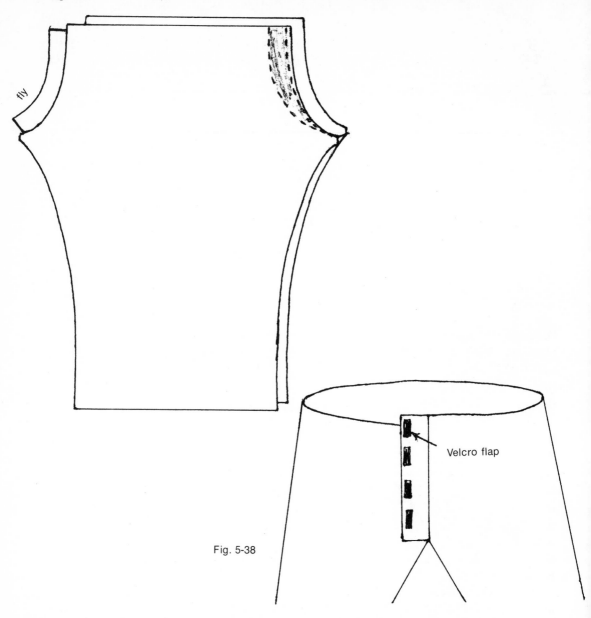

fly

Fig. 5-38

Velcro flap

include a 2-inch flap for the fly as shown. Fig. 5-36.

7. Sew the two legs together at the rear; take in for better fit or leave as is. Fig. 5-37.

8. Sew Velcro tabs to flap and front of pants to close fly. Fig. 5-38.

9. Add a draw hem to the waist or in-stall belt loops. Finish cuffs to length and style desired.

10. Inspect all stitching. Look for loose seams, puckering (a problem with this type of construction), and missed stitches. Repair as needed.

6

Shelters

For backpackers, to tent or not to tent is often a major question. Some rugged traditionalists scorn the use of a tent entirely. They claim that a tent stifles freedom and smothers adventure, and that it overinsulates the user and prevents him from experiencing the real outdoors. To them, shelter means natural shelter—windfalls, trees, caves, or perhaps a bivouac or lean-to constructed from whatever nature provides. Of course, for those who take this seriously, it can also mean getting cold, wet, and downright miserable—but a little suffering is supposed to be good for you.

Others, who agree with the traditionalists on their dislike of tents, but who also dislike getting cold, wet, and miserable, compromise slightly by carrying a tarp, poncho, or plastic sheet. Any of these can be quickly turned into a skimpy but serviceable bivouac that will keep out the worst of the bad weather.

Then there are those who—rain or shine—always carry a tent. They view the traditionalists as fanatics and masochists,

and are more than willing to trade a little less adventure and freedom for a lot more comfort and a little extra weight. And, of course, there are those who worship comfort above all else—they're the ones who think that roughing it is taking their self-contained tent-trailer off the highway to some place that doesn't have a disposal station.

And so the controversy goes. Which way is the right way? You'll have to decide for yourself, but speaking as one who has tried and enjoyed all of these approaches, here are my thoughts on the subject of shelters.

Man really is one of the toughest, most adaptable creatures on the face of the earth. For thousands of generations he made do without artificial shelters (caves, trees, and the open air suited him just fine). In fact, a sizable percentage of the world's population still hasn't realized that anything more is necessary. So man can survive outdoors quite well without a shelter, if he knows what he is doing, if he respects nature, and if he is lucky.

Roughing it, going cave man, or getting back to basics, call it what you will, survival-style camping is gaining in popularity. Books, courses, and even established schools will try to teach you how to survive in the wilderness with a bare minimum of gear. Part of this training is how to find and utilize natural shelter, and how to improvise some very decent shelters from available materials.

I am very much in favor of this. I feel every outdoorsman should know as much as possible about survival in the outdoors. Learn the survival techniques for shelter building if possible and practice them, with discretion, if you really must; however, don't use them unless you have to. Log cabins and lean-tos have their place, but backpackers and campers are no longer pioneers. When camping leave the axe at home, and whenever possible carry a lightweight shelter along instead.

Designing and building your own tent can be a complicated, difficult, and critical job. A number of factors must be taken into consideration (fabric tear strength, porosity, stress distribution, aerodynamics, etc.), so for this reason I suggest that the amateur stick closely to the standard and proven designs. Sophisticated design and innovative thinking have their place, but when it comes to tents leave that to the experts. Beautiful, unorthodox, and highly sophisticated designs that are reliable, roomy, and light are available (notably the superb tents from North Face), but these are beyond the capabilities of the average do-it-yourselfer.

For more details on tent construction and design, and for some interesting ideas for your do-it-yourself tent, you might look into *Backpacking Equipment: A Consumer's Guide* by William Kemsley. Kemsley's book includes evaluation and comparisons on many of the leading commercial tents. You will find it worthwhile reading.

PONCHOS, TARPS, AND TUBES: BIVOUACS

On weekend trips or for overnighting I generally leave the tent at home, but I usually take such trips only if the weatherman is cooperating. For short excursions I find a tent a hindrance—it slows me down with extra weight in my pack, and it affects my mobility. Instead, I carry a poncho, for use as a garment or ground sheet, and if the occasional shower does manage to catch up with me, I can pitch the poncho as a bivouac and wait it out. Since I rely on this setup only when expecting decent weather, I rarely have to suffer for long under such a drafty, leaky shelter.

I prefer the poncho for use as a bivouac for one reason—a poncho will do almost everything a tarp or tube will, and you can wear the poncho as a rain garment, too. This important advantage is also the poncho's chief disadvantage—when the poncho is being used as a shelter you are deprived of your personal rain garment. A lightweight breathable nylon wind jacket weighs only ounces and can be carried along for those times the poncho is set up as a shelter. The light nylon keeps out rain for short periods, it's adequate for camp chores and short trips away from your shelter, and it will be useful in other situations, too.

Ponchos come in different sizes and styles, with some of them cleverly modified to make into much better shelters. The regular poncho (about 84×54 inches) is the most common type. It makes an adequate rain garment, but a somewhat skimpy shelter. The frame pack poncho is larger (about 108×60 inches) to allow it to fit over a pack. The extra fabric at the back may be snapped up when not used with a pack, and its larger size makes it much better for use as a shelter.

Frostline offers a kit to turn a poncho into a nice one-man bivouac. The kit consists of a snap-in floor and a set of poles. Details for constructing a poncho are given in Chapter 5, Project 5-2.

A tarp is a rectangle of material, usually waterproof, that has many uses on a camping trip. You can use one as a ground sheet, a sleeping bag cover, or as a versatile, light, easy to pitch shelter. When choosing a tarp for use as a shelter, get one about 10×10 feet, and look for one with grommets along the outside and reinforced ties at strategic spots near the center. These ties allow the tarp to be pitched in a variety of ways that are often a great improvement over the usual lean-to or pup-tent pitches.

For use by backpackers, lightweight nylon tarps, plastic sheeting, polytarps (plastic sheeting reinforced with a grid of fibers), or the heat-reflecting space blankets are all quite good. Good quality nylon should last you several years. Reinforced plastic sheeting should last at least a couple of seasons, but if using ordinary plastic sheeting, or the emergency pocket-size space blankets, expect to buy a new one for every trip. With careful handling plastic sheeting may last a few weeks, but it is not reliable. However, it is cheap and readily available. Get it in the thicker sizes, and get the opaque (black or green) for some privacy and slightly more durability.

A tube tent is a polyethylene tube that may be pitched on a ridgeline to form a pup tent. The weight of your body and equipment keeps the floor in place, but since the sides are not pegged down a good wind means a lot of flapping. Tube tents do have a significant advantage over tarps—a weatherproof joint along the bottom and a floor—but every time you use a tube you run the risk of cutting or puncturing the fragile floor. If you use a tube for more than a short trip, get in the habit of placing the same part on the ground each time; otherwise, your shelter will soon resemble a shower stall.

Tube tents are usually found only in stores specializing in lightweight camping gear, but you could easily make one from readily available plastic sheeting. Two-inch tape may be used with a 10×10-foot piece of sheeting to make a one-man tube. For a two-man tube use a 10×12-foot piece (circumference).

A shelter made from a poncho, tarp, or tube will never be as weatherproof as a good tent, but with ingenuity and the right accessories you can usually rig up something that shuts out the worst. If you are serious about bivouacing, always carry lots of line (I like 550-pound-test nylon parachute line) because sooner or later you will run into a situation that requires it. If you carry a set of lightweight pegs and poles (or walking stick), you can pitch your shelter in a hurry, without relying on trees. This is sometimes very important. And if you use a tarp regularly, invest a few dollars for some Versa Ties or Visklamps, for attaching guy lines to lightweight tarps without grommets. They make the job much easier.

BACKPACKING TENTS

For longer trips, where weather predictions may be unreliable and where waiting it out is impractical, I carry a lightweight, fully enclosed backpacking tent as insurance. A few nights spent under a poncho in mosquito season or in heavy rains will quickly convince you of the desirability of a fully enclosed shelter. A light, inexpensive, single wall, waterproof backpacking tent with adequate ventilation and properly designed flaps and netting is ideal for such trips.

A backpacking tent is usually a small (suitable for one to three people), light (weighing between 3 to 8 pounds), and highly portable unit. Tents that fit this definition come in many different styles and shapes, range in price from $10 to $150, and can range in quality from junk right up to tents almost suitable for expedition use.

A backpacker will be using his tent primarily for sleeping in, so smaller tents may be adequate. If you do your camping in areas where rain is overabundant, you might want to invest in a larger tent, to allow for actually living inside it for longer periods, and to store your gear inside with you. In most cases a tent with a floor size of 5×7½ feet should be more than enough for two, with room for three if friendly. Remember, the smaller the tent, the lighter the tent, and the less weight you will have to lug around on your back.

A well-designed and well-constructed tent of this type will provide excellent protection from insects and rain, while at the same time providing adequate ventilation for comfort. These tents will stand up to moderate winds, quite a bit of abuse, and some may even be used (with discretion) for winter camping. A good backpacking tent is probably your best bet

A backpacking tent. This tent is from Ridgeline and has coated waterproof walls, I-poles, 12-inch side walls with zippered vents, and is light, roomy, comfortable, and inexpensive.

for a first tent, even for large families, and is recommended as the tent most suitable for most people.

Single Wall or Tent and Fly?

One thing to think about is whether or not you want a single-wall tent or a double-wall tent (tent and fly). A single-wall tent is usually made of waterproof materials throughout, and relies on windows and vents to control the condensation caused by the evaporation of body moisture in an enclosed space. With these tents make sure that all vents and windows are covered by flaps and by insectproof screens. The vents should be large in size and adjustable, but even in cold or windy weather you may be forced to leave them partially open to avoid condensation. For moderate conditions these tents can be entirely suitable, but for severe conditions they may not be as comfortable. A single-wall two-man tent will weigh about 2 pounds less than a similar tent of double-wall design and will cost a lot less too, so consider both their advantages and disadvantages before deciding.

Many backpacking tents are made with a double-wall design. The inner wall is breathable, and usually will protect only against wind and light rains. For maxi-

Double-wall (tent and fly) design allows moist air to escape through the walls. This one-man tent has walls made of netting, which makes it very nice for summer.

mum protection a waterproof, nonbreathable fly is pitched over the tent. The space between the tent and the fly allows water vapor inside the tent to escape through the walls, rather than condensing on the inside and dripping. If you are going to use your tent in colder weather, then the double-wall design is much more practical. You can close up all the vents

Side vents on a single-wall, waterproof tent.

and still get fewer problems from condensation. In addition, the space between the walls acts as insulation, making the double-wall tents much warmer. Or if the weather is especially nice, you may decide to carry only the tent or the fly alone.

Shapes

The most efficient shape, in terms of volume enclosed by the least fabric for a good backpacking tent is the sphere. Half of a sphere gives us a dome, which is a nice shape to use for tents. Unfortunately, this most efficient shape requires a very complicated and inefficient arrangement of poles and supports to maintain. North Face has introduced an interesting geodesic dome tent they call the Oval In-Tention. This beauty is a technical marvel, but I definitely wouldn't advise a do-it-yourselfer to attempt one.

A much more practical compromise between efficiency and simplicity is the design commonly called igloo, dome, or semidome as represented by the tents from Jan Sport. These tents are not true domes, but for all practical purposes they are just about as roomy, and a lot easier to make. The flexible fiberglass frames push outward on the tent fabric to create a free-standing tent with a stressed skin, which makes for a tight pitch and efficient spilling of wind. The frame also has enough flexibility and rigidity to absorb wind gusts without too much distortion, but in really heavy weather all tents should be braced out with guy lines.

Another efficient shape that has been receiving a lot of attention lately is the half-cylinder. These hoop tents are fairly strong, but the large vertical sides stop a lot of wind. Most of these designs use flexible fiberglass poles, and I have seen such

A dome tent that is free standing, compact, and easy to pitch. This one is the Altra Two Person Tent with rainfly and vestibule fly. (Photo courtesy ALTRA, Inc.)

tents lean over and shake around even when guyed out. The hoops just don't have the wind spilling or shock absorbing characteristics of the domes.

With rigid aluminum poles the hoop tent is a different proposition entirely, providing lots of space, real headroom, and walls that are vertical at the floors for maximum usability of space. The basic hoop tent may be modified somewhat for more efficiency or better wind-shedding

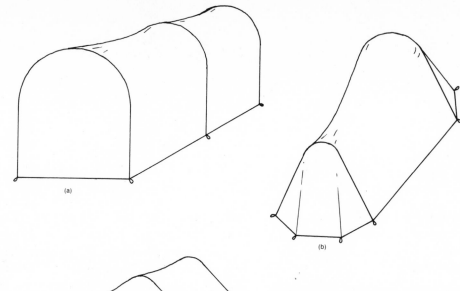

(a)

(b)

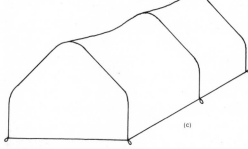

(c)

Hoop tents are roomy, simple to make, and if rigid
poles are used very strong.

capabilities. With ⅝-inch aluminum rigid
poles to keep the shape, there is little distortion or flopping. Several well-known
companies are making some quite success-
ful tents along these lines.

The most popular shape of all for a tent
is the traditional A-tent or pup tent, which
is fairly easy to make at home. This style
of tent has proven itself through the years,
and lately has been coming in for some
interesting modifications that improve it
even more. The simple pup tent, with A-
or I-poles, has its merits (strong, fairly
light for volume, sheds wind and rain
very well, easy to make at home, versatile)
but it also has its bad points (lost space at
peak and near sides, sags unless cut with

catenary* at peak, requires pullouts at
sides for strength and efficiency, ends are
subject to wind load, guy line at front is
awkward).

The A-shape is the one I recommend to
do-it-yourselfers. This design can be made
into a simple, inexpensive tent, entirely
suitable for general backpacking, or with
extra care and attention to detail, it could
be made suitable for use as a mountaineering or expedition tent. The projects section of this chapter has plans for a simple

* Catenary cut refers to the fact that a line strung
between two points will naturally hang down due to
its own weight. Look at any telephone line for an
example.

Various modifications of the basic pup tent.

Left:
High at one end for headroom, low at feet for more efficiency and less weight.

Middle:
Squared peak gives extra usable headroom.

Right:
Vertical side walls with pullouts give extra usable space at sides.

but adequate little two-man tent that could be made in a single-wall, I-pole version for lightweight warm-weather backpacking, or made as a double-wall, A-pole-at-each-end version for winter camping and mountaineering. It can be a fine tent either way.

Frames

There are several ways to rig frames for this relatively simple and straightforward pup-tent shape. The simplest setup is with I-poles at each end. This gives fairly good stability (the top of the triangle is supported on all four sides by seams or guy lines to turn the pole effectively into a pyramid), but all the stress is concentrated on a single vulnerable area. I-pole failure is quite common, especially with the less expensive tents that use softer and cheaper poles. Even with the best tents, gusty winds can sometimes break or bend

these poles or rip out the pole and tent joint at the top.

A-poles are almost twice as strong as I-poles, so are recommended if heavy winds are a factor. Strength, however, is not their only advantage. By using A-poles at the ends, you are using one of nature's strongest building forms—the triangle—to support your tent. The triangle at the end of your tent is rigid in its own plane, so side distortion and flapping are minimized. You will also find it a lot easier to enter and exit your tent without having to twist yourself around an I-pole that falls right in the middle of the door. And the tent is supported along a much larger area (sleeves), eliminating ripped-out poles in most cases.

If you want to make your A-tent free-standing and eliminate those clumsy guy lines at the ends, then consider either a ridge pole or else tilt the poles. The ridge pole strengthens the tent and allows it to be moved around as a unit, but the tilted poles don't require any extra parts. Both of these modifications should still be guyed and pegged out in heavy winds.

If you are interested in the stressed skin designs, consider what a broken or lost pole could do to you. With some of the more complicated external framed tents,

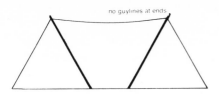

Tilt A-poles out to make tent free standing and to eliminate guylines at ends.

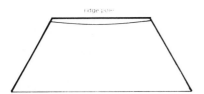

Add ridge pole to strengthen tent, and to make it free standing.

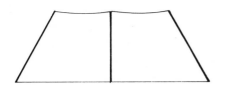

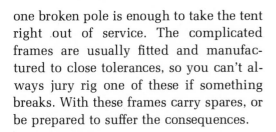

Fiberglass wands in sleeves; under tension, they reduce flapping and add to interior space.

A mountain tent. This one is a Sierra Designs Glacier. This tent has breathable walls (with fly), A-poles, catenary cut, vertical cut side walls, two entrances, a vestibule, a cookhole, and features quality construction throughout. The properly designed zippered entrance can give adjustable ventilation at the end, and is very convenient to use.

one broken pole is enough to take the tent right out of service. The complicated frames are usually fitted and manufactured to close tolerances, so you can't always jury rig one of these if something breaks. With these frames carry spares, or be prepared to suffer the consequences.

MOUNTAIN TENTS

For the severe conditions encountered in mountaineering and winter camping, a well-made, top-quality tent is a necessity.

Snow, cold, high winds, and heavy rains are handled reliably only by a properly designed, well-made tent. Anything less may let you down just when you need it most. If you are expecting such conditions forget any delusions about roughing it with a poncho or a cheap tent; "experiencing nature" is one thing, but survival is another.

Mountain tents (also known as expedition tents, high-altitude tents, and winter tents) closely resemble backpacking tents, but because mountain tents are expected to stand up to severe conditions, they are generally made with greater care and attention to detail. Also, since they are to be used by serious backpackers and mountaineers, they have features that the average person rarely needs and cares little about. These extras make the mountain tents much sturdier, more livable, and considerably more expensive.

While mountain tents are available in different styles and shapes, the most popular design is still the two-man, double A-frame. These tents usually feature a catenary cut, two entrances, and a bathtub floor, and many have such options as cookholes, snow flaps, frostliner, vestibule, etc. Mountain tents range in price from $100 to $300, and are usually worth every penny of the cost to those who really need them. For the average backpacker, who will never take advantage of all the extra features in a mountain tent, a good backpacking tent is a better choice because it's a few pounds lighter and much cheaper.

The first and foremost consideration when choosing a mountain tent should always be reliability—a tent that fails just when conditions are at their worst can mean bad trouble in the wilderness. Reliability is a function of materials, workmanship, and design. Many tents are advertised as "suitable for mountaineering"—and they are, in light winds—but for serious use get the best tent you can afford. Genuine mountain tents are made from only the finest materials, heavily reinforced at all probable failure points, and they are double or triple stitched for extra strength. And they are simple, well-thought-out designs that have been extensively tested as to their suitability before they ever get on the market. Distrust any new design until it has been thoroughly field tested by you, no matter how desirable some of its features may seem in the store.

Even a well-designed tent can blow apart or collapse if not made of the proper materials, or if put together with sloppy workmanship. Tents made from top-quality, lightweight ripstop nylon have stood up to some really fierce storms, so the materials available today will do the job if put together properly. Unhappily, craftsmanship nowadays carries a very high price tag, so if you want your tent put together properly, be prepared to pay for it. Or try making your own. A quality tent can be made at a fraction of the commercial prices. This is one place where you really can save a lot of money with do-it-yourself.

Size

A mountain tent should be somewhat larger than a backpacking tent; if the weather turns really bad you may have to spend a few long days cooped up in one. Boredom starts to set in, claustrophobia takes over, and even your best friend can become a real pain when you're confined for a few days in a too small tent. On the other hand, a mountain tent that is too large is inefficient (you heat your tent with body heat, which works nicely for small tents, but not so nicely if the volume is too large). Also, if care is not used when designing a larger tent, the wind loads on large panels can become higher than ripstop nylon can take.

Mountain tents are available in sizes that may be theoretically more efficient than two or more smaller tents, but in practice it has been found that a couple of small tents provides more versatility, especially in areas where space may be at a premium, and also allows various combinations that are not available with one large tent (if the party splits up, for example). The optimum size for efficiency, versatility, strength, and portability is the two- or three-man size. A floor size of $5 \times 7\frac{1}{2}$ feet is just about ideal, but usually these tents will have additional space for storage in the vestibules.

Tents, Flys, and Frostliners

For a serious mountain or winter tent the double-wall (tent and fly) design is the only suitable one. At higher altitudes and colder temperatures condensation becomes more of a problem, and if you have to cook in your tent (not recommended) or hang wet clothing out to dry inside it, then you will need all the ventilation you can get. Such situations are not uncommon in winter camping or mountaineering, so get a tent with breathable walls.

If the tent is to be used extensively for cold-weather camping, then consider a frostliner as a very desirable option. A frostliner is a lightweight inner tent made from absorbent cotton fabric that soaks up moisture which otherwise would condense on the inside of the tent walls and freeze. Without a frostliner these ice crystals usually shake loose with every bump or flap of the tent walls; you can have a snowstorm inside your tent as well as one outside. When the frostliner gets too wet or too iced up, remove it and either hang it out to dry or shake it to remove the ice. Frostliners also provide another layer of air between you and the cold, so they add considerable insulation and warmth to a winter tent.

Frostliners and flys on most tents are removable, for versatility, but a few specialized tents have the fly sewn directly to the tent. On such models make sure that there is adequate space between the walls and the fly for insulation, and to allow for some air circulation, to remove condensation from the inner wall. If the fly touches the walls of the tent at any point, the tent becomes in effect a single-wall tent and condensation can take place there.

If the tent is to be used for below-freezing weather only, some authorities recommend leaving the fly at home to save weight. They point out that you don't get much rain below freezing, so a fly is not necessary. I prefer to carry the fly for winter camping for several important reasons. Snow can melt on contact with your tent, so some waterproofing is desirable. Then there is the insulation factor—a tent with a fly is warmer than a tent without one. Also, some tents are made from fabric that is overly breathable, to aid in reducing condensation, and these tents may be far from windproof without a nonporous fly for protection. Take a look at the wind chill chart on page 34; you need only a little wind to get a lot of cold.

Finally, there is the strength/wind spilling factor. A tent pitched properly with a fly is much stronger than a tent without one. For maximum strength the fly should always be attached to extra pegs placed slightly farther out than the tent pegs. You may also find that the fly pitches much more tautly than the tent itself, which is a great help in eliminating flapping tent walls. Carry the fly: it is worth the extra effort. A fly with an extension (either detachable or sewn on) is an excellent accessory for any breathable tent, and the addition of such a fly goes far toward turning a backpacking tent into one suitable for more serious winter or expedition use.

One final word on winter camping and breathability: If you decide to ignore all the advice and try winter camping in a single-wall, nonbreathable tent, be very careful about ventilation. Zippers have frozen and snow has been known to drift over vents, and people have suffocated in such conditions.

Shapes

When it comes to mountain tents there are fewer shapes to choose from; the reliability factor rules out some of the more exotic designs.

Currently both dome and hoop tents that are suitable for serious expedition and mountain use are available commercially. These designs, if properly executed, can be as strong, light, and stable as the A-tent, and also can be much roomier due to their more efficient use of space. However, from the do-it-yourselfer's point of view, neither of these designs is as easy to make as an A-tent.

For optimum strength and resistance to wind and snow loads, a tent should be taut and tight when pitched. Many tents cannot be pitched tight without overstraining the materials, but in the best tents considerable care is taken in design, layout, and fabrication to ensure a taut pitch. A loose tent is a flapping tent, and a tent that flaps can tear itself apart from the strain. Even if this doesn't occur, the flapping makes the tent much colder (moving air is cold air) and much less livable (it's difficult to sleep in a flapping tent; the noise and commotion may be somewhat less than soothing).

The standard A-tent can be made relatively tight if certain steps are taken. Most important, the ridge line seam must be cut with catenary. The amount of catenary to use is variable, but ¼-inch sag per foot of ridge is suitable for lightweight nylon tents. The sides can also be given a better cut. This involves a lot of extra work, but it may be worth it; such tents are among the tightest and nicest pitching of the A-tents. Since this design allows vertical side walls with an A-frame, it is also somewhat roomier than the standard types.

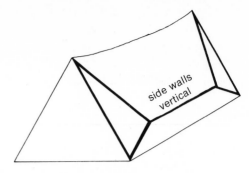

Vertical cut side walls; extra panels deflect wind nicely and allow the use of A-poles at ends.

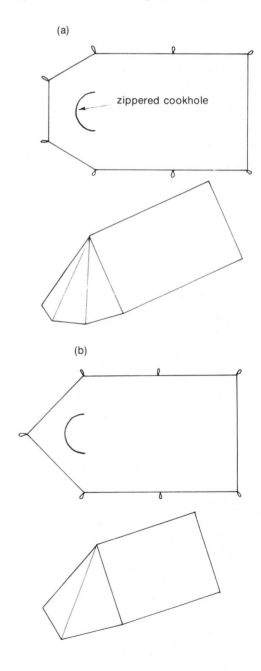

(a)

zippered cookhole

(b)

The two most common vestibule shapes for A-tents.

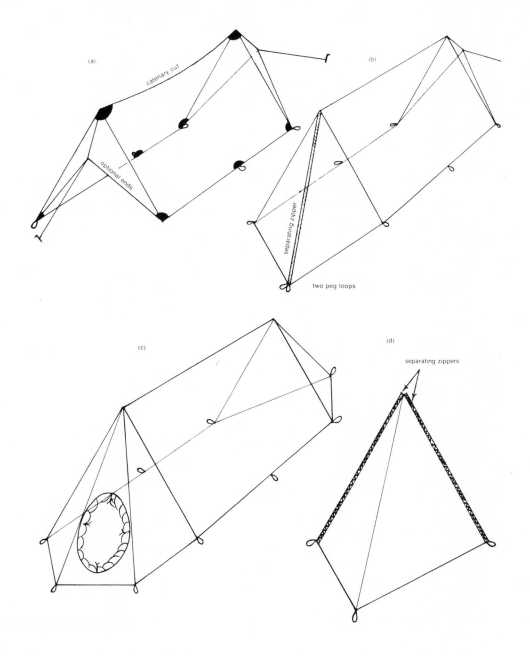

(a)

catenary cut

optional ends

(b)

separating zipper

two peg loops

(c)

(d)

separating zippers

Tent flys for A-tents.

Almost all A-tents, intended for serious winter or expedition use, are outfitted with vestibules, which help considerably in adding to a tent's ability to stay up in high winds. I feel that A-tents without a vestibule (fitted instead with a fly that extends over the same area) provide more versatility without any important drawbacks. This is the arrangement I recommend to those of you making or buying a tent for all-around use. If the tent is to be used mainly for winter camping, then a more specialized design with a sewn-on vestibule may be more suitable.

Frames

The frame of a mountain tent is subject to all kinds of abuse, and is expected to survive such indignities as hundred-mile-an-hour winds, all-night snow falls, and the occasional encounter with near-sighted mountain goats. The standard arrangement for mountain A-tents has for years been a double A-frame of rigid aluminum alloy tubing. These poles are slipped through fabric sleeves at the ends of the tent, and joined at the top with some kind of fitting. At the bottom they should fit into pockets or grommets fastened to the corners of the tent. Otherwise, if the tent is pitched on snow, the poles will sink. I prefer the web pockets as the grommets sometimes all too easily tear out from the strain.

For extra versatility and for emergency use you can rig an A-tent to accept both A- and I-poles. For lightweight backpacking you can use the I-poles. Or if your A-poles get broken on a lengthy trip, you can still jury-rig some I-poles that will keep the tent up. If you are making your own tent, consider this feature.

For super heavy-duty use you can rig an A-tent with three sets of poles instead of

Fittings for the top of a set of A-poles; the first three are ideal for the do-it-yourselfer, while the last one is available commercially as a replacement.

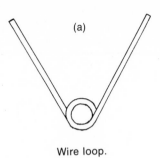

(a)

Wire loop.

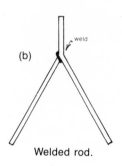

(b)

Welded rod.

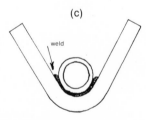

(c)

Sixty-degree pipe coupling with ring added for ridgeline.

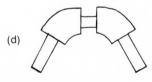

(d)

Cast plastic or aluminum; the plastic flexes enough to allow different angles.

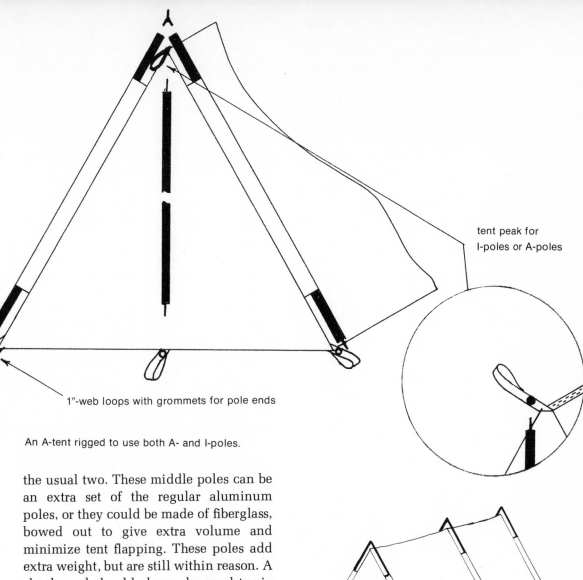

tent peak for
I-poles or A-poles

1"-web loops with grommets for pole ends

An A-tent rigged to use both A- and I-poles.

the usual two. These middle poles can be an extra set of the regular aluminum poles, or they could be made of fiberglass, bowed out to give extra volume and minimize tent flapping. These poles add extra weight, but are still within reason. A shock cord should always be used to rig the guy lines and the frame for severe wind. The shock cord absorbs most of the strain, and pullouts are cushioned from heavy gusts.

For the ultimate in a taut pitch, a stressed-skin design has distinct advantages over a standard tent and frame. With a stressed-skin tent the poles are flexible and under tension when erected. Such a unit absorbs wind gusts, just like the shock cord, with give in the frame. The proper balance between too much give (floppy tent, weak frame) and too little

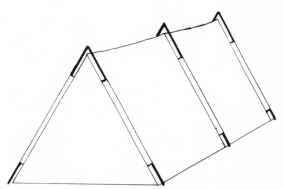

An A-tent can be rigged with three sets of A-poles for extra strength, and to eliminate side flapping.

(broken pole joints) is critical with such designs. Jan Sport offers flexible tent pole sets in fiberglass or aluminum that are of possible use to the do-it-yourselfer, but only actual use in the field will prove whether these poles are suitable for your application.

Most of the stressed-skin designs are also freestanding. This means that they can be pitched without guy lines. Whether or not they should be pitched this way is another question. For moderate conditions freestanding tents may live up to their name, but when heavy winds come up they must be guyed out and braced just like any other tent design. The flexible frames will absorb only moderate amounts of wind before pole breakage, tent distortion, and possible tent failure. If this doesn't impress you, then consider the fact that whole tents have been known to fly away at inopportune times—sometimes carrying irreplaceable gear (and even on occasion their unwary owners) over cliffs or on some exciting rides.

Special Features

The real difference between a backpacking tent of the highest quality and a tent designed for serious mountain or expedition use shows up in the special features that a mountain tent has. The mountain tent is designed to serve as a genuine home for extended periods of time, under any and all conditions. For these reasons mountain tents have such features as bathtub floors, double entrances, cookholes, snowflaps, and extra conveniences such as internal pockets.

Most quality tents are made with a bathtub floor, but for mountain tents this should be a required feature. For camping on snow or in wet conditions, a bathtub floor is the one that will keep out the wet. There should be a minimum of ground level seams, and every seam exposed to possible leakage should be coated with a flexible waterproofing compound.

Tents designed for cold-weather use should have two entrances. This provides for a second exit if one gets drifted over or frozen shut. If living in the tent for extended periods, you will find this back door an almost indispensible convenience. This second entrance should be at the opposite end of the tent from the main one (not a tunnel entrance sewn into the main door). Otherwise, snow could cover both doors at once, and the convenience of having two doors isn't of much value at all.

Entrances for a mountain tent can be either the zippered flap type or the tunnel type. The usual arrangement is one of each—the zippered flap for convenience, the tunnel for reliability. If you wish you could use zippered entrances at both locations—the chance of both zippers freezing at the same time seems remote— or you could use two tunnel entrances. Tunnel entrances are considerably easier to make than the zippered type, and have the added advantage of being more weatherproof to use. In addition, two tents with tunnel entrances can be joined together to give you a two-roomed tent. This is sometimes very useful.

If the tent is to be used exclusively for cold weather, then you could leave out the usual mosquito netting over the openings or make it detachable. Otherwise every vent, window, or entrance must be covered with tightly woven netting that closes completely. Without such netting, bugs can and will get in to make your nights miserable.

Most good mountain tents provide for extra ventilation with vents. These vents may be of the tunnel type, or the top part of a properly designed zippered door may be left open slightly. If the tent is provided with such vents they should be placed just under the peak, to promote the exhaust of

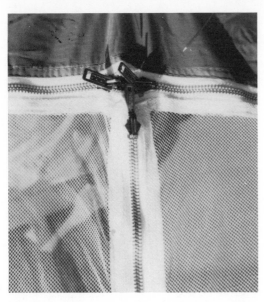
All vents, entrances, and windows must seal tightly with insect netting.

warm, damp air, and to keep rain and snow from getting in.

If you decide to risk cooking inside your tent (sometimes necessary), then a cookhole provides a place to do so without too much of a mess. Hot stoves have a way of sinking into snow, tipping over, and starting fires, so be careful here. It is always a good idea to have a vent located high over the cookhole to exhaust the warm air. Many poorly designed tents have a cookhole that is placed too close to a tent wall—remember even "flameproof" nylon burns. I prefer to use a floorless vestibule fly combination for my tents. This allows cooking outside the tent without problems.

For serious winter use on ice or rock, many mountain tents come equipped with snow flaps that may be detachable or sewn on. If making snow flaps for your tent I suggest you make them detachable (they sometimes freeze in place and must be left behind), and I recommend using coated waterproof fabrics that won't absorb water and aggravate the freezing problem.

For extra convenience, and for organization, most good tents come with pockets sewn to the walls. These are very useful for storage of small items. These pockets are easy to make, and could be sewn on during construction or added later. If you make one of them large enough it can even take the place of a stuff sack, allowing you to store the tent inside its own built-in pocket.

CAMP TENTS

Camp tents (family tents) are larger than backpacking tents or mountain tents, and are generally designed to be pitched for longer periods of time. Some are made of canvas and are suitable only for car campers, but a few manufacturers specialize in lightweight, portable, nylon designs that are ideal for use as base tents for expeditions, and for larger backpacking parties. These multiperson designs often weigh less per person than two smaller tents, but of course their versatility is not as great. When designing or building large tents you can run into a number of extra problems. If using lightweight materials, keep the panels as small as possible and reinforce extensively with 1-inch tape or lap-felled seams.

There are many shapes and sizes to choose from here, but again the A-tent can be the do-it-yourselfer's best choice. REI offers a nice four-man A-tent they call the Grand Hotel. This tent is a standard A-design enlarged to 80 inches wide, 88 inches long, and 52 inches high. The materials used are 1.9-ounce ripstop for the walls and coated taffeta for the floor. This design seems ideal for a do-it-yourselfer needing a light, compact four-man tent.

If you need something larger, consider the tipi—perhaps the easiest and roomiest design for the do-it-yourselfer. And such tents made of lightweight fabrics are backpackable. With the tipi though, you will probably have to cut poles at the camp site, which may not always be possible.

Portable geodesic domes are now available that are light enough to be backpacked when taken down, and as large as a real house when erected. Unfortunately these units are more building than tent, but for large semipermanent installations they may be ideal. Jan Sport offers a light, portable six-man version of their stressed-skin dome and possibly this could be more your style. There are also several hoop designs that are roomy enough for larger parties and light enough for backpacking. Look around and see what you can find.

MATERIALS, TOOLS, AND PROCEDURES
FOR TENTS

MATERIALS

It is very important that you use the best materials available for your do-it-yourself tent. The material costs are a relatively small part of the total cost involved; your labor is a much more significant contribution. Don't waste all that labor by skimping on materials.

Fabric

For tent walls a fabric that is light and strong is needed. In general, the best fabric to use for breathable tent walls is 1.9-ounce ripstop nylon (with a tight weave and a firm hand) that has been treated to make it water repellent. Nylon taffeta is a somewhat tighter fabric that also makes excellent tents, and Dacron ripstop is another alternative.

For the floor a fabric is needed that is waterproof, abrasion resistant, strong, and tough. For sturdy tent floors that will give good life and not weigh too much, 2- to 3-ounce double-coated nylon taffeta is ideal. The coating should be urethane, or some equivalent, that will not crack, separate, or deteriorate with use. For expedition tents or winter tents you might use fabric as heavy as 4 ounces. For a lightweight tent 1.9-ounce urethane-coated ripstop will last several years with care.

For the tent fly, or for walls in a nonbreathable tent, a strong, light, coated fabric that will withstand the wind, rain, and sun is needed. Material as light as 1.5 ounces is used successfully for these applications, but I feel that 1.9-ounce polymer coated (e.g., Temper Kote) ripstop nylon is the ideal fabric. Polymer coatings are somewhat stretchier than the usual urethane types, which means polymer coatings don't detract much from the tear strength of the fabric. This is a very important consideration with the lightweight fabrics used here.

For vents, windows, and doors, some type of insect netting is necessary. I like to use knits here. Good examples of a knit will be woven tight enough to keep out any bugs, loose enough to see through, strong enough to survive, and flexible enough to give with any major strain and then return to their original shape when the pressure is removed. Or, if you prefer, you could use marquisette netting instead. Knits and netting are available in nylon, Dacron, or polyester, so take your choice.

Thread

I use a thread made from polyester and cotton for all my tents. This thread supposedly has the strength of a synthetic and the ability of cotton to swell when wet, to fill needle holes. It is also somewhat more suitable for use on home sewing machines than stronger, stretchier nylon. If nylon thread works well in your machine, you could use it. I coat all tent seams with Kenyon K-Kote sealer in any case, so threads for a tent are judged only by what feeds best.

Hardware

Zippers are an important component of a good tent, and in a tent they get a lot of use and abuse. I use #5 Delrin zippers from YKK wherever I need a zipper that takes a pull with tabs on both sides (doors). For windows, vents, and wherever tight curves are a factor, I prefer large YKK coil zippers. These are not readily available to me with tabs on both sides. Since the coil zippers are somewhat smoother and more weatherproof than the Delrin-toothed style, I would use them throughout if I could get proper sliders for them. Make sure your zippers are on a synthetic tape; cotton tape can rot out long before the zipper wears out from use.

Pegs can be made from various materials and in various styles. You should have several sets to suit whatever conditions you will be encountering. Pegs can be bought or you could make your own. For additional information about pegs, see the "Options, Accessories, and Modifications for Tents" section of this chapter.

Lines for all my tents are made from 550-pound-test parachute cord. This is a woven nylon line that fits tent line tighteners well. It has more than enough strength for this application. This line will not rot or unravel like the lines commonly found on cheap tents. If you already have a cheap tent, switching over to these lines can be a worthwhile improvement. Flame seal all ends with this type of line to prevent fraying.

Poles are traditionally made from aluminum alloy tubing. For small tents ⅝-inch, .028-wall, 6061-T6 aluminum alloy tubing is ideal. This material is readily available and fairly cheap. For flexible poles for a stressed-skin design, solid or hollow fiberglass is being used, along with small-diameter aluminum tubing of a harder, springier composition (7001 aluminum).

TOOLS

You will need a sewing machine in good working condition to make your tent. With all those long seams and large panels, a large table will be a definite asset, as will an assistant. Make sure your sewing machine is properly set up before starting; there is a lot of stitching here and minor problems can become major hassles on a big job.

You will need pencils, chalk, a carpenter's square, a tape measure, a protractor for measuring angles, a long straightedge, and a large space to work on for layout. Work as accurately as you can when laying out your tent. A fraction of an inch out can mean an annoying wrinkle or a weak stretched seam; do it right.

You will also need some tools if making your own poles. A hacksaw, file, popriveter, solder, or epoxy glue may be useful. If buying poles you may still need some tools to trim them to size. If getting grommets installed commercially, make sure they use a type that will fit your pole ends; of course, it's also important that they do a good job.

PROCEDURES

A tent is one place where lack of craftsmanship is glaringly obvious. A quality tent is a thing of beauty and precision, with panels that pitch tautly and seams that accept their proper share of the stress and no more. If care is not used in layout, cutting, and sewing, a tent will not pitch tightly and it will be much weaker, no matter how well designed or how good the materials. This is a job that must be done carefully and properly if you are going to end up with a good tent.

If you have any doubts about how your tent should go together, then don't hesitate to construct scale models before starting in on the real thing. A model drawn in two dimensions on paper, then taped together to give you a three-dimensional representation, can be invaluable in understanding what goes where, and how. You could also construct a scale model from cheap fabric (an old sheet) if you feel you need practice in the sewing techniques.

When doing the actual sewing, go carefully and slowly. Make each seam as if it were the most important part of the tent. Seams are used in tents for reinforcement and transmission of stress, and if they are not made properly they will usually fail from the severe strains imposed on a tent by the wind. Pin all seams before sewing to ensure that the panels will end up even. Nylon is a very stretchy material and just because you cut the panels straight doesn't mean they will end up straight when you are finished sewing. The seams must be straight, sewn with tight, straight stitches, and triple or double stitched for greater strength.

All seams should be of the lap-felled type for extra strength. The lap should work like a shingle, with the top layer folding over the lower layer to provide a waterproof seal. This is especially important on all horizontal seams, which will collect water and leak if not made properly. All seams should be carefully sealed with a flexible waterproof sealing compound. I use Kenyon K-Kote Seam Sealer for this; it is compatible with most Kenyon coatings and does a very good job.

Whenever attaching pullouts, or for any other high-stress areas, reinforce the thin fabric of your tent with patches of extra material, sewn on to spread out and accept the strain. The peaks and corners of any tent will last longer if an extra layer of fabric is used there for reinforcing. Try to incorporate all pullouts into a seam, which will accept and spread out strain quite nicely, or else use round sewn-on patches. Sew all pullouts to both layers of such patches, then seal the stitch holes.

For an excellent practice project that will be useful, easy to make, and that will teach you all of the techniques needed for making your tent, try making a poncho (Chapter 5, Project 5-2). Another good practice project is to make the fly for your tent first.

OPTIONS, ACCESSORIES, AND
MODIFICATIONS FOR TENTS

Fly

Making a fly is really very simple. Get fabric in 60-inch width if you want to minimize your sewing, then sew two pieces together along their length. Use a catenary for this seam. After that, reinforce the corners and side pullouts with patches, then fold over the fabric twice along the edges for a finished seam. Sew on the web pullouts (recommended over grommets which sometimes rip out) and you are finished. If you want to include a vestibule extension with the fly, it can be easily made and added on.

Pegs

Pegs for lightweight tents come in many different sizes, shapes, patterns, and materials. Different conditions require different types of pegs for best results. For general camping almost anything will do—twigs, steel wire, plastic, all will do the job. For ordinary conditions I find the commercially available plastic pegs best for versatility, security, and light weight. They are cheap too. For use on rock or ice, specialized pegs are recommended. These must be strong enough to stand up to repeated pounding into hard materials, and for this application high-quality steel is the best choice. For soft snow you need a wide peg. One and one-half inch aluminum corner molding makes a strong, lightweight peg for this application.

Poles

The best way to get a set of poles for any tent of standard design is to buy poles from one of the stores specializing in backpacking equipment. Strong, light-weight pole sets are available through many stores as an accessory or replacement part. If you can find what you need in the stores, then buy it; it won't cost more than a few dollars over what you would have to pay for the materials to make a set. Usually you will be able to find a set of poles that will be suitable, even if you have to trim a bit or add in an extra section.

If you are working with a nonstandard design, then you will have to make your own poles. In this case 5/8-inch 6061-T6 seamless aluminum alloy tubing is probably the best material for smaller tents; .028 wall is light and strong enough, but this tubing is available in various wall thicknesses and you could use .035 wall for extra strength. For larger tents you will probably find 7/8-inch tubing best.

For tents using flexible poles I strongly recommend trying to find commercially made poles that are adaptable. These poles are designed specifically for the conditions that tent poles will encounter, and will usually do a much better job than anything you could throw together at home. If cutting fiberglass to shorten a flexible pole, watch out that the ends don't split. Use a fine-toothed saw and cut very carefully.

If you want a one-piece pole that is much stronger than any segmented pole, a ski pole cut to the right length is ideal. For winter camping you could design your tent to use your ski poles for a frame, but this limits your mobility when camp is set up. For summer use a cut-down ski pole makes a superb walking stick that will come in handy in many ways. Segmented poles are a compromise forced on the backpacker by considerations of size and portability. The fewer sections a pole has, the stronger and more rigid it will be. Consider your pack size when making tent poles, and if possible use fewer long sections instead of many short ones.

Every joint in a tent pole is a weak spot and a potential failure point. In fact, almost all pole failures take place at the joints. There are various types of pole joints available, with each manufacturer claiming his is the best. The arguments they use to support these claims are of interest, and understandable, only to a stress engineer, so we will ignore them. Any of the commonly used pole joints are acceptable if carefully fitted and made of the proper materials. Sloppy joints are the sign of poor quality poles, but we are limited here by the fact that poles will get

Poles are critical to a tent, and pole joints are critical to the poles.

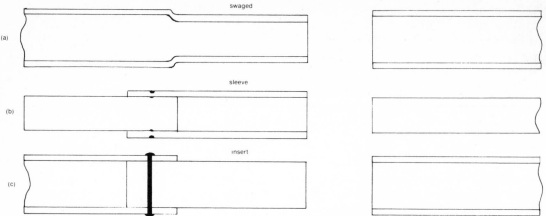

swaged

(a)

sleeve

(b)

insert

(c)

Top:
The swaged type of joint—special machinery is needed to make them.

Middle:
The sleeved style of joint—common with fiberglass poles.

Bottom:
The insert type of joint—easy to make at home, and perhaps the best design in any case.

dirty and seize up if tolerances are too close.

The insert type of pole joint is probably the easiest to make at home, and some people feel it is the best design in any case. Make the inserts about 4½ inches long and leave about 2½ inches protruding. Rivets, solder, or epoxy can be used to keep the insert in place. You could easily fit your homemade poles with shock cords, which are available from several sources in kit form. Shock cords are a real convenience when setting up, and keep the pole sections from scattering all over the place. Remember to smooth all rough or sharp edges of your poles to keep them from cutting the shock cords, and to ensure proper and smooth operation when setting up or disassembling.

___

PROJECT 6-1: TWO-MAN A-TENT

Length—88 inches
Width—58 inches
Height—50 inches
Weight—4 pounds (without fly, poles, pegs)
Capacity—two men plus gear, or three men

Design

This is a very simple, adaptable design that will give you a decent tent with a minimum amount of work. These plans are for a tent suitable for backpacking and general camping. For an expedition tent take extra care when sewing, and add in any options, accessories, or modifications that you feel are appropriate. For reliability and strength all seams should be lap felled, double or triple stitched, and all corners and pullouts should receive extra patches of fabric to reinforce these areas of extra stress.

Following the given plans and dimensions will give you a compact, easy to

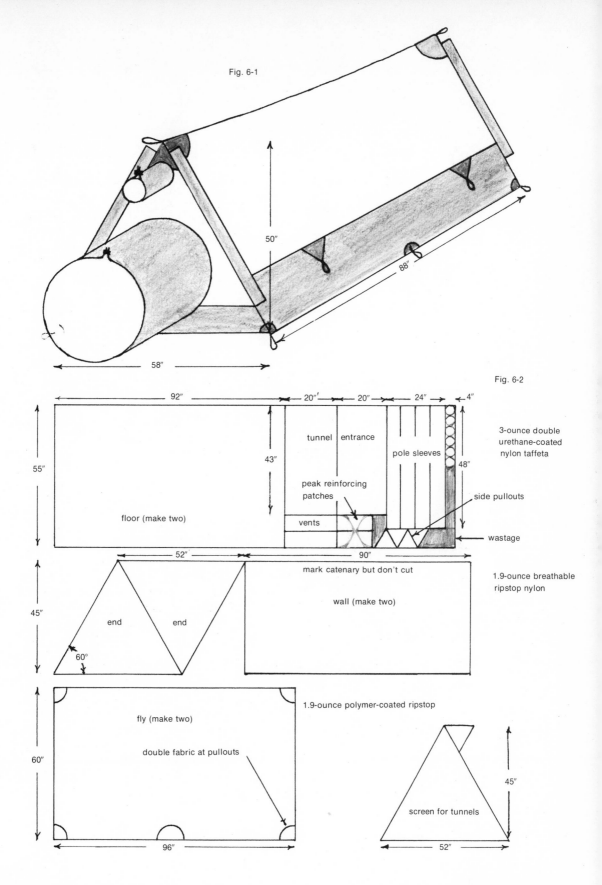

Fig. 6-1

Fig. 6-2

50″

88″

58″

92″   20″   20″   24″   4″

55″

43″   tunnel entrance   pole sleeves

48″

floor (make two)

peak reinforcing
patches

vents

side pullouts

wastage

3-ounce double
urethane-coated
nylon taffeta

52″   90″

45″

mark catenary but don't cut

wall (make two)

1.9-ounce breathable
ripstop nylon

end   end

60°

fly (make two)

double fabric at pullouts

1.9-ounce polymer-coated ripstop

60″

96″

45″

screen for tunnels

52″

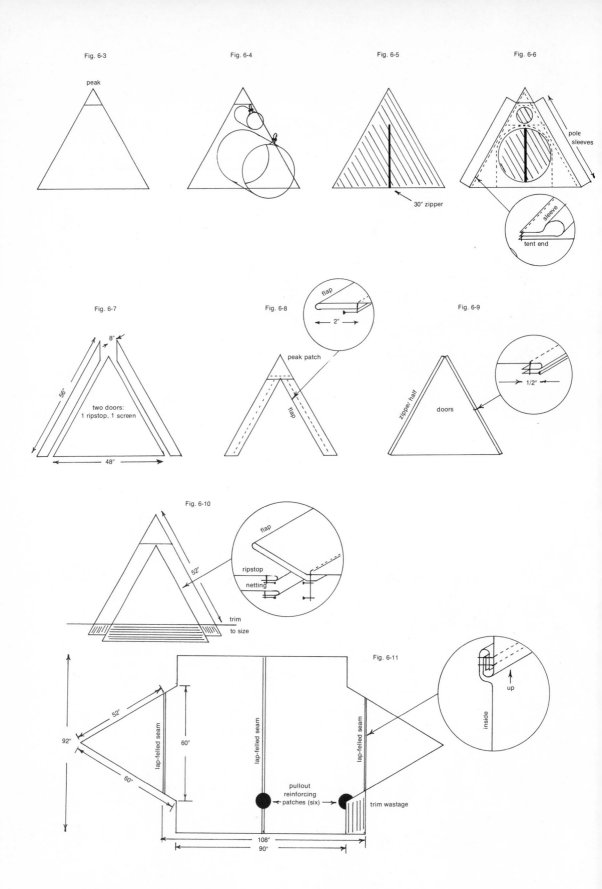

Fig. 6-3

peak

Fig. 6-4

Fig. 6-5

30" zipper

Fig. 6-6

pole sleeves

sleeve

tent end

Fig. 6-7

8"

56"

two doors:
1 ripstop, 1 screen

48"

Fig. 6-8

flap

2"

peak patch

flap

Fig. 6-9

zipper half

doors

1/2"

Fig. 6-10

52"

flap

ripstop

netting

trim
to size

Fig. 6-11

flap

inside

up

52"

92"

60"

lap-felled seam

60"

lap-felled seam

lap-felled seam

pullout
reinforcing
patches (six)

trim wastage

108"

90"

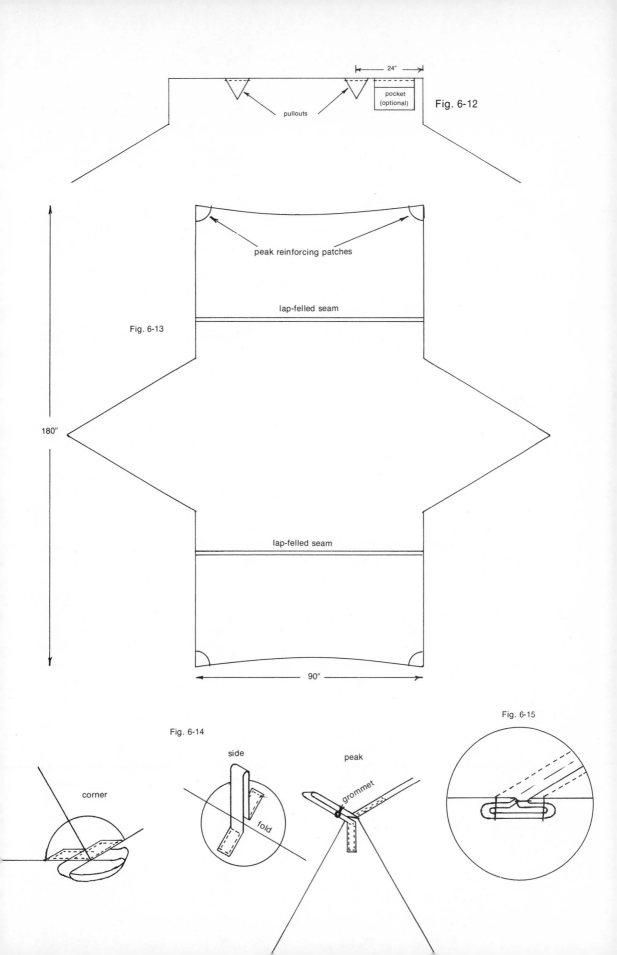

24"

pullouts

pocket
(optional)

Fig. 6-12

peak reinforcing patches

lap-felled seam

Fig. 6-13

180"

lap-felled seam

90"

Fig. 6-14

corner

side

fold

peak

grommet

Fig. 6-15

make tent. If you have a larger family, then two such tents can be joined together with extra tunnel entrances to provide a two-roomed shelter for four or five. Or if you prefer a larger tent, the dimensions can be scaled up to give a large A-tent suitable for four. (See the REI Grand Hotel for an example of a four-man A-tent.)

These plans are kept as simple as possible, for ease of construction, but this simple design can be improved considerably and made more sophisticated by the addition of a few easily added modifications. Here is a list of the most desirable options, accessories, and modifications that will add the most to your tent:

1. For general camping, and especially if the tent is to be used in cold weather, the tunnel-type entrance is suitable. This type of entrance is considerably easier to make than a zippered entrance, and is more reliable in freezing weather. If the tent is intended exclusively for warmer weather, then a zippered door provides better ventilation and more convenience.

2. An extra entrance adds extra convenience and livability to any tent. This extra entrance could be another tunnel, or it could be zippered. A tunnel-type entrance may be easily added to your tent during or after construction.

3. Make the fly with a vestibule extension, either sewn on or detachable. This will make the tent roomier, and much more suitable for use in severe conditions.

4. While this tent could be made as a single-wall design (lighter, cheaper, and easier to make), the double-wall design (tent and fly) is recommended. The double-wall design provides more comfort and livability in severe conditions, and unless you intend to use your tent exclusively in warm weather, the double-wall design is preferred.

Materials

Fabric. If making the tent with breathable walls you will need three different types of fabric:

Floor—7 yards of 55-inch 3-ounce double urethane-coated nylon taffeta

Walls—8 yards of 45-inch 1.9-ounce breathable ripstop nylon

Fly—6 yards of 60-inch 1.9-ounce polymer-coated ripstop nylon

You will also need about 60 inches of 45-inch-wide netting for the windows and the vents.

If you are worried about fire in your tent, flame-resistant fabrics and netting are available from Sierra Designs. While the tent will still burn if exposed to an open flame for too long, such materials do considerably decrease the safety hazard. Use flame-resistant materials for a winter tent that will be cooked in.

Webbing. 1-inch nylon webbing makes excellent peg loops and pullouts; 12 feet should be enough for a tent.

Hardware. You will need three cord clamps for the tunnel entrance and the two vents. If you prefer a zippered entrance you will need four 48-inch-long #5 zippers (Delrin or coil type) equipped with sliders that have pull tabs on both sides. These zippers should have at least one end that separates. You will also need one 36-inch zipper with a double pull slider for the screened entrance. About 50 feet of ⅛-inch (550-pound-test) nylon parachute line is needed for the tunnel drawstrings and tent lines. If making your own poles you will need 24 feet or ⅝-inch, .028-wall, 6061-T6 seamless aluminum alloy tubing. You will also need a short length of ⁹/₁₆-inch brass tubing for the inserts (the length needed depends on how many segments your poles have; 4½ inches per joint). Commercial poles are available that are adaptable, though you may have to buy extra sections as most of them make up into poles that are too short.

Options, accessories, and modifications require their own extra materials. Be sure to consider them when calculating material amounts.

Construction

1. Read Chapter 4 for information on tent design and Chapter 3 for information on materials, tools, and procedures. If you are modifying the given plans in any way, make sure you think through your changes before starting. Practice with the materials, tools, and procedures until you are familiar with them. Carefully read the following instructions and make sure you understand them thoroughly before you actually start making the tent.

2. Lay out the pieces on the fabric. Work on a large, smooth surface such as a floor, and take care that the patterns are drawn accurately. A large triangle made full size (stiff paper, cardboard, ⅛-inch fiberboard) will help considerably in laying out the end pieces. Light nylon fabric is very stretchy, so be careful not to distort it when drawing, measuring, or cutting. Fig. 6-2 shows the recommended layout.

3. Cut out all pieces, collect all hardware, webbing, etc. Since finished seams are used throughout, flame sealing or serging is not required.

4. Sew the two halves of the tent floor together with a lap-felled seam. You should now have a rectangle of fabric 108×92 inches.

5. Make the front end of the tent. Sew the triangular reinforcing patch to the in-side of the end with a finished seam. Fig. 6-3. Sew the two halves of the tunnel entrance into a tube with a drawstring hem at one end. Sew the tunnel-vent piece into a tube with a drawstring hem at one end. Locate and pin the tunnels to the end piece. Leave at least a 2-inch clearance between the tunnels and the edges of the end. Mark the tunnel holes in the end (1-inch seam allowance), cut out the holes, then sew the tunnels to the end with lap-felled seams. Fig. 6-4.

Cut the screen and insert a zipper as shown in Fig. 6-5. Sew the screen to the end as shown in Fig. 6-6. Do not sew along the bottom edge of the screen below the tunnel. The screen hangs down at this point and patches of Velcro may be sewn to the screen and the end to provide a seal along the bottom. Sew the pole sleeves to the ends as shown.

6. Make the back end of the tent. This may be an exact duplicate of the front (repeat step 5), or only a vent may be used. If the tent is to have a double entrance, or if a zippered entrance is desired, Figs. 6-7, 6-8, 6-9, and 6-10 show the optional zippered door. When the end is completed, trim to proper dimensions. One hint when installing zippers in tents—measure carefully and pin the zippers to the fabric before sewing. Otherwise the fabric can stretch enough to throw the zippers out of proper alignment.

7. Sew the two ends to the floor with lap-felled seams. Use 1-inch seam allowance, and make sure you fold the seams properly so that they act like shingles to shed water. Fig. 6-11 shows the proper shape and dimensions.

8. Sew the circular stake reinforcing patches in place (Fig. 6-11) and trim off any waste.

9. Sew the side pullouts to the floor

edge as shown. Fig. 6-12. Now is the time to sew in the optional pockets if desired.

10. Sew the side panels (walls) to the floor with a lap-felled seam. Make sure the seam is folded properly to shed water. Fig. 6-13. Sew on the side/peak reinforcing patches to the inside of the walls as shown.

11. Sew on all web pullouts and stake loops. Watch the fold lines for location (see Fig. 6-14); e.g., the floor measures 60 inches wide, but the floor ends up 58 inches wide when finished. Don't install any grommets till you have tried the poles and finished tent for fit.

12. With the tent inside out, fold the sides up along the ends, pin, then sew from the bottom corners to the peak. Use lap-felled seams here, and take care that everything works out evenly. Sew the ridge seam from peak to peak. Use about 2 inches of catenary here, and again take care that everything lines up evenly. Pinning helps. The ridge seam should be another lap-felled seam, only this time center it rather than folding it to one side. Fig. 6-15.

13. Make the poles (if you haven't purchased a set) as detailed in the text. These poles should be about 60 to 66 inches long, and should form a 60-degree angle at the peak. The poles should be trimmed and fitted to the tent until they set up properly. Exact dimensions will vary due to seam allowances, sleeve width, etc.

14. Inspect the tent for any loose seams, wrinkles, and puckering, correct, then pitch the tent and inspect it again. If care was taken in layout, cutting, and sewing, then the tent should pitch taut and tight.

15. Make the fly. This should be self-explanatory: lap-felled catenary cut ridge seam, reinforced corners and pullouts, edge folded twice to finish. The fly should be fitted to the tent, which can vary in finished dimensions by quite a bit. If you want to take a chance on fit, and especially if you need practice at sewing, the fly could be made first.

7

Sleeping Bags

A sleeping bag is one of your most expensive and most important pieces of equipment. Remember, you will be spending approximately one third of your time outdoors in one. A few nights spent shivering in a cold sleeping bag can ruin an otherwise pleasant trip. On the other hand, using a sleeping bag that is much too warm is just as bad—you end up sleeping on top of the bag. Then, driven back inside by the cold night air, you spend your nights sleeplessly oscillating between too hot and too cold. Or you may spend a lot of time and money choosing and buying the lightest, most efficient, best quality down-filled backpacker's bag—and perhaps end up on a canoe trip with a friend. When the bags get wet, which is to be expected on a canoe trip, you end up shivering through the night, while the experienced canoeist is warm and comfortable in his fiber bag. Or you may go backpacking with a cheap, heavy, fiber-filled bag, which weighs up to 5 pounds more than a good down bag. After struggling up the hundredth hill with that extra

weight, you won't really care what bag you crawl into that night. You'll be so exhausted that a bed of nails would do.

To avoid all of these hassles, get the right sleeping bag. But there are so many different kinds and shapes of bags—rectangular bags, barrel bags, tapered bags, mummy bags, and double bags; space-filler cut bags, differentially cut bags, and contoured differentially cut bags; down bags and fiber bags; three-season bags, summer bags, expedition bags, and combination bags—it is difficult to know which bag is the right one for you. This chapter should help you decide.

For several years now sleeping bag design has been fairly stable, with manufacturers making many small detail changes rather than a few revolutionary ones. Certainly, the bags we have now are much better than the ones we had ten years ago, but the nonexpert would be hard pressed to describe the differences. However, with top-quality down becoming scarce, there have been very noticeable improvements in synthetic fills, and in the designs utilizing them. These materials are still fairly new, so the designs using synthetics are not as sophisticated as those using down. With all the attention focused here, look for this to change. If a synthetic that lofts as well as down is ever found, look for down to become obsolete. In the meantime, here are a few things to consider when choosing or designing an efficient and comfortable sleeping bag.

SHAPE

The shape of the bag has a lot to do with how warm it will be, and with how comfortable you will feel inside it. The larger the internal volume of the bag, the more space that must be warmed by your body heat, and the more room for air currents and breezes to travel around in. Therefore, a tight bag is an efficient bag. But many people (and I am one of them) find it very difficult to sleep in a bag that is too tight. A bag that is too constricting can cause claustrophobia in some people, which can keep them awake and uncomfortable just as effectively as the cold. So sleeping bag shapes must be a compromise—a toss-up between efficiency and roominess—and each person will have to decide on his own which is best for him.

The critical areas in fitting the bag are the shoulders, hips, and feet. The circumference of the bag at these locations affects comfort a great deal. In addition, the length of the bag is very important—too short and you stick out into the cold, too long and you waste insulation and heat at the bottom. The best rule of thumb for fitting a bag is to get the smallest one you feel comfortable in.

Rectangular

The simplest, cheapest, and heaviest bags are the ones known as rectangular bags. They are usually made with a wraparound zipper, which allows them to be opened up for use as a bedspread or extra quilt. These bags are rarely hooded, and they are always made with a space-filler cut. Such bags are quite good for milder weather, indoor use, or car camping, and wherever weight and warmth are not critical. For the person who thrashes around in his sleep, or for someone who is very stout, a rectangular bag may be a good choice because of its roominess.

Semirectangular

Semirectangular or "barrel" bags are basically similar to rectangular bags, but to save weight and to decrease the internal volume the bottom half is tapered. This makes them somewhat more efficient than rectangular bags, but they should feel almost as roomy. The semirectangular bag should be wide at the hips to allow you to draw up your knees if you wish, and wide at the shoulders to allow you to turn around inside the bag. Many people find them the best compromise between lightness, efficiency, and roominess.

Most semirectangular bags have a wraparound zipper and a simple flat cut foot, but some are available with a boxed foot and a full-length zipper down one side. A few have hoods attached, but most do not, though some are available with an optional detachable hood. Again, the space-filler cut is used for such bags because it is much easier to make, and because with a roomy bag the differential cut is not that much more efficient. The semirectangular shape is the one I prefer for my bags. The simple layout and ease of construction are very strong points, but the one that sells me is the roominess. I simply cannot be comfortable in a mummy or tapered bag that is tightly fitted.

Tapered

Tapered bags take into account the fact that your feet need less space than your shoulders. They taper from the top to the bottom. This makes for a light, efficient bag, but one that may be somewhat constricting. With tapered bags, when the knees come up you must bring the whole bag with them. Some people find this objectionable.

The cheaper tapered bags are flat cut at the foot, with a wraparound zipper, but some have a boxed foot or a zipper down one side (full length or half length). They may or may not have a hood, and are available in either a space-filler cut or a differential cut.

Quite a few manufacturers sell these bags as liners, to extend the warmth of another bag. They are usually made small, to fit inside a regular-size outer, and to get the most efficiency out of this design. For a do-it-yourselfer interested in making his own sleeping bag, a tapered bag can be nearly as light and as efficient as a mummy bag, and it can be considerably easier for him to make.

Mummy

The mummy shape is generally recognized as the most efficient for a sleeping bag. These bags are made to conform as closely as possible to the shape of the body. They are contoured from hips to feet, and also from hips to shoulders, where they are usually snugly fitted instead of having a wide opening closed with a drawstring. These bags are the most expensive—the work involved in making

A mummy bag follows the shape of the body as closely as possible. However, the mummy bag is not a good project for a do-it-yourselfer unless you're using a kit from one of the kit manufacturers. (Photo courtesy Eastern Mountain Sports)

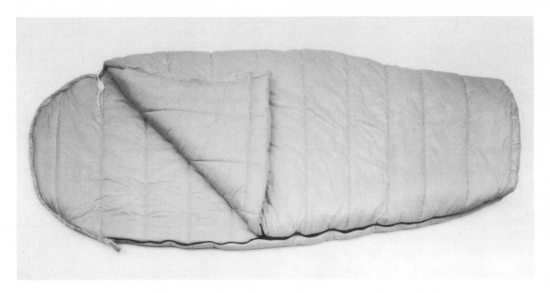

a decent mummy is much greater than that involved in one of the simpler designs. They literally have to be "tailored."

To get the most efficiency out of a mummy bag it must be tightly fitted, which many people find undesirable. Since mummy bags are designed to be efficient, the vast majority of them feature such details as a boxed foot, fitted hood, channel block, well-baffled zipper (half length or full length), and differential or contoured differential cut (although there are a few mummy bags made with a space-filler cut).

I don't feel that a mummy is a good project for a do-it-yourselfer—the slight increase in efficiency comes at the cost of a lot of extra work. There are other bags available that will be just as warm, but which will weigh a few ounces more, and which will be much easier to make. For this reason I do not include any plans for a mummy bag. If you wish to make your own mummy bag, several of the kit manufacturers include them in their lines.

Doubles

The double sleeping bag gets its popularity from the fact that it is warmer to sleep with someone else. And one double bag usually costs and weighs less than two singles. But, of course, they are only practical for those who always go camping together.

There are several high-quality doubles on the market, usually taking the form of a super-wide mummy, with two short zippers, a closure in the middle, and some form of double hood. There are also many ways of joining two single bags to form a roomy, if somewhat inefficient, double. I feel the increased versatility with two singles more than makes up for any increase in efficiency found with the doubles.

The bivouac or "shorty" bags are for those who want the absolute ultimate in light weight. Mountain climbers especially like these bags, which are used with an expedition parka for bivouacs on long climbs. There are several designs available that may be worn as pants, and then the legs may be zipped together for sleeping. Bivouac bags are great for kids and shorter adults, or for extra warmth as a liner. Many top-quality bivouac bags are made with fiber insulation instead of with down—the fiber provides reliable insulation, even in wet conditions.

Cut

Sooner or later someone is going to conduct scientific experiments to solve the controversy regarding the optimal way to cut the shells of sleeping bags, but until then we will have to make do with the information now available. Here are some facts and theories on shell design.

Space-Filler Cut

With this type of cut the inner and outer shells have the same circumference. When they are sewn together to form a sleeping bag, the inner shell drapes around the sleeper, filling up space. The space-filler cut is used primarily for cheaper bags (it is easier to make), for roomier bags (the semirectangular and rectangular bags don't really benefit from a differential cut), and some people even use it for top-quality mummy bags (they say the space-filler cut reduces the internal volume of the bag, which reduces the body heat required to maintain warmth).

Regardless of any theoretical advantages or disadvantages, the space-filler cut

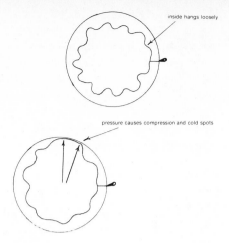

Space-filler cut—easy to sew, and may be just as warm.

is the easiest to make. That is why I recommend it for any bag you will be making yourself. If you are purchasing a bag and want one that is the ultimate in efficiency, then give a thought to the cut but, personally, I suspect it doesn't really make much difference.

Differential Cut

With a differentially cut sleeping bag the inner shell has a smaller circumference than the outer. This means that, theoretically at least, when you press an elbow or knee into the inner shell, you cannot compress it against the outer shell and cause a cold spot. The vast majority of sleeping bag manufacturers feel that a differentially cut bag is warmer, but no one has yet proved it or established exactly how much warmer. If you feel this theoret-

ical advantage is worth the extra work, you can make your bags with a differential cut. Simply add 6¼ inches to the circumference of the outside shell for every 1 inch of shell thickness. (This means that if your bag has a shell thickness of 3 inches then the outer should be about 18¾ inches larger than the inner.) Gather your baffle material evenly when sewing so as to take up this difference along the inner shell. A good trick is to mark the baffle material in quarters and pin or tack to the inner to ensure that the gathering comes out evenly.

There is much more that could be said about the differential versus space-filler controversy—the differential cut is more difficult to make, and it is effective only with tight fitting bags (with larger bags the shell stands away from the sleeper, promoting cold air currents). However, many people feel the differential cut is better for a restless sleeper, and that the close contact of the shell with the sleeper in a space-filler design promotes excess sweating.

Contoured Differential Cut

While the differential cut may have its advantages, the proponents of the contoured differential cut point out that your body is not round, you are not built like a

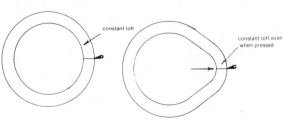

Differential cut—resists compression.

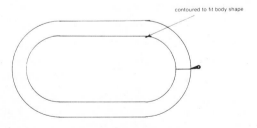

Contoured differential cut—matches the contour of the body as closely as possible.

piece of pipe. The contoured differential bags are cut to conform as closely as possible to the contours of the body. In this way they hope to achieve even insulation everywhere, which means even warmth.

Perhaps this is the ultimate in shell design, but for the person interested in making his own, I feel it is simply too much work. The contoured differentially cut bags involve intricate sewing, careful fitting, and complicated design. They are beyond the capabilities of the average do-it-yourselfer. However, if you are experienced at sewing and don't mind the hard work involved, you may want to try your hand at one of these bags. Several of the manufacturers offer kits every bit as sophisticated as the best of the "ultimate" bags, and if you do your part they may turn out even better.

COMFORT/THICKNESS

Regardless of what type of cut is used to construct the shells, the whole purpose of a sleeping bag is to provide insulation between you and the cold. The two shells (with fill between) are there to provide thickness to insulate you. But how thick is comfortable? And exactly how uncomfortable is cold?

Comfort is a personal variable that involves too many factors for us to pin down precisely, but studies have been made correlating thickness to comfort. The most widely quoted figures come from the U.S. Army's research, and these are given below. However, most people feel these figures are not too realistic. Look in the sleeping bag sections of a few mountain shop catalogs for some more reasonable ones—and then forget them. Although the manufacturer's comfort figures are as honest as he can make them, you are one factor over which he has no control. Your

physical condition, how you camp, where you camp, your metabolic rate, degree of exhaustion, when you ate, what you ate, and so on, do make a big difference.

THICKNESS OF INSULATION REQUIRED FOR COMFORT (IN INCHES)

Effective Temperature °F.	Sleeping
40°F.	1.5 inches
20°F.	2.0 inches
0°F.	2.5 inches
−20°F.	3.0 inches
−40°F.	3.5 inches

These figures are approximate but are a good base for an average healthy person.

CONSTRUCTION

Sewn-Through Construction

The easiest and oldest way to construct a sleeping bag is simply to quilt pieces of fabric together and stuff with some light, bulky filler. This makes into a reasonably good bag for moderate conditions, but the rows of quilting put there to hold the fill from shifting are cold spots. Thickness is warmth, and wherever the stitches compress the fabric and filler, there is cold. With a sewn-through bag, the less stitching the more warmth.

There are several ways to make a quilted or sewn-through sleeping bag. Sewn-through bags are not as efficient as baffled bags, but they are still fairly light for their warmth. They are quite suitable for moderate conditions. For example, Project 7-2, a down-insulated sewn-through semirectangular bag, is quite comfortable for some people right down to

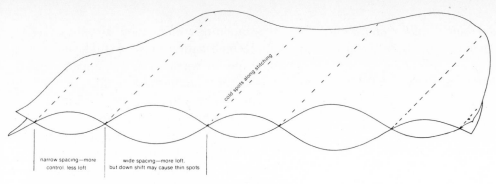

A sewn-through or quilted bag; the seams are cold spots.

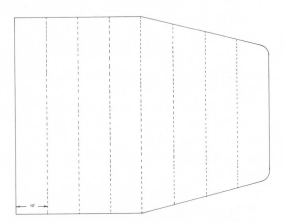

Concentric seams are easy to make; few seams to give problems with cold or down leakage. Ten-inch spacing gives best compromise between loft and control.

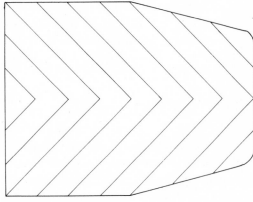

Chevron seams—extra work, good down control, but the points are potential failure spots.

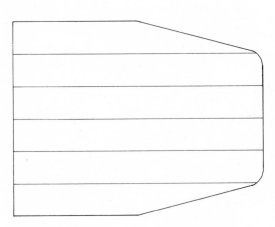

Longitudinal seams—down bunches at foot, so avoid.

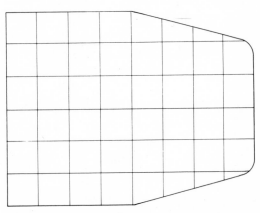

Rectangular seams—extra seams mean extra work, more cold spots, and more potential down leaks, but provides very good control.

30°F., and it weighs only 2 pounds and 10 ounces. Sewn-through bags are also ideal for use as liners.

The biggest advantage of the sewn-through sleeping bags is that they are very easy to make. I offer one design (Project 7-2) of this type that could be made in an evening even by a beginner.

Double-Quilted Construction

The double-quilted method of constructing sleeping bags is quite similar to the sewn-through method, but two layers of insulation are used. This way the thin spots of one layer are offset by the thick spots of the other layer, providing even insulation throughout.

This was how the older winter bags were made—with the two layers permanently sewn together along the edges. These bags were warm enough, but they were heavy. They have since been made obsolete by the more efficient baffled designs (lighter for a given thickness).

COMBINATION BAGS

Today the double-quilted design is used only in a modified version (two separate bags, an inner and an outer, which may be separated or combined as desired). This is the modern combination sleeping bag. Such combination bags are still heavy, but they are so versatile and adaptable that this is not thought to be significant.

The combination bags can be the most versatile setup available. You can have a sewn-through inner for warm weather and a baffled outer for three-season use that may be combined into a single bag that is suitable for really cold weather. You could have a fiber-filled inner for wet conditions and a down-filled outer for maximum loft with minimum weight that could be used separately or combined into one bag that is fairly light, but still fairly effective if wet. Or you could zip your two bags together into a large double—the lighter bag on top for warm weather, the heavier bag on top for colder weather.

This is the type of bag I prefer for my personal use, and the system I recommend. It gives the greatest range of service for the least cost or work. Projects 7-1, 7-2, and 7-3 are all designed to be used as a combination-bag system that should be versatile enough to suit almost anyone. If you are an experienced camper who specializes in one form of camping, then a more specialized bag might be found that is more suitable for your activity. But for the average person interested in a general-duty bag for use over a wide range of conditions, I think the combination bags are ideal.

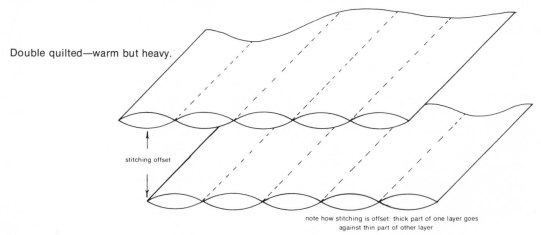

Double quilted—warm but heavy.

stitching offset

note how stitching is offset: thick part of one layer goes against thin part of other layer

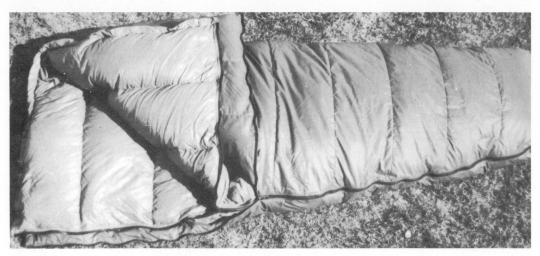

Sewn-through inner inside a baffled outer; a combination bag.

Box-Baffled Construction

The box-baffled design is an improvement over the simple sewn-through types. By using gussets sewn to the inner and outer shells, the sewn-through seams and cold spots can be eliminated, in theory. In practice it has been found that down has a tendency to work its way out of the corners, leaving thin spots along the gussets. For this reason the box baffle is not as popular as other baffled designs.

Slant-Box Baffled Construction

With the slant-box baffled construction (slant wall, slant tube, parallelogram), the gussets are sewn at an angle. This has two advantages over the regular box style: First, the thin spots along the gussets are offset by the thick spots of the next section, which cuts down considerably on cold spots along the gussets. Second, the parallelogram shape will not restrict down loft; when stuffed the parallelogram will change shape allowing the down to loft fully.

The slant-box construction is the most popular of the baffled types. It is used extensively for quality lightweight bags and three-season bags, and some people even say it is the best style for the heavier winter bags. The slant box provides maximum loft with a minimum of panel weight, and there are some who feel that it provides the greatest warmth per pound of total bag weight. If you space the baffles 6 to 8 inches apart you will get good down control, good loft, and a minimum of panel weight. If you space the baffles closer, you will get better control but more panel weight. If you space the baffles much wider than 8 inches, you may find down shifting, and cold spots can become a problem.

For the do-it-yourselfer, the slant-box construction is a good choice. The baffles may be cut as simple strips of material and sewn in place. If the differential cut is used, things can get a little more complicated, but by marking, pinning, and gathering, you can make the baffles come out neatly.

V-Baffled Construction

The V-baffled design is widely regarded as the optimum for maximum thickness with minimum fill weight. It uses almost twice as much paneling as the slant box, but the Vs do such a good job of controlling down shift that less down is needed. The V tubes will not expand to allow full loft, as do the parallelogram tubes, so careful measurement of down is necessary for maximum efficiency. However, the V design seems to maintain loft longer under difficult conditions (long usage, dampness), so it is widely used for expedition bags, where loft retention is critical.

For the do-it-yourselfer, who must work with rather crude tools, the increased theoretical efficiency with the V tubes is offset by the difficulty in accurately partitioning out the down. If making your own you are quite likely to overfill or underfill, which can be important with a V design. The slant-box design is less critical here, which makes it the better choice for a home builder. If you feel you need an ultra-efficient design for a winter bag, you could use the V type. Space the baffles 7 to 9 inches apart for lightness, with good control. If you use down that is commercially prepackaged by weight, then you may be able to improve on fill consistency.

Fiber Constructions

When synthetic materials are used as fill instead of down, different constructions should be used to get maximum efficiency with them; the designs meant for down often won't work. Here are a few representative types for Fiberfill II and PolarGuard.

Quilted. As with the quilted down bags, the inner and outer shells are sewn to-gether. With the quilted fiber bags, however, there is usually a layer of compressed insulation between the seams, which provides some extra thickness. Some of these bags may look like cheap sewn-through down bags—with widely spaced seams running around the bag. With these bags the extra stitching actually lowers the warmth rating of the bag by causing unnecessary thin spots.

Double Quilted. Again, this is very similar to the design for down-filled bags, but to save weight the inside shells (backing) may be some ultralight material such as cheesecloth. Fibers will not shift as badly as down, so a lighter material may be perfectly acceptable here.

Sandwich. This is basically a double quilt with a third layer between for extra thickness. The sandwich construction is suitable for three-season or winter bags, in either Fiberfill II or PolarGuard. The center bat of insulation is usually edge stabilized rather than quilted.

Slant-Box Baffled. This is the North Face "Batting Baffle" system, which gets good marks for its loft/weight ratio with Fiberfill II. The bag is constructed with slant-wall box baffles that are made from fiber batting.

Edge Stabilized. PolarGuard is a continuous filament fiber batting with high stability. Some manufacturers don't use quilting at all with this fiber; they feel it will resist shifting and lumping without it. Instead, they sew the bats to the shell around the edges (zipper seams and drawstring hem).

Fiberfill II must have a backing, and it gives slightly less loft than PolarGuard, which does not need to have a backing, and which has the best loft of the synthetics. Both these materials will do an excellent job if you use them the way they were intended. With the Fiberfill, quilt at regular intervals (8 inches seems about right). With the PolarGuard quilt as desired, or use the edge-stabilized design.

SPECIAL FEATURES

Shape, cut, construction, and fill are the major factors involved in evaluating or designing a sleeping bag, but it is the special features—the detailing, the ingenuity of the designer, the degree of sophistication—that separate a mediocre bag from an exceptional one. The fine details, things like zipper flaps and channel blocks and tuck seams, can and do make a difference. If you are interested in such exotic details, read on.

Tuck Seams

There are several ways in which tuck or "hidden" seams may be used, but they involve twice as much work, since each seam should be sewn twice. On some bags the fabric is folded over along a seam edge to give a tuck seam, but this is not as strong as the double-sewn style. The double stitching reinforces itself, as detailed in Chapter 3, and is good insurance against baffles ripping out under hard usage. In addition, the seams are not exposed to wear or snagging, and this can lengthen the life of the bag considerably. Tuck seams on a sleeping bag are one of the most reliable outside indications of quality throughout.

If you are considering using tuck seams on a do-it-yourself project, be careful; tuck seams may change the way in which the item will have to go together. Think things through carefully before rushing in; a bit of practice to iron out the details is advised. If you do use tuck seams, you will need about ½ inch extra seam allowance for every seam. On a sleeping bag with a lot of baffles, this can add up to a considerable amount, so don't forget it.

Channel Block

A channel block is a baffle set opposite the zipper that divides the down tubes roughly in half. This is to prevent down from shifting inside the tubes. Unfortunately, many people like to be able to shift the down around inside these tubes, so the channel block is not an unqualified advantage. On bags without one you can "chase" down from the bottom for those cold nights when you need more loft on top. For warm nights, down can be shifted to the bottom, leaving you a thinner and cooler top. I prefer bags without a channel block, but this is a personal decision. For the do-it-yourselfer, a channel block is

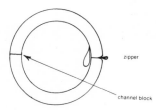

A channel block prevents down shift inside the tubes.

extra work that could be avoided. None of my designs has a channel block, and you would be well advised to leave them that way.

Baffle Materials

There is some controversy among bag manufacturers as to what material should be used for the baffles. Some use ripstop, some use marquisette netting, and some use a knit. The people who prefer the ripstop point out that it positively prevents down migration from one baffled section to another, and that the baffles will be as strong as the rest of the bag. Those who use marquisette say the netting clogs up with down and helps prevent down shift inside the baffles, which may occur with smooth, slippery ripstop. The ones who use a nylon or poly tricot knit point out that baffles are constantly being pulled and pushed out of shape, which is hard on the seams and the fabric, and that good knits give with the strain, then "remember" their original shape and return to it when the strain is released. Take your pick according to whatever argument appeals to you.

For do-it-yourselfers, remember that baffling edges also can fray. If you use ripstop nylon, you will have to finish every single cut edge inside the bag. This can run into a lot of work, so I recommend using the poly tricot knit, if you can find it. I also like the idea that the knits will give with any strain. Whatever you use for baffles, treat your bag with care. Bags that are handled roughly will tear out baffles no matter what they are made from.

Zippers

Some winter bags are made without zippers; the user merely slithers in from the top. This is a neat idea that you might consider for any ultralight, superefficient bag. A zipper is a potential source of cold, it can weigh quite a few ounces, it can fail when you need it most, and it is not absolutely necessary. All in all, some very good arguments for leaving it out. However, if convenience is more important to you than efficiency, then a zipper is desirable. What style of zipper installation to use depends on where you draw the line between convenience and efficiency.

The most convenient, and the most versatile arrangement, is the wraparound zipper. With this style the bag can be

Two bags with wraparound zippers; the most versatile arrangement.

opened up and used as a quilt. If the zipper is a separating type, then two bags with matching zippers can be zipped together to form a double, with the zippers at the sides. If the zipper has two sliders, then the foot may be opened up for ventilation on hot nights. Unfortunately, with all that zipper exposed to the outside, this can be the coldest type to sleep in.

The full-length zipper runs down one side of the bag. If the zipper is a separating type you can zip two such bags together, if they are a right and a left. Right and left refer to which side the zipper is on, and one of each is needed to make a pair. With this style of double the zipper runs down the middle, which can get annoying if each person desires a different degree of ventilation.

The half-length zipper runs half way down one side. The shorter the zipper, the more efficient the bag, but the less ventilation available for warm weather. The half-length zippers usually do not allow pairing, and are used primarily for highly efficient cold-weather bags or for liners. Some bags are made with the zipper on top. These are not as common as they once were.

For a look at the details involved in choosing a zipper, see Chapter 3, "Materials," and the materials section of this chapter.

Zipper Flaps

Zippers are a source of cold. The job of the zipper flap (draft tube) is to insulate the sleeper from any cold getting into the bag at this location. There are several types of zipper flaps, depending on the degree of sophistication of the design. Zippers jam often on these flaps, so many manufacturers now sew a strip of stiffening material to the tube to keep it from snagging. If you get a left and right set of bags, check to see that you get a top and bottom set of zipper flaps. Some manufacturers overlook this detail. The natural location for the draft tube is at the top, hanging down over the zipper, but if the tube is well designed and well stuffed a bottom flap might be just as warm. A zipper flap may be attached to almost any bag without one or installed during the construction process on the bags you make yourself (Projects 7-1 and 7-2).

Drawstrings

Drawstrings are used at the top of most bags to adjust the degree of ventilation. On cold nights, tightening the drawstring can make quite a difference. For some reason most drawstrings are attached in the middle of the bag and emerge near the zippers. This is a big disadvantage if the bags are to be paired. For a better arrangement see how I attach the drawstrings to my designs (pages 223–224). A cord clamp is a nice detail here; it saves untying knots, which can be annoying and even dangerous.

Hoods

Since the head and neck regions are responsible for much of the heat lost from the body, it makes sense to insulate them, too. A properly designed hood will do just that, and will further reduce any air currents at the top of the bag. The hood should close up completely, except for a space at the front to breathe through. This space is important; your breath carries water vapor which, if exhaled inside the bag, will decrease the efficiency of down insulation. A quick-release cord clamp is a good idea here, too. Make sure you can work it from inside the bag. A detachable hood will not be as warm as one that is

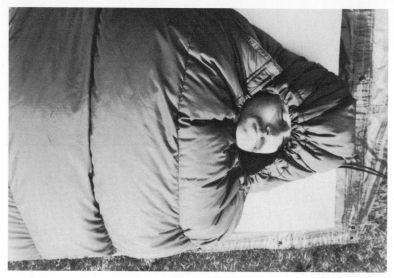

A hood is necessary for maximum efficiency in cold weather.

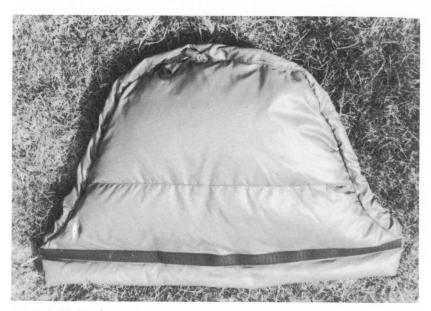

A detachable hood.

permanently attached, but it will help considerably. This hood will fit almost any bag (check the dimensions before starting), and it is the ideal warm-up project for a sleeping bag.

Another item that you may find desirable is a collar. These are available in kit form from Frostline and Holubar. If you use a combination bag, with a separate inner and outer, the inner will function well as a collar. A collar positively seals off the bag from drafts or heat loss through the top of the bag.

Boxed Foot

The boxed-foot arrangement is a continuation of the mummy principle; the contours of the body are matched as closely as possible for maximum efficiency. With-

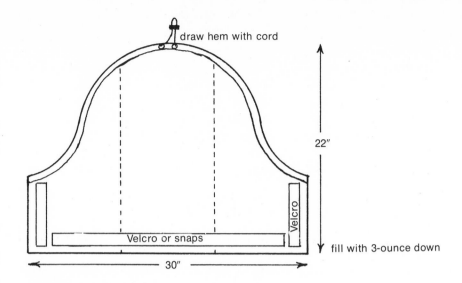

draw hem with cord

22"

Velcro

Velcro or snaps

30"

fill with 3-ounce down

A detachable hood; a useful accessory for those bags without one.

An oval boxed foot; makes the bag warmer and roomier. A full-length zipper works well with these types.

out a boxed foot your feet tend to compress the insulation at the bottom, causing a cold spot at one of your most vulnerable locations. For a do-it-yourselfer, the flat-cut foot is much easier to make, especially with a wraparound zipper. With a full-length zipper a boxed foot is a sensible addition that wouldn't be too hard to in-

stall. Two ovals with a baffle across could be sewn in if desired. This is a good way to make the bag seem longer without actually increasing the length.

MATERIALS, TOOLS, AND PROCEDURES FOR SLEEPING BAGS

MATERIALS

The materials that go into a sleeping bag are highly specialized, and the right fabric, insulation, and zippers may not be readily available locally. If this is the case, a letter to one of the kit manufacturers or one of the bigger mail-order mountain shops will get you the things you need.

Fabric

The fabric used for a sleeping bag shell must meet a number of stringent requirements: It must be light (heavy materials compress the insulation, lessening efficiency); it must be strong (a bag is subject to a lot of abrasion and snagging in its lifetime, and the fabric must be able to stand up well); it must be porous enough to breathe, but it must be tight enough to be as downproof and as windproof as possible (moving air is cold air); it must be water resistant to keep out light rain and dampness; and it should be easy to clean and care for.

The fabrics that come closest to meeting all of these requirements are ripstop nylon and light nylon taffeta. Ripstop, in ¾-ounce to 1.9-ounce weights, is the preferred material for sleeping bags, though there are some who feel the heavier weight of the taffeta is justified by its increased resistance to abrasion. When choosing a ripstop for down-insulated items, get one with a high thread count. Such a fabric will be stronger (tear strength), and it will be less porous (windproof and downproof). Also look for some indication that it has been treated to improve its downproof qualities and its dirt and water resistance. Never use a coated fabric for a sleeping bag unless you understand the principles involved. Though there are a few bags on the market with coated shells, these are still highly controversial. The material used for baffling can be ripstop, marquisette netting, or tricot knit.

Insulation

Chapter 3 gives a concise summary of what you need to know about insulations for sleeping bags. If you decide on down, get a good grade from a responsible supplier. With sleeping bags, which require a fairly large amount of down, you should be able to notice the difference between cheap and good down immediately (the cheap down will have less loft), and

you would certainly notice it in the long run. With clothing, which uses smaller amounts of down, down quality is not quite as critical.

Just one point of interest about the fibers that has not been mentioned previously: EMS has Fiberfill II for sale that is prequilted to 60-inch-wide ripstop nylon. The price is reasonable, and it will save you a lot of hassles. This is what I use for Project 7-1, and for some of my insulated clothing. Check the EMS catalog.

Thread

For use on down-insulated items I recommend a poly core/cotton wrapped thread. This thread is strong and the cotton wrapping seems to clog the needle holes, keeping down leakage through the seams to a minimum.

Hardware

My designs utilize a separating zipper about 96 inches long, which is not likely to be available locally. I recommend a #5 Delrin here, in a double-slider, one-slider-with-two-pulls model. Just ask for a sleeping bag zipper in that length if the details confuse you; most suppliers will know what to send.

The #5 Delrin is the best choice for a number of reasons: it is lighter than metal; it won't conduct cold like the metal zippers; the large teeth are plenty strong; the teeth are snag resistant, and if they do snag they rarely harm the fabric; this type is becoming standard, which is important for zipper compatibility (doubling).

If you want to spend a few pennies wisely, invest in one of the spring-loaded cord clamps for the drawstring. These can be worked with one hand, and they are fast and convenient. If you need your pennies you can make something just as usable out of leather. Two holes close together in a piece of leather make a friction lock. Whatever you do, forget about knots. Trying to untie a slipped knot with one hand, in the dark in a hurry, is not an enjoyable experience.

TOOLS

Make sure your sewing machine is properly set up for the job at hand. Practice on a scrap of material until you are satisfied. Sleeping bags are no place for loose or crooked stitches; if the needle goes where it shouldn't and you have to rip out seams, you leave holes that will leak down forever. Do it right the first time.

PROCEDURES

See Chapter 3 for how to handle the fiber insulations and for advice on handling down. With an item as large as a sleeping bag, a helper is very handy, and so is a large table to work on. The three bags I offer as projects are designed to go together with an absolute minimum of work. I have stressed ease of construction over sophistication, and I don't regret it at all. Following the given plans will lead to some pretty nice gear, but if you are a real equipment freak and want more sophistication, you can add to these designs—they are meant to be as versatile and adaptable as possible—or you could buy one of the kits, which are sophisticated enough for even the most fanatic. Following is a list of options, accessories, and modifications that might help you build exactly what you need.

OPTIONS, ACCESSORIES, AND MODIFICATIONS FOR SLEEPING BAGS

Sleeping Bag Cover

A sleeping bag cover can serve two useful functions: it protects the bag, and it makes the bag warmer. If you do much camping without a tent, a sleeping bag cover is a desirable option; it keeps dirt and moisture out of the bag, and protects the fragile shell from snags and abrasion. A cover is much cheaper to replace and much easier to clean than a sleeping bag.

Many people also find a cover, or a liner, a good method for extending the warmth rating of the bag. While the actual thickness of the light cover, or liner, is negligible, it will immobilize air trapped between the layers of fabric, adding about 10 degrees to the effectiveness of your bag. The trouble with liners, though, is that unless they are securely attached to the inside of the bag, they can twist themselves around you, which can be interesting to say the least. However, they do protect the inside of the bag from the worst source of dirt—you. For the same protection and warmth, without the hassles of a liner, sleep in a clean sweat suit.

A sleeping bag cover should be plenty large, or else it may restrict down loft and actually lower the warmth rating of the bag. Some have built-in pads, some have pockets for removable pads, and some have one side coated for water repellency. Don't use a fully coated sleeping bag cover. Your body gives off moisture in the form of perspiration which must get out; otherwise you will stew in your own juices.

The sleeping bag cover shown in the illustration fits in well with the combination bag system described in the projects section. On really warm nights it and a

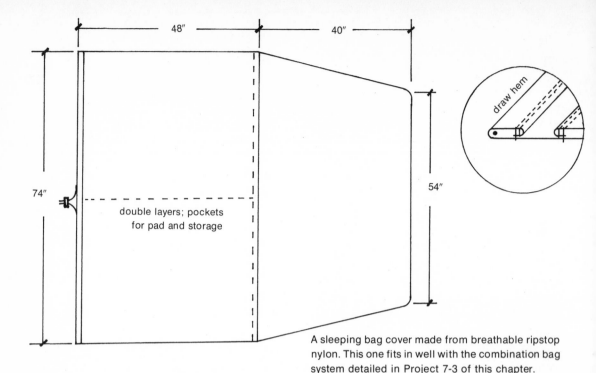

A sleeping bag cover made from breathable ripstop nylon. This one fits in well with the combination bag system detailed in Project 7-3 of this chapter.

pad may be all you need. Such a cover is also a good warm-up project for one of the sleeping bags.

Stuff Sack

A sleeping bag is a fragile piece of equipment. It should be handled carefully, and stored and transported inside a pack compartment or stuff sack for longer life. If making a pack you could design in a compartment to carry your sleeping bag, or you could make a stuff sack. Plans for stuff sacks are included in Chapter 4.

Pads

In cold weather a sleeping bag is only as good as the pad underneath it. It's a fact that thickness is warmth, and your weight will usually compress the insulation under you to an insignificant amount. Cold will then creep up from the ground

into the bag and you. To avoid this problem use a pad made of foam, either open or closed type, which resists compression better than down or fibers.

Open-celled foams are softer, breathable, and they absorb water. Closed-cell foams are firmer, nonbreathable, and waterproof. With the open-cell foams a waterproof ground sheet should be used to keep moisture out of the bag. The closed-cell types may be used directly on damp ground or snow with no problem. A ⅜-inch or ½-inch Ensolite pad (closed cell) will provide sufficient insulation for use directly over snow. A 2-inch polyfoam pad (open cell) will provide about the same amount of warmth. The poly is bulkier, but more luxurious. The Ensolite is thinner and less comfortable, but slightly lighter. Take your choice—comfort or efficiency.

Several bags are available in a two-layer construction—high lofting down or fibers on top, compression-resistant foams or fibers on the bottom. This arrangement makes a lot of sense; you may be able to leave the pad at home with these types, saving considerable weight, but they are bulkier, so check out the compressed size before buying. Most of the good ones are still within the range of interest of a backpacker.

Detachable Hood

While detachable hoods are not quite as warm as permanently attached hoods, bags with detachable hoods are much more versatile. A bag with an attached hood means carrying extra weight in warm weather, when a sleeping bag is used most often, while a detachable hood may be left at home, or carried only when needed. The design shown on pages 218 and 219 can be fitted to nearly any non-hooded bag, and it makes a good accessory. It also familiarizes you with all facets of sleeping bag construction, so it is a very good warm-up project. To attach such a hood to the bag, use Velcro or snaps on the hood and the bag's drawstring hem. Make sure the Velcro or snaps do not interfere with the operation of the draw-string. The hood can be made baffled, but a sewn-through construction is simpler and is warm enough.

Drawstring Hem

Many sleeping bags are made without a drawstring at the top, and some are made with drawstrings that emerge near the zippers, which is a big disadvantage for pairing. A drawstring that emerges in the center makes for a much warmer double bag. This way the gap between the two sleepers is not left open to the cold. Construction and installation details for such

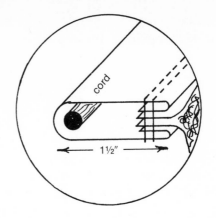

Drawstring hem construction details—cross section.

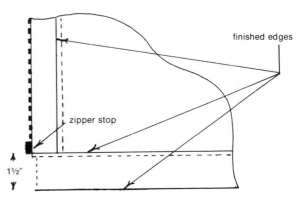

Drawstring hem—edges.

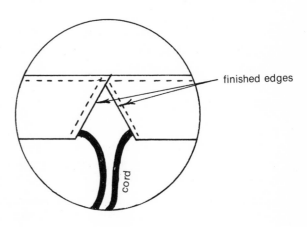

Drawstring hem—center.

a drawstring hem are shown. This may be attached to any bag with little difficulty.

Zipper Flaps

Projects 7-1 and 7-2 are designed to be used as summer bags or as liners for a combination bag. For this reason no zipper flap is necessary. Project 7-3 is meant to be used as a three-season bag or as an outer for a combination, so it has a double zipper flap with two zippers. If you want two types of bags to be compatible, extra thought should be given to zipper installation and zipper flaps. Several arrangements for zipper flaps could be used. Check out some commercial bags for ideas, and see Project 7-3.

Clothing To Wear

The layer principle of dressing, which provides warmth and versatility with clothing (see Chapter 5), can also keep you warmer while sleeping. You sleep warmer in pajamas than without them, so you should choose your camp clothing with this in mind. For example, instead of carrying an extra pair of pants and an extra shirt, carry something like a sweatsuit (top and bottom). It may be worn by itself while your other clothes are airing out, it may be worn as long underwear for extra warmth, or it could be worn as pajamas. This way you get maximum efficiency out of your clothing, and you can also save on sleeping bag weight; sleeping in clothing means you can carry a lighter/colder bag. But make sure the clothing you sleep in is clean and dry; wet clothing means a wet sleeping bag, and dirty clothing means a dirty sleeping bag if you disregard this advice.

PROJECT 7-1: SEWN-THROUGH FIBER SLEEPING BAG (FOR SUMMER, FOR WET CONDITIONS, OR FOR USE AS A LINER IN A COMBINATION BAG)

Weight of bag—3 pounds, 10 ounces
Length (inside)—74 inches
Circumference—Shoulders: 58 inches
—Hips: 58 inches
—Feet: 38 inches
Loft—3 inches (sewn through, with smooth outside shell)

Design

This bag is made from Fiberfill II that has been prequilted to 60-inch-wide ripstop nylon and a light nonwoven backing. The prequilted feature cuts down tremendously on the work and the hassles involved in using Fiberfill II (prequilted Fiberfill II is available from EMS). The bag could be made from ordinary nonquilted fiber bats, but this would involve a lot of tricky, extra work. Or you could use PolarGuard, which doesn't have to be quilted, and an edge-stabilized construction, which eliminates quite a few inches of sewn-through seams (cold spots).

If you follow the given design you should end up with a nice, roomy, summer bag, light enough for backpacking, but not as light as a down bag. The main advantage of using fibers as insulation is the fact that they retain their warmth when wet, while down does not. This makes fiber bags the ideal choice for canoeists and those living in damp climates. If a warmer bag is desired, then you could make the bag using the double-quilt construction. This requires another layer of quilted insulation/ripstop instead of the ripstop shell. Such a bag will have 5 to 6 inches of loft, and will be suitable for three-season use.

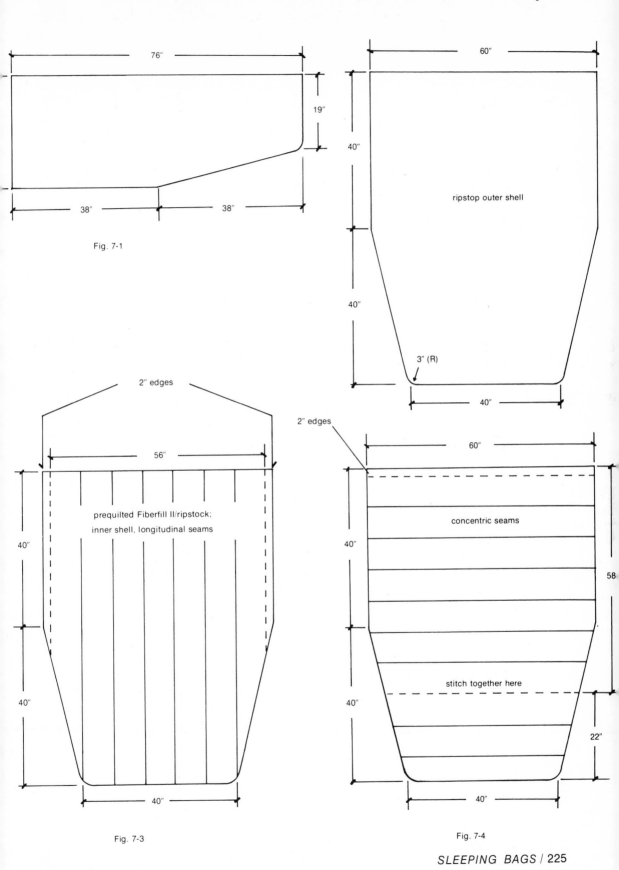

Fig. 7-2

76"

19"

38"

38"

Fig. 7-1

60"

40"

ripstop outer shell

40"

3" (R)

40"

2" edges

56"

prequilted Fiberfill II/ripstock;
inner shell, longitudinal seams

40"

40"

40"

Fig. 7-3

2" edges

60"

concentric seams

40"

58"

stitch together here

40"

22"

40"

Fig. 7-4

inside out

Fig. 7-5

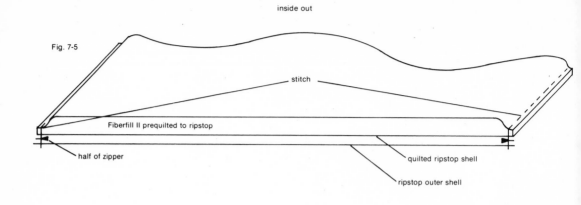

stitch

Fiberfill II prequilted to ripstop

half of zipper

quilted ripstop shell

ripstop outer shell

Fig. 7-6

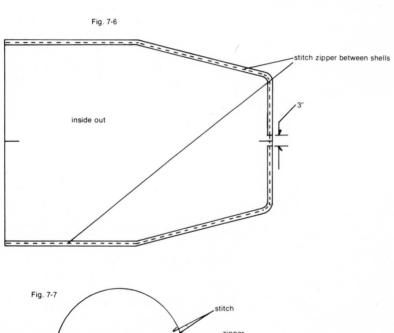

inside out

stitch zipper between shells

3"

Fig. 7-7

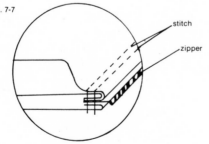

stitch

zipper

Materials

Fabric. The outer shell requires 84 inches of 60-inch-wide ripstop fabric. Nylon taffeta may be used here for extra durability, but keep the weight of the fabric between 1.9 and 2.5 ounces. Use only breathable (noncoated) fabric for sleeping bags. Don't worry about downproofing with the fiber insulations.

Insulation. I recommend the prequilted Fiberfill II for this application, but if you prefer PolarGuard use it instead. Do not use nonquilted Fiberfill or Fiberfill II bats unless you have had experience working with these materials. Otherwise you may run into a lot of problems. You will need 84 inches of 60-inch-wide material.

Hardware. You will need a zipper that is long enough to wrap around the foot and up the side to the top. I recommend a #5 Delrin zipper, two-way separating, one slider with two pulls. The ones I use are 96 inches long. You will also need a cord clamp and 72 inches of cord for the drawstring, which is a very worthwhile option.

Construction

1. Read Chapter 3, "Procedures" to familiarize yourself with the techniques involved. Note especially the advice on sewing fiber-insulated items. Carefully read through the following instructions, and make sure you understand them before beginning.

2. Lay out the outer shell as in Fig. 7-2. Cut out the shell.

3. Lay out the inner shell of prequilted fiber/ripstop. The simplest way to do this is shown in Fig. 7-3. The concentric seam construction, as shown in Fig. 7-4, requires more work and more material, but it results in a nicer bag.

4. Sew around the layout lines, about ½ inch inside, then cut out the inner shell. By sewing before you cut the shell out, you save yourself some problems later. It will help if you pin the layers in place before sewing.

5. If your machine will sew a serging stitch, serge all the cut edges of the ripstop outer shell. Serging is not practical for the insulated inner shell so flame seal as detailed in Chapter 3. Be especially careful here; Fiberfill II will burn. Try to keep the fibers out of the flame while still melting the edge of the ripstop backing.

6. With the inner and outer shells inside out, and with the zipper halves between them, sew the zipper halves to the edges of the shells. Fig. 7-5. Pinning is necessary here to keep everything lined up while stitching. There should be a 3-inch gap at the bottom between the zipper ends. Fig. 7-6.

7. Turn the shells right side out, then sew alongside the zipper teeth with two rows of stitches. Fig. 7-7. Be careful here as the Fiberfill II will tend to roll and pucker. Use pins and go slowly.

8. Attach a drawstring and drawstring hem to the top. You may have to trim the zipper and reinstall the zipper stops. If desired, you can use a cord clamp for adjustment.

9. Inspect the bag for loose stitching, puckering, rolled seams, etc., and correct.

Weight of fill—1 pound, 8 ounces of down
Weight of bag—2 pounds, 10 ounces
Length (inside)—74 inches
Circumference—Shoulders: 58 inches
              —Hips: 58 inches
              —Feet: 38 inches
Loft—4 to 5 inches maximum (sewn
through)

Design

This sleeping bag is very easy to make;
even a beginner should be able to complete one in a single evening. The sewn-
through construction, space-filler cut,
simple zipper installation, and a minimum
of detailing make this bag a pleasure to
work on. Yet this bag is probably one
of the best for the beginning backpacker
or average camper. With 1½ pounds of
down it will keep you warm through
nearly any summer night (at low altitudes),
and this is all that most people will ever
need. If you follow the given plans and
dimensions, you should end up with a
very nice, light, roomy, and completely
versatile bag.

Because there is no channel block in
this design, the bag will be usable over a
wider range of temperatures; simply fluff
more down into half of the bag and use it
on the top or bottom, as conditions dictate.
The two-way wraparound zipper, which
opens from the bottom for ventilation, contributes a great deal to the bag's comfort in
warmer weather. The drawstring closure
at the top helps keep warmth in on colder
nights, giving this bag a fairly wide comfort range. With the optional detachable
hood, a good pad, and a light sleeping
bag cover, you could even do some
mild cold-weather camping or summer
mountaineering. And with this sewn-
through bag inside a three-season bag, you
could sleep through the coldest nights in
comfort.

This bag is specifically designed to be
used as one part of a combination bag
(1½-pound sewn-through inner, 2½-
pound baffled outer). It may be used as a
liner, to extend the warmth rating of the
outer bag by about 30 degrees. Or you can
zip the two bags together, giving you a
large, roomy double. The heavier bag
could be on top for cold weather, or the
lighter bag on top for warmer weather.
The double will retain the bottom ventilating feature, and the location of the drawstrings away from the zipper will allow
you to close off the gaping hole found
when most such bags are zipped together.

The given dimensions are for a bag to fit
the average-size person. If you are 5 feet,
11 inches or taller, then a hood is required,
or you could increase the size of the bag to
suit. If you feel you need a warmer bag, do
not attempt to obtain more loft by overstuffing. This will simply waste expensive
down, without giving increased warmth.
If you need a warmer bag, go to a baffled
design, such as the one shown in Project
7-3, or consider one or all of the following
options.

Recommended Options

A hood is a highly recommended accessory for this bag. If you make a removable
hood, which attaches with Velcro or
snaps, the warmth of the bag will be increased by a significant amount. For details on constructing and attaching such a
hood, see pages 152 and 153.

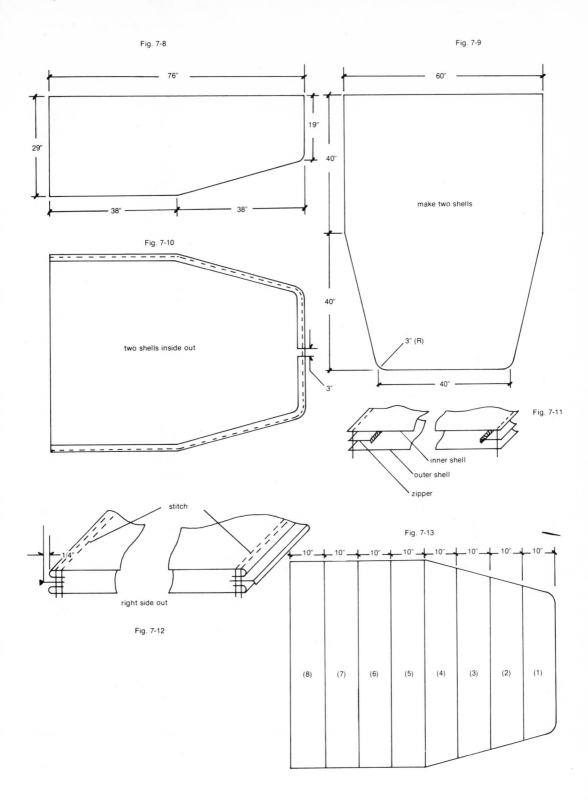

Fig. 7-8

76"

29"

19"

38" 38"

Fig. 7-9

60"

make two shells

40"

40"

40"

3" (R)

40"

Fig. 7-10

two shells inside out

3"

Fig. 7-11

inner shell

outer shell

zipper

stitch

1/4"

right side out

Fig. 7-12

Fig. 7-13

10" 10" 10" 10" 10" 10" 10" 10"

(8) (7) (6) (5) (4) (3) (2) (1)

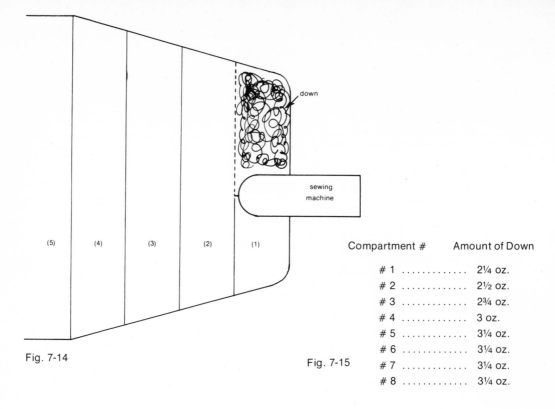

Fig. 7-14

Fig. 7-15

Compartment #	Amount of Down
# 1	2¼ oz.
# 2	2½ oz.
# 3	2¾ oz.
# 4	3 oz.
# 5	3¼ oz.
# 6	3¼ oz.
# 7	3¼ oz.
# 8	3¼ oz.

Because the bag is designed to be used as a summer bag, or as a liner for a combination bag, there is no zipper flap. If you plan to use this bag by itself in colder weather, then you may find a zipper flap desirable. However, such a flap interferes with the flap on the outer bag when used as part of a combination double.

To extend the range of your bag even further into cold weather, and to provide protection from dirt, a sleeping bag cover is a useful accessory. This cover incorporates a pocket for your pad, and also a pocket for storage of clothing, which can be used to provide additional insulation if desired.

Materials

Fabric. The recommended fabric is a good quality, high-thread-count ripstop nylon, which should weigh about 1.9 ounces per square yard, and should be treated to be downproof and stain and water resistant. Heavier fabrics will compress the down, and lighter fabrics will not be as durable. If the material has been calendered (shiny surface), decide in advance which side you want to show, then lay out accordingly. You will need about 14 feet of 60-inch-wide fabric.

Insulation. A good grade of down should be used. I use both goose down and duck down for my sleeping bags, depending on what is readily available. For the nonexpert it is very difficult to measure much difference in loft or durability between quality examples of the two. Get good down from a reliable supplier, and don't worry about the theoretical difference between the types of down. One and a half pounds of down gives a good loft to this design, but as little as 1 pound could be used for a thinner, colder, cheaper bag.

Thread. I strongly recommend a cotton wrapped/poly core thread for this application. This design has a lot of seams, which are a potential source of annoying down leakage, and the cotton wrapping seems to clog the holes best. The poly core thread is also strong, which is an important consideration with a sleeping bag, especially one with exposed seams.

Hardware. You will need a zipper that is long enough to wrap around the bottom and up the side to the top. I recommend a #5 Delrin, separating, with two sliders. They are hard to find locally, so you may have to mail order. The ones I use are 96 inches long and have one slider that has two pulls. You will also need a cord clamp and 72 inches of cord for the drawstring at the top. This is a very important part of the sleeping bag, and it is easy to install, so don't leave it out.

Construction

1. Read Chapter 3, "Procedures" to familiarize yourself with the techniques involved. Carefully read through the following instructions, and make sure you clearly understand each stage of the construction before beginning.

2. Lay out the inner and outer shells on the fabric. If you use 60-inch-wide cloth you will not need to piece them together. Fig. 7-9. Cut out the two shells.

3. If your machine will sew a serging stitch, serge all the edges on both shells. If you have no serging stitch, finish the edges by flame sealing them, as detailed in Chapter 3.

4. Starting from the foot of the bag, leave a 3-inch gap between the zipper ends and sew the zipper halves to the edges of the shells. Make sure the shells are inside out while this is taking place. Figs. 7-10 and 7-11.

5. Turn the shells right side out, then sew alongside the zipper teeth with two rows of stitches. Fig. 7-12. Don't fold the fabric too close to the teeth or the slider may bind on it. Stitch across the gap between the zipper end.

6. Mark your quilt lines every 10 inches, as shown in Fig. 7-13. Use chalk or something else that will rub off.

7. Sew three quarters of the way across the bag along quilt line 1, at the foot. Stop the machine with the needle down. Without taking the bag out of the machine, stuff the required amount of down into section 1. The easiest way to do this is with a Ziploc bag, or else with commercially packaged down. Once the package is well inside the sewn part, pop the seal and remove the bag, leaving the down in place with little mess or bother. Then finish sewing across the quilt line. Fig. 7-14.

8. Repeat step 7 with each quilted section. Fig. 7-15 gives the recommended amounts of down.

9. Attach a drawstring and drawstring hem to the top. You may have to trim the zipper and reinstall the zipper stops. If you are so inclined, you can use a cord clamp for adjustment here.

10. Inspect the bag for loose stitching and down leakage.

PROJECT 7-3: BAFFLED DOWN SLEEPING BAG (FOR THREE-SEASON USE, OR FOR USE AS AN OUTER IN A COMBINATION BAG)

Weight of fill—2 pounds, 8 ounces
Weight of bag—4 pounds, 6 ounces
Length (inside)—76 inches
Circumference—Shoulders: 68 inches
　　　　　　—Hips: 68 inches
　　　　　　—Feet: 48 inches
Loft—6 to 7 inches

Design

Read the section on "Design Considerations for Sleeping Bags" in this chapter to help you evaluate various features. I recommend the slant-box baffle construction to the home builder, but you could make this bag with V-baffles if desired. All of my bags are made with a space-filler cut, which is much easier to sew and just as warm with a loose fitting bag. I prefer the semirectangular shape for its roominess, but if you are not bothered by a tight bag you could just as easily make it tapered. If you want a warmer, longer bag, you could install a boxed foot and a hood. In other words, you can make this bag any way you like. Make sure you read the section on "Options, Accessories, and Modifications" before starting construction.

If you follow the given plans and dimensions, you should end up with a warm, roomy, versatile bag, suitable for three-season use and a wide range of activities. With 2½ pounds of down it will keep you warm through some pretty cold nights, and if you need more warmth you can slip in an insulated liner (Projects 7-1 and 7-2).

This bag is designed to be as versatile as possible; with no channel block you can fluff down into the top for cold weather, or into the bottom for warm weather. The two-way wraparound zipper contributes much to the bag's comfort in warmer weather—the zipper opens from the top for ventilation—and the centrally located drawstring at the top improves efficiency in cold weather. The double-zippered zipper flaps provide a good seal along the vulnerable zipper seams, and also work well as a zipper flap for a combination double bag. In fact, this bag was specifically designed to be used as part of a combination bag system.

The given dimensions are for a roomy semirectangular bag. If the bag is not going to be used with an insulated liner, then you could reduce the circumference by quite a bit (subtract 10 inches and use only 2 pounds of down). You could also leave out one-half of the double zippered zipper flap (a single flap with only one zipper is adequate if the bag is not used as a double). The length should be adequate for people up to 6 feet tall; those taller than that can lengthen the bag or add a hood and a boxed foot. Don't try to gain more loft by overstuffing with down; 2½ pounds is more than enough. If desired you could use less down for a lighter, cheaper, colder bag (2 pounds is a practical minimum with this design).

Materials

Fabric. The recommended fabric is a good quality, high-thread-count ripstop nylon. This should weigh about 1.9 ounces per square yard, and should be treated to be downproof (Kendown), and stain and water repellent (Zepel). Do not use coated materials. If the fabric has been calendered (shiny surface on one side),

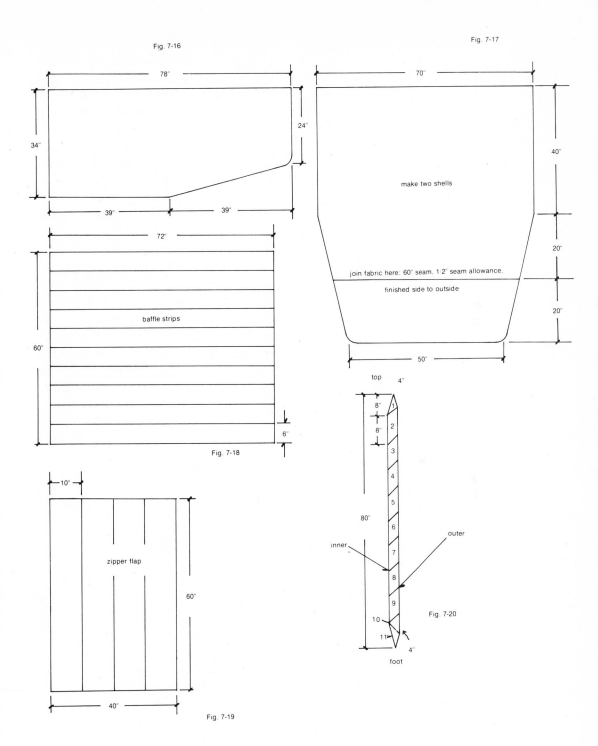

Fig. 7-16

Fig. 7-17

78"

34"

24"

39"   39"

72"

baffle strips

60"

6"

Fig. 7-18

70"

make two shells

40"

20"

join fabric here: 60" seam. 1 2" seam allowance.

finished side to outside

20"

50"

top   4"

8"   1

8"   2

3

4

80"   5

6

inner   7

outer

8

9

10   Fig. 7-20

11   4"

foot

10"

zipper flap

60"

40"

Fig. 7-19

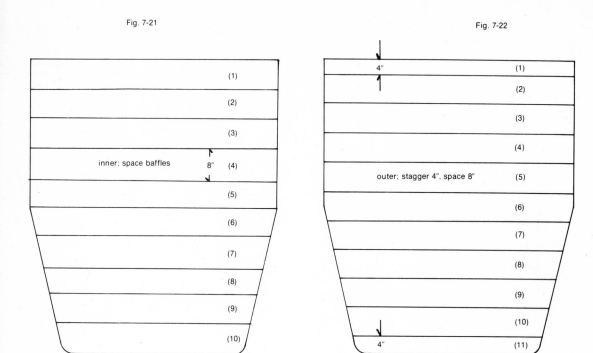

Fig. 7-21

inner; space baffles   8″

(1)
(2)
(3)
(4)
(5)
(6)
(7)
(8)
(9)
(10)

Fig. 7-22

4″

outer; stagger 4″, space 8″

4″

(1)
(2)
(3)
(4)
(5)
(6)
(7)
(8)
(9)
(10)
(11)

Fig. 7-23

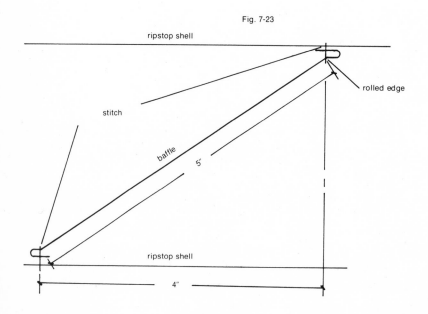

ripstop shell

rolled edge

stitch

baffle   5″

ripstop shell

4″

Fig. 7-24

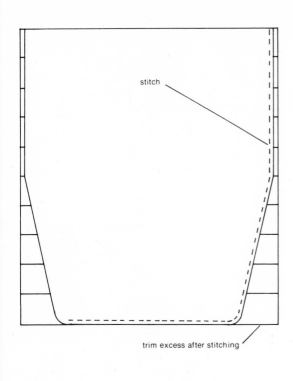

stitch

trim excess after stitching

Fig. 7-25

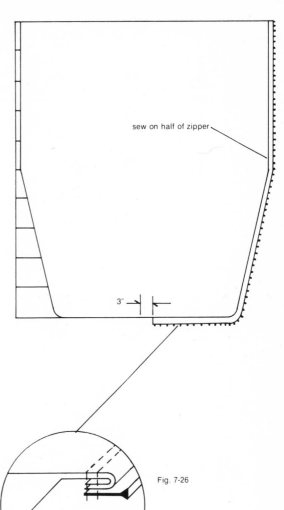

sew on half of zipper

3"

Fig. 7-26

Fig. 7-27

Compartment #	Amount of Down
# 1	1.5 oz.
# 2	4.25 oz.
# 3	4.25 oz.
# 4	4.25 oz.
# 5	4.25 oz.
# 6	4 oz.
# 7	3.75 oz.
# 8	3.5 oz.
# 9	3.25 oz.
#10	1.5 oz.
#11	1.0 oz.

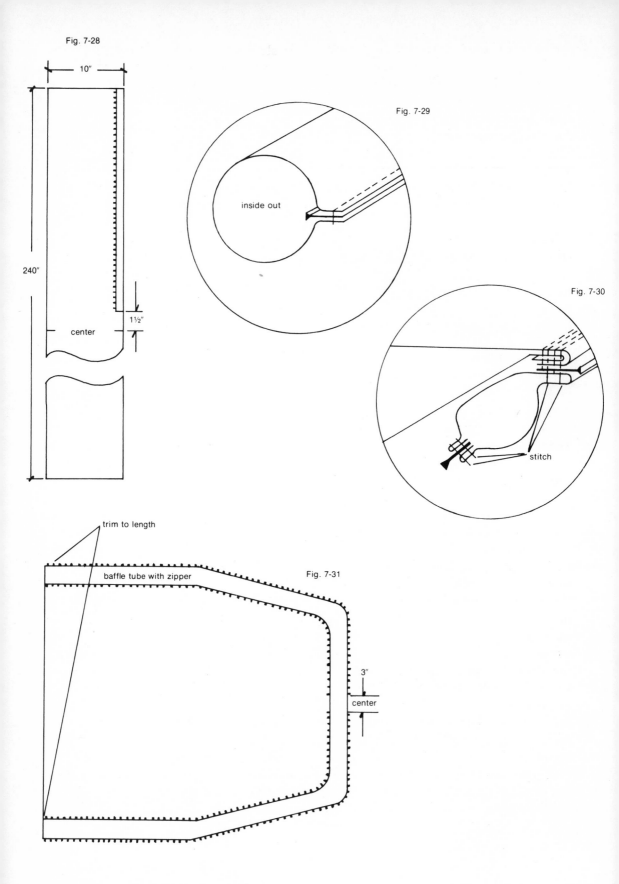

Fig. 7-28

10"

240"

center

1½"

Fig. 7-29

inside out

Fig. 7-30

stitch

trim to length

baffle tube with zipper

Fig. 7-31

3"

center

decide in advance which side you prefer, and lay it out so that this surface is exposed. You will need about 16 feet of 60-inch-wide fabric for the two shells, and about 40 inches of 60-inch-wide fabric for the double zipper flaps.

You can make the baffles from ripstop, netting, or tricot knit. You will need about 72 inches of 60-inch-wide material for the baffles.

Insulation. Use a good grade of down, either duck or goose, from a reputable supplier. For the do-it-yourselfer consistency at filling is more important than any theoretical differences between the types of down. As long as you use quality down you should have no problems; 2½ pounds of down gives good loft with this design, but you could go as low as 2 pounds.

Thread. I recommend cotton wrapped/polyester core thread for this application. This design has a lot of stitching, which is a potential source of annoying down leakage, and the cotton wrapping seems to do a good job of sealing the needle holes here.

Hardware. This design calls for two zippers, though it could be made with just one. If you stay with the wraparound design you will need zippers about 96 inches long. If you modify the bag to use a full-length zipper, you will need one about 80 inches long. A full-length zipper works well with a boxed foot. I recommend #5 Delrin zippers for sleeping bags. Get the ones that separate, with two sliders, one slider with two tabs (one inside, one outside). These zippers are hard to find locally, so you may have to mail order.

You will also need 80 inches of cord for the drawstring, and a cord clamp for adjustment. This is a very important part of

the sleeping bag, and it is simple to install, so don't leave it out.

Construction

1. Read Chapter 3 to familiarize yourself with the materials, tools, and procedures involved. Note especially the information on handling down. Carefully read through the following instructions, and make sure you clearly understand each stage of construction before you start.

2. Lay out the inner and outer shells on the fabric. If you use 60-inch-wide material you can piece the shells together as shown in Fig. 7-17. Lay out the zipper flap tubes and the baffle strips as shown in Figs. 7-18 and 7-19. Cut out these parts.

3. If your machine will sew a serging stitch, serge all the fabric edges. If not, flame seal the edges as detailed in Chapter 3. If you use tricot knit or some nettings, you may not have to flame seal the baffle edges.

4. Mark your baffle stitch lines on the insides of the two shells. Stagger the lines as shown in Figs. 7-20, 7-21, and 7-22.

5. Sew the baffle strips to the two shells as shown in Figs. 7-20 and 7-23. Use ½-inch seam allowance, and for a neater job roll the edges of the baffles as shown. Stitch the two layers of shell fabric together at the top.

6. Stitch along one side of the bag, then trim off the excess baffle material. Fig. 7-24.

7. Install one-half of the zipper as shown. Figs. 7-25 and 7-26.

8. Stuff with down and then finish the other side (steps 6 and 7). Fig. 7-27 shows a table for dividing the down by weight, but some balancing out is still to be expected. Try for even loft throughout the bag. This can be difficult for a home craftsman without expensive equipment.

9. Piece together a zipper flap tube. Sew in two zipper halves, as in Figs. 7-28 and 7-29. Turn the zipper flap tube right side out, stitch along zipper, then attach to edge of bag. Figs. 7-30 and 7-31.

10. Trim the ends of the zipper flap tube to length, stuff with about 4 ounces of down, then sew shut. You may have to trim the zipper ends and reinstall the zipper stops.

11. Sew on a drawstring and drawstring hem, as detailed on pages 223–224. You may have to trim the zipper and reinstall the zipper stops. A cord clamp is highly recommended here for adjustment of the drawstring.

12. Inspect for loose stitching, raw edges, and down leakage.

Project 7-4: Bivouac Bag (see Chapter 5, Project 5-6, for details on a pair of fiber-insulated pants that make into a bivouac bag).

Acquiring Your Equipment

Acquiring your equipment is very simple. First, you assess your equipment needs (see Chapter 2 for some advice). Second, you study and evaluate equipment to find the gear that best suits your needs—which is what the chapters dealing with specific equipment are about. Third, you acquire this equipment, either by buying, renting, making it from a kit, or do-it-yourself.

I'm pretty enthusiastic about do-it-yourself as the ideal source for equipment, but there are other alternatives and some of them make good sense. For example, in my workshop I have a little yellow day pack—made from good materials, but cheaply sewn—which I picked up for $2.98 in a bargain basement.

When I costed out the materials necessary to duplicate my little pack—after the seams had pulled out around the bottom shoulder straps—I found it would cost me about $4, and of course my time. Not content to merely copy, I made up my own plans, and eventually they evolved into the design for my Fresh Air Day Pack. If I figured out exactly how much the even-

tual product cost me, I think it would be at least ten times the $2.98 I would have had to spend for another cheapie. In practical terms I would probably have been much better off to stock up on about five of the cheapies, which conceivably could have lasted me a lifetime.

As a general rule, however, do-it-yourself usually does manage to save you money. If you go about it properly, do-it-yourself is consistently the cheapest source of good equipment, but there are cases—if budget is the main concern—where do-it-yourself just cannot compete with mass merchandising, discounts, and genuine bargains. Let's take a look at some of the ways to acquire good equipment without having to spend a fortune on it.

BARGAINS

Before I discovered do-it-yourself I was just another impoverished camper, dedicated to window shopping and hunting the elusive and wary "genuine bargain." I

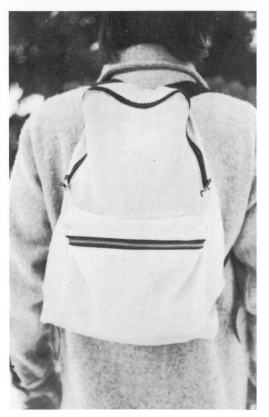

A $2.98 "bargain" day pack.

still enjoy the hunt, though I no longer take it quite as seriously as I once did. As a dedicated (if semiretired) bargain hunter, I think my experience may be valuable to the reader.

Some of you may be affluent enough to be able to outfit yourselves completely in the best commercial gear available, and not feel the bite. If you are one of these lucky individuals you don't need this book—just run down to the highest-priced store in town and buy the best of everything. You will have some pretty good gear, no doubt about that. But for the rest of us, who have to count every cent, here is what I have learned from several years of penny pinching, scrounging, and, of course, expeditions into those bargain basements.

Remember, there are lots of places to get your gear other than the specialized mountain shops, though these people are the ones to go to for consistent quality gear, informed advice, and customer satisfaction. Although in the long run they are the best commercial source of gear, for the informed, careful shopper on a budget, there *are* alternatives.

Doing Without

You really don't need every single piece of new and expensive equipment in the catalogs to enjoy yourself camping. I know that there will be many who disagree with that statement, but I'll let it stand—history is on my side. People have been camping for a lot longer than the mountain shops have been in business. The next time you get the overwhelming urge to buy that shiny new doodad that you absolutely must have to enjoy camping, think about your cavemen ancestors; they didn't have shiny new doodads and they seemed to get by. In fact, they didn't have a down sleeping bag, or a down parka, or a neat and ingenious little stove—and they still got by.

What I'm suggesting is that you don't have to go overboard on equipment to enjoy camping. Take a good look at your old gear if you have any. Do you really need a new one, or can it be fixed? Believe me, it is no shame to show up in the woods with patched-up gear. Quite the contrary, some of the most experienced campers around become so sentimental about "scruffy old reliable" that they keep their gear alive for centuries longer than necessity, or budget, dictates. In fact, there seems to be an unspoken competition in reverse snobbery going on, to see who can show up with the most decrepit looking, but still serviceable, gear.

Scrounging: An Alternative

If you are a brand-new camper, then you have no gear to recycle or repair. In this case borrow from your friends until you learn the ropes. Most acquaintances will let you try out their gear. But if your friends start losing themselves in the brush every time you meet them on the trail, it is time to think about gear of your own.

Once you discard the somewhat dubious ethics of use it, throw it away, then a lot of alternatives to shiny new gear present themselves. Clothing is probably the most obvious place where campers save money by scrounging around. If you don't believe me, stand on a well-used trail and watch the people come by. A lot of them look like leftovers from the Boer war, but it doesn't seem to cut into their fun at all. If you want to look like the best-dressed camper of the year, then by all means spend your money on fancy clothes designed specifically for camping. But be careful—too much of this camping-type clothing is designed more for style than for the trail. And if you really use the stuff, it will not remain stylish for long. Actually, the scruffier you look, the more experienced you look in the bush.

When ransacking closets for clothing good enough for camping, don't worry too much about what it looks like; concentrate instead on proper fit (too big is just fine up to a point) and proper function (wool pants are great, but some other fibers are cold in the wind). Above all, pick out gear that will last you through this trip and at least a couple more.

If you want to get involved in winter camping, then the problem gets tougher. You can't take just anything when your comfort and possibly safety depends on your clothing. Expensive down clothing is relatively inexpensive through do-it-yourself, but even less expensive is the winter gear made from polyfoam. Check out R. C. Rethmel's book *Backpacking* "Appendix I," for some very good, and cheap, ideas.

A good pair of boots is commonly thought to be one of the three most important pieces of gear a backpacker can own (the other two are a tent and a sleeping bag). A good pair of boots is also one of your most expensive purchases, but I am reluctant to advise you to scrounge here. However, I do know people who backpack in moccasins and sneakers, and they say it is great. If your feet can take it, hold off on buying boots until you really need them.

For easy trails and canoeing I like to wear my Wallabee crepe-soled moccasins, and I recommend them highly. Unfortunately, they cost almost as much as a pair of lightweight boots designed specifically for hiking, so economy is not really a consideration here. Don't ever use leather-soled street shoes when walking in slippery stuff. The crepe does a fair job in most conditions, but nothing is as good as a genuine lug sole (Vibram) for all-around traction in any conditions.

Another excellent place to save money is with the camping kitchen. If you decide that you need gear to cook with, a lot of the expensive lightweight and specialized cooking kits can be duplicated from what you have at home. This is a slightly heavier but much cheaper way to go. The nesting cook kits have a big advantage in that they are designed to stow away in a minimum of space, but look in the kitchen cupboard before you go out and buy pots specifically for camping—you might get lucky and save yourself around $20. Tin cans will work as cook kits, but personally I don't thing they are worth the bother.

Good stoves are expensive, so think about cold meals on short trips. Perhaps an inexpensive alcohol or Sterno-type single burner will fit your needs. If you are cutting down on costs you don't really need freeze-dried foods, but they aren't all that much more expensive, and the convenience and light weight are big arguments for them. Look around supermarkets before you head for the camping stores; sometimes you can find dehydrated or freeze-dried food at your local market at much less.

Rentals

Almost every specialized equipment store has gear that they will rent out, even to beginners. Expect to put down a healthy damage deposit, and then off you go. For the occasional, once-a-year-type camper, this is undoubtedly the best way to do it. You get very good gear, and the costs are nominal. Bring the stuff back clean, and admit to any damage without them beating it out of you; you never know when you might want to rent it again. Also inquire if the store has a rent-to-own policy. If they do, this means that your rental fees can be deducted from the cost of the tent, bag, etc., that you are using or perhaps applied toward new gear. This is a fantastic way to compare equipment, and then to buy from experience.

Time payments and credit purchases are similar to rent-to-own, but check out the loopholes before you sign—credit can

Item	Deposit	Rentals		
		1–3 Days	6–8 Days	12–15 Days
Tents				
2-man backpacker	10.00	6.00	10.50	13.00
3-man backpacker	10.00	7.00	11.50	14.00
Packs				
Frame pack	10.00	4.50	7.50	10.00
Day pack	5.00	2.00	4.00	6.00
Sleeping Bags				
Fiberfill II	10.00	3.00	6.00	9.00
Summer down	10.00	4.00	7.00	10.00
Stoves				
Svea 123	5.00	2.00	3.00	4.00
Optimus	5.00	2.00	3.00	4.00
Pot Sets				
Single	2.00	1.00	2.00	3.00
Family	5.00	2.00	3.00	4.00
Rain Wear				
Ponchos	5.00	2.00	3.00	4.00
Canoeing				
Canoes	20.00	14.00	22.00	30.00
Paddles	5.00	1.50	4.50	7.50
Life jackets	5.00	1.00	3.00	5.00
Car rack	5.00	1.00	3.00	5.00

be expensive. Rented gear is generally a better deal, especially when you consider that you may not have a place to store your gear for those months that you will not be using it. And you will not have to worry about making payments on time. Just drop in a few weeks before your next trip to reserve the gear for the dates you will need it and pay only for the actual time you have it. It makes a lot of sense to me, and to the multitudes who do it this way every year.

On page 242 is a sample list of rental fees from a mountain shop. For example, the two-man tent they rent out is the North Face Sierra, which retails for approximately $180. At only a little more than a dollar a day rental, you would have to rent your tent for a period of six months to equal the cost of buying one. Did you use your tent for six months last year? Or since you bought it?

Used Gear

While you are in the store looking at all that gear you would like, but can't afford, ask them if they ever sell the rental gear at the end of the season. If they do, and if you can wait, you can pick up some really good gear for next to nothing. Remember, this gear has already paid for itself over the season, so you can usually haggle on the price. In many cases the gear is still in excellent condition, but of course it is also a case of buyer beware—there's very little chance of a refund on used gear.

You might also check them out for a trading board, which is a list of used gear available from private sources. Some stores even have used gear they sell on consignment for other people, or perhaps gear they have taken on a trade. Expect to pay a bit more for such deals; the store has to get its cut, too. If the store does have a billboard listing private deals, this is your best bet. There are no middlemen between you and the seller, and the chances of stumbling over a bargain are very good. Again buyer beware, but the stores are pretty straight, and most people selling privately are not trying to put one over on you. Ask both about a written guarantee. Very few will give one, but if they are willing, by all means take it.

Clubs, organizations, and even shopping mall parking lots sometimes have a used sporting-goods sale, which is a very good place to shop. Don't confuse these with regular flea markets that carry everything; look for advertisements that specifically say sporting goods. The prices at such events are often ridiculously cheap, especially at those sponsored by a charity that sells donated gear (a lot of which comes from those impulsive closet- and basement-cleaning forays we all get into now and then).

Surplus

Everybody seems to have their own pet opinions on surplus equipment for backpacking, and many experienced backpackers refuse to have anything to do with "army green." They say it is too heavy, too old, and poorly designed. The one thing that surplus gear does have going for it is that it is durable. The army absolutely hates any equipment that wears out in less than a century or two of really hard use. I think the reason for this is the paperwork involved—obvious to anyone who has ever tried to convince a supply clerk that his boots really were worn out.

Since I put durability at the top of my priorities when evaluating equipment, I

Army surplus combat boots.

a lot less than the best quality civilian outdoors clothing, and it lasts just as long. Since the armed forces like to be fashionable too, their uniforms change relatively often, and then they are stuck with millions of tons of "obsolete" clothing that is brand new, and of the best quality. And if you want to dress stylish, check out how in the greens are on the trail and on the street. You won't be out there all alone, that's for sure. Incidentally, if you get surplus combat pants don't use those giant cargo pockets on the thighs for anything more than maps. Each step with weight up there is wasted energy.

Clothing is about it for surplus gear for backpacking for me, although I do like the army canteen and cup, which stores away

am willing to put up with the many faults of some surplus gear because of its fantastic longevity. I still have two sweaters that are over ten years old, which I wear regularly; and for years I used my issue combat boots for backpacking. For general-duty camping and wherever weight (or color) is not a factor, surplus gear can do the job for a lot less.

In general, only two kinds of gear find their way into the surplus stores: the gear that the army considers too worn out to be useful (and, believe me, the army takes a lot of convincing on this) and the gear that has not kept up with the advances of time (obsolete gear). It is the gear that the army considers obsolete that we are most interested in. This stuff may be brand new, never issued equipment, and this is what is preferred.

Clothing is the best place to think surplus. Canadian and American surplus clothing is pretty good, and I wear quite a bit of green on the trail. Army green costs

Canadian Army surplus canteen and cup. Note webbing with Velcro flaps.

around the canteen and inside the canteen carrier. But before you buy such a rig, check out the weight. Remember, the quality of surplus gear is great, but the gear itself is often heavy and archaic. Not only that, but since the greens became a fad on the street, good surplus clothing prices have skyrocketed. If the prices are reasonable the clothing is a very good buy, but watch out for imitations that are made from cheaper materials, designed to cash in on the surplus look.

Smart Shopping

About the best thing I can say here is look around before you buy. Store A may want $150 for a certain sleeping bag. Store B may just happen to have a sale on, and have the exact same item with the same manufacturer's guarantee, for $99.99. The trip across town to find out will not be that expensive, and besides, bargain hunting is a lot of fun.

Try to hold off purchasing whatever you want until it goes out of season. Remember, a lot of shops sell backpacking stuff in the summer and switch over to skis for the snow. They hate to store leftovers for the winter—it costs them money—so they will sometimes cut their prices substantially in the fall.

Another thing to watch for is discontinued merchandise. Although the camping-gear manufacturers are not as bad as the car people, every now and then they do update their line. The old stuff is still as good as ever, but it usually gets cheaper. Just use discretion here. For instance, a discontinued model of a sleeping bag that does not have new-fangled, super-duper design is usually just as warm this year as it was last year, when then it was the new-fangled, super-duper model. It is still a good buy.

But what about parts for your old-model gear when they wear out? If the manufacturer is a good one, parts and service for the obsolete gear will remain available, but ask about this before buying. Actually, the really good equipment will not depreciate too much no matter how long it stays on the shelf. On discontinued merchandise you generally get full warranty, but it is meaningless if the manufacturer doesn't supply your particular store with the parts, so watch out here. As far as warranty and seasonal sales go, it should make no difference, but it sometimes does. If you see a sign that says "No Refund on Sale Merchandise," start worrying. If you see a sign that says "No Refund Or Exchange on Sale Merchandise," you should leave the store at once. If you see those signs at any time, they are good arguments for shopping elsewhere.

The people who specialize in selling top-quality equipment may charge more than the local bargain basements. They do so because they give better customer service and satisfaction. Just one tip on refunds: keep your bills until the item dies of old age. In general, no bill means no refund, and you can't blame the stores for this—they do lose a lot of gear to "rip-offs."

The part of scrounging I enjoyed the most was skulking around dingy basements in pursuit of the elusive genuine bargain. I keep hearing "You get what you pay for," which does have some truth to it, but I have bagged quite a few of those rare bargains in my time. Just because a piece of good stuff somehow finds its way into "disreputable" surroundings, there is no reason to shun it. If you see top-name merchandise at ridiculous prices in basements, then by all means grab it.

If you know equipment, you can enjoy yourself when shopping or scrounging

A double-layer, down-insulated parka purchased for $52.95.

check out the instructions, and perhaps to rob them of some particularly good idea. For those of you not interested in designing your own, kits have a great advantage over "start from scratch" do-it-yourself. The kit people have been at it for a while now, and their designs are every bit as sophisticated as the very best commercial designs. They supply the development and research that is a big part of the finished product. And every single one that I am familiar with has a written policy of satisfaction guaranteed or money refunded, and they live up to it, too. Some will even go as far as refunding postage on returned items, which is not the way to make money, but the way to keep the customers happy. That is just the kind of people they are.

The instructions for the kits have been developed with a lot of customer feedback, and they are excellent. The kit people like to tell everyone that their instructions can be easily understood by beginners—and they're right. If you do get stumped, which is not too likely, then they will bail you out with phone advice or a refund. This is a major advantage over strict do-it-yourself.

Another advantage the kits have is their convenience. All parts are already gathered into one bundle, whereas getting all the materials together can sometimes be a problem with do-it-yourself. The prepackaged down, for example, is a real time and nerve saver. Even if you are considering strict do-it-yourself, at least look to the kit people for your down. They have it in convenient little packages, in various sizes (by weight), which are just right for nearly any project.

Where do-it-yourself has an advantage over the kits is when you want something truly different or new. While the kits can be customized to some extent, they are all

without getting burned. If you don't, then leave the hunt to others, and shop where customer service is more than a sign on the wall. Most large department stores have a sporting-goods section that handles good backpacking gear at reasonable prices. Unfortunately, these stores often have clerks who don't know what they are talking about and who hardly know a backpack from a folding cot. What they do know, however, is that a happy customer is a spending customer; thus these places will go out of their way to give exceptional service on such things as warranty, refunds, and exchanges. They have better prices than the exclusive mountain shops, too. If only they would hire clerks who knew what they were doing, that would be my idea of the place to shop.

Kits

Even though I usually like to start from scratch, I have used a few kits, just to

The jackets and rain gear shown on the four children were made from Holubar's Kits for Kids.

Each of the items in the photo was made from Frostline Kits. From left to right: Mountain Parka, Trailridge Tent, Hatch-Back Sack (does not include frame), Down Vest, Cougar Sleeping Bag.

This Deluxe Rain Parka is easy to make from the Altra Kit. (Photo courtesy ALTRA, Inc.)

rather orthodox in design and materials. Although they do have a pretty good selection, which is improving all the time, the kits are even more restricted in the choices available than is regular commercial gear. For the real innovator, pure do-it-yourself is the only way to go.

Both kits and strict do-it-yourself can produce excellent gear at great savings, but you have to do your part. Remember, any form of do-it-yourself is superior to buying it, but the choice between which do-it-yourself—kits or strict—is not quite as clear cut. They both have some advantages. Personally, I will stay with strict do-it-yourself; I find the extra rewards well worth the extra efforts.

Remember also that you save more with do-it-yourself from scratch, you can have anything you can think up, and it is a lot more fun, especially the staying up all night to figure things out yourself. But for those people not sure of their abilities, I can recommend the kits to start with.

Kit Suppliers

Here is a list of the firms currently making kits, but new people are coming in every year, so keep your eyes open.

ALTRA, INC.
5441 Western Avenue
Boulder, Colorado 80301

Small selection, they guarantee the quality of their products and your satisfaction. If you encounter a problem you can't solve, you can phone them and one of their designers or experienced home sewers will talk you through your predicament.

CALICO KITS
P.O. Box 1222
1275 South Sherman
Longmont, Colorado 80501

CANADIAN NORTH AGENT
Box 1050—Station B
Ottawa, Ontario K1P 5R1

The only Canadian kit company—so far.

COUNTRY WAYS, INC.
3500 Highway 101 South
Minnetonka, Minnesota 55343

EMSKITS
1041 Commonwealth Avenue
Boston, Massachusetts 02215

They have most of the materials, and a good selection of gear. They use Dacron Fiberfill II in their insulated articles. They also charge a $3 handling fee for returns on opened kits. A division of Eastern Mountain Sports.

FROSTLINE KITS
Frostline Circle
Denver, Colorado 80214

The oldest firm, with perhaps the greatest selection. They carry almost all the items you need for do-it-yourself, and they handle down-insulated items. They sell nothing but the kits and materials.

HOLUBAR KITS
P.O. Box 7
Boulder, Colorado 80302

Good selection, same guarantee as their finished products, and they do have materials, even if they are not in the catalog. Their catalog includes made-up articles of high quality; compare the prices for an idea of just how much you can save with kits.

MAKIT
P.O. Box 571
Whittier, California 90608

Small selection, good price for a sleeping bag insulated with PolarGuard. They have PolarGuard for sale, along with a fair selection of materials. Their items are available finished.

PLAIN BROWN WRAPPER
2055 West Amherst Avenue
Englewood, Colorado 80110

SUNDOWN
2700 Highland Drive
Burnsville, Minnesota 55337

Good selection, they handle down-insulated items.

Two of the oldest and biggest kit people—Frostline and Holubar—give special discounts to groups. Holubar allows nearly any group a discount (Boy Scouts, Girl Scouts, other youth groups take note), but to qualify for the Frostline group discount, you must be involved with a home economics sewing class. Frostline says that over 1,000 schools across the United States (and a few in Canada) are using their kits as sewing projects in home economics.

## 9

Use, Maintenance, and Repairs

USE AND MAINTENANCE

There are two ways to do things: you can put a little extra time and care into using and maintaining your equipment properly, or you can put a lot of time or money into repairing or replacing it later. The choice is yours. To simplify matters greatly, remember that equipment life depends on the materials used, and the use and care that these materials receive. Chapter 3, "Materials," gives information about the specialized materials common to lightweight camping equipment. A thorough knowledge of these materials, their properties, and their individual weaknesses is a good place to start.

The materials used in lightweight camping gear have been called miraculous; certainly they are stronger, lighter, and tougher than anything we have ever had before. They may truly be miraculous, but they are not indestructible; they may still be destroyed by improper treatment. (For example, Delrin zippers are perhaps the toughest, most reliable made, but did you know that Delrin melts at about

330°F.? You hardly want to learn about this while drying your clothes around a campfire!) It is your job to learn the proper ways to use and care for your equipment.

When it comes to maintenance, the biggest part of your routine will be the inspection of your equipment—before you use it and after use. Since quality backpacking equipment is designed to be rugged, it will generally take a great deal of wear before actually failing. And when it does start to fail, you will usually have plenty of warning if you know where to look. A regular program of inspection will therefore eliminate almost all of your equipment failures in the field.

The second largest part of your maintenance routine will be cleaning—mostly cleaning up after your trips for storage, but also some cleaning in use. The main concern here is with the right kind of cleaning, for improper cleaning has ruined a lot of gear. For example, it is generally acknowledged that more sleeping bags have been ruined through improper washing than any other way. But there are still those who toss their expensive sleeping bags into an agitator washing machine, blissfully unaware of the dangers involved—and then they end up with a ruined bag. There's no doubt that proper cleaning can be important to the life of your gear, but too many campers don't know exactly what constitutes proper cleaning.

The proper use, care, and maintenance of your gear—the proper techniques and habits to learn, the best ways to clean your gear, the things to look for that signal impending failure—can get quite complicated. That is why so many choose to forget or ignore the problem. But, hopefully, this chapter will answer most of your questions and simplify things considerably.

PACKS

Pack Bags

Use. Pack bags are designed to be tough and to last for a long time. The fabrics used in good quality packs will rarely wear out from abrasion without years of heavy use; however, the bags can sometimes fail in other ways. The most common failure points are the bottom seams, and with a soft pack, the seams joining the straps to the bag. By beefing up these weak spots you can make your pack bag last almost forever.

On a pack that uses zippers, as most designs do nowadays, another potential weak spot may exist. When zippers were first introduced they received some bad publicity because of their lack of reliability in this heavy-duty application. This has changed. The modern nylon-coil and Delrin zippers used today have almost completely eliminated zipper failure. If

you don't overload compartments, and always hold the zipper together while you close it, your zippers should outlast the rest of the bag.

Because packs are tough, they get treated roughly. Usually they can take it, but here are some special things you should watch for:

Don't load your pack to the limit, grab it by a strap and jerk it around. While the straps may have sufficient strength to carry more than you could ever stuff in, sudden jolts could tear them loose. Don't leave your pack on when climbing through barbed wire fences. While Cordura and other pack fabrics do have very high tear strengths, they are definitely not invulnerable. Don't drop your pack off a mountain, or even throw it off the bed of a truck. While the seams may be strong enough to last and last in normal use, such abuse can split them wide open as they try to change shape. Don't load your pack with some hard object and then transport it with this object rubbing against something on the outside (like a truck bed). The fabric will be caught between two abrasive areas with no way to escape; it can wear through in a hurry.

Inspection. The place to watch in the soft packs is the bottom corners. The abrasion the bag receives is often concentrated here, and the fabric can wear out. Watch also the seams along the bottom; they are usually the first to go. Check how the bag/strap seams are holding up. They are designed for extra strength but they can fail. If the zipper gives you any problems replace it immediately, before things get worse. Inspect occasionally for broken teeth or worn tape where the slider rubs against it, especially around the curves. If you have any partition floors, see how they are holding up.

In pack bags the usual problem places are still there, but there are a few new ones depending on the specific design of the bag. Check especially the attachment points for hanging the bag on the frame. In the cheaper designs that use the top frame horns enclosed in sleeves, the bag is being supported by a relatively flimsy arrangement; expect a lot of trouble here if you carry heavy loads. In packs using the more common grommets and pins, inspect the grommets for signs of tearing loose. This is not too common on the good packs, but it can happen. If your bag is the top-loading type that has a hold-open frame along the top, inspect for abrasion along the edges. This is quite common in packs that are transported lying down, with the bag to the bottom.

Cleaning. Never wash nylon in strong detergent; it can strip out the water-proofing and possibly even weaken the fabric. Use only mild soap, warm water, and a small brush. If the bag is impossibly dirty, send it to the dry cleaners, but remind them that it was waterproof (water resistant) when it left, and that you expect to get it back the same way. If you are near coniferous trees keep an eye out for pitch or sap on the bag, which can harden into a really ugly cleaning job and weaken the nylon fibers by chemical action if the sap is left on long enough. Keep in mind that a clean pack is more water resistant than a dirty one, it will not rot, and the mice, squirrels, etc., won't find it such an appealing breakfast.

Pack Frames

Use. The vast majority of pack frames are made from tubular aluminum, so we will concern ourselves mainly with them. The most important thing to remember about aluminum tubing pack frames is that aluminum is soft. Some alloys are harder than others, but the common ones found in pack frames can bend, dent, abrade, or occasionally crack.

If the frame uses the most common system, it will have welded joints. The quality of the joints pretty well determines the quality of the frame on these types. (See Chapter 4 "Frames.") The trick is to get a solid joint without annealing (softening) the surrounding area. If not done properly, there will be an area around the welds softer than the rest of the tubing. Since this area is also one of the high-stress points on a pack frame, bending can occur here quite easily.

This is one of the best arguments for using some form of nonwelded frame joints, and many manufacturers offer ingenious solutions to the problem. These nonwelded joints, however, have their own unique problems—specifically, how well they hold, how much they flex, and how long they will last. Whatever system is used to hold the joints together, the aluminum tubing can still bend, dent, abrade, or crack if abused. Nearly every frame that is retired gets that way through abuse, not old age. The solution is to take a little extra care when trying to get your heavy pack from your feet to your shoulders. Practice makes perfect, and may save you the cost of a new frame.

When transporting or shipping your pack watch out for abrasion between the frame and any hard object. Aluminum is soft and therefore it bends, abrades, and dents easily, and each dent is a potential failure point as it weakens the tubing around it, so stow your pack carefully. One of the biggest advances in frame design was the discovery that body-contoured frames were more comfortable than straight ones. This is why your frame has those nice curves in it. If you want to keep those curves, don't put a heavily loaded pack frame side down in your trunk and bounce it over several miles of rough road.

Inspection. The joints are the weakest spots so watch them closely. Cracked welds mean out with it, or if it is a good frame, contact the manufacturer; most good ones have warranties and repair facilities, and they should be able to fix it cheaper and better than your local welding shop. On the nonwelded joints be especially watchful. These joints have their advantages, but there are many different kinds, with their own special quirks. You may have to tighten a screw occasionally, or perhaps replace some fitting. This may cost only pennies, but it can make all the difference on the trail. It would be a good idea to stock up on a spare joint fitting when you buy the frame. Most of these designs are fairly new, so ultimate reliability is still to be seen, though they should do the job.

Bends may or may not be repairable at home. Some of the alloys are pretty brittle so don't play around too much here. Your best bet would be to contact the manufacturer. If the frame bent, you probably bent it, so expect to pay for the repairs.

Dents are weak spots in tubing. You will have to judge the degree of damage and decide if the dents are serious or merely cosmetic. Keep your eye on them.

Aluminum abrades easily. This is a major problem in a vibrating truck bed or car trunk if the frame is in contact with something hard. It is also a smaller problem on the trail if some hard object rubs continuously against the frame. Watch for shiny spots indicating wear and if serious enough, pad the area with tape.

Cleaning. Aluminum can be anodized by a process similar to natural oxidation (rusting). If you have ever used nonanodized aluminum you know that it gives off a dirty grayish powder that stains nearly anything rubbing against it. Anodization is a slightly harder surface layer that does not rub off so easily.

In the nonanodized frames expect some staining, but this is not a major problem. Don't try and make your frame more stylish by polishing the dull surface layer of oxidation off; aluminum oxidizes in contact with air and that coating will keep coming back no matter how much you polish. You can paint over aluminum to prevent this problem, but the paint wears off eventually.

Never polish the anodized frames. This could remove the thin layer of anodization, and you defeat its main purpose for being there. Some anodizing leaves the frame a pretty color. If you are tempted by this, remember that scratches will occur, and they will stand out much more on a colored background than on a natural one. Clean both types of aluminum with a damp rag and don't use abrasives (mud is an abrasive).

If your pack straps are cotton, keep them clean and dry and watch for rot. If the straps are nylon web or padded nylon fabric, wash as you would ordinary nylon. Warm water, a small brush, and mild soap will make most harnesses look almost as good as new.

CLOTHING

Boots

Use. Just about every how-to-go-camping book ever written gives information on the proper selection, use, care, and maintenance of boots. The thing to remember about boots designed for the outdoors is that they are tougher than their more civilized relatives. This makes them tougher to break in, and if they are not chosen carefully and broken in properly, this makes them tougher on your feet. Personally, I favor the take-your-time approach to breaking in boots, so I can't make judgments about the other methods that are supposed to work faster. There are lots of stories about how to break in your boots quickly. There are also lots of stories about people ruining their boots while trying to break them in quickly.

On proper boot care, most experts agree that more boots are ruined by improperly drying them than from any other cause. "Cooked" boots and boots with mud left on them dry out too much, and the leather becomes brittle and cracks. Never dry your boots with heat hot enough to cause your skin discomfort. Better yet, never use heat; use crumpled newspapers stuffed inside to draw out most of the water—and have patience.

Clean your boots with a stiff brush and cool water whenever they get too dirty. When they have dried thoroughly, give them the waterproof treatment recommended for the specific type of leather they were made from. See the recommendations that are usually included with good boots, or quiz the nearest shoemaker. The general rule is oil for oil-tanned leather; silicone for chrome-tanned leather. I use Sno-Seal on my boots, but it is a nuisance to put on since it or the boots must be heated slightly.

Almost every book I have read proclaims loudly and frequently that socks are just as important as boots for proper foot care and comfort. I believe it. Since I started using wool socks for hiking, I find them so comfortable and superior to the synthetic, thin kind that I now wear thick wool all the time, summer or winter, hiking or lounging. In some situations I wear two pairs of socks, one thin inner, and a thick wool outer. This changes according to immediate conditions (feet swell, boots stretch). Even on fairly short hikes I carry at least two pairs each of inners and outers, not so much to replace dirty socks, as to replace the occasional wet ones. At such times clean, dry socks are worth their weight in gold.

Inspection. If you keep your boots clean and waterproof them regularly, they should last for years. Watch out for deep cracks in the uppers that mean the leather is drying out, or perhaps that you "cooked" them once too often. The uppers should outlast several soles with proper care, and several soles should last a long, long time. Watch the stitching for worn-out threads, especially if you do any climbing, and always watch the sole-boot seams on glued boots to make sure they aren't coming off. If your soles do wear out finally, a local shoemaker or perhaps one of the specialists can make your old boots nearly as good as new for a lot less, and you won't have much trouble breaking them in again.

Cleaning. Like I said, boots that have mud caked and dried on them lose moisture. And boots that lose too much moisture become brittle and crack. Keeping your boots clean is not merely for appearances; it helps them stay alive longer. Clean regularly with a stiff brush and cool water, and when dry treat them to make them waterproof. There are several different types of sprays or powders that can keep the insides of your boots smelling nice and sweet. Try them if you like.

Keeping wool socks clean on a long trip is sometimes a problem, especially if you wash them in cold water. Some people use their hand soap, but of course there are many special potions that will do a better job. Whatever you use, wash them often; washing loosens up the compressed areas you have trampled down, and washing socks regularly is the social thing to do. If you forget to do so, your friends may take matters into their own hands and wash them for you—with you still in them.

Rain Gear

Use. Rain gear is designed to keep you dry and comfortable when the world is wet. I find that the ventilated poncho provides me with more comfort—even if it is slightly wetter comfort—than do the tighter rain jackets. In some conditions, however, the poncho is almost worthless and even dangerous. Driven rain will find every little crack in your defenses and will eventually work its way to you. The flappy poncho just will not provide the protection that a cagoule or jacket will in these conditions. In windy conditions a poncho can also billow and catch air, and can throw you off balance at a critical moment. Bicyclists and climbers beware.

A trick that makes a poncho much more manageable in windy conditions, without sacrificing too much of its ventilation or protection, involves folding the poncho under until it is just a few inches wider than your shoulders. Then you secure the poncho around your waist with a belt or rope, using the extra material as a wrap around the section below your arms. This way your lower arms may get wet, but the rest of you stays very dry, and ventilation seems to be adequate.

I like to use rain chaps (individual legs) rather than a pair of waterproof rain pants.

I find that the chaps give just as much protection, and they provide much better ventilation. Make them wide enough to put on over your boots, and make sure that they are short enough to avoid tripping or snagging on ground-level obstacles. Make them from tough 3.1-ounce polymer taffeta; the ripstop chaps just don't stand up too well. Chaps should not be taken off when the rain stops because there may be a lot of water on low vegetation.

Inspection. Almost every type of rain gear will leak, but often you won't know it until you are out there in the rain getting leaked on. It is almost impossible to tell where these leaks are coming from, though as a general rule the seams are the worst culprits. Coating all seams with a flexible waterproofing may provide some relief.

Next, look at the design of the garment. Brims around a poncho or jacket hood are not just decoration; they are supposed to direct rain away from your face, not down your neck. Ventilating flaps can also let in wind-driven rain, so make sure rain wear stresses several small openings rather than a few large ones that can flap or billow.

If it is an older garment subject to much use, look for abrasion spots that have worn away the waterproof coating. These may not be very obvious to the eye, but they can be the source of some very hard to trace leaks. Rips and tears in the fabric should be obvious, and they should be fixed immediately, before they spread further, possibly forcing you to buy a new garment when a small repair at the right time could have saved it.

Cleaning. Coated materials, of which most rain garments are made, should be washed carefully—warm water, mild soap, gentle cycle on the washing machine, etc.—or the coating may separate from the fabric. If you decide to send it to the dry cleaners, make sure you mention that the material is waterproof or water repellent, or else you may not get it back that way. Most larger dry cleaners can restore water repellency to fabrics in which the original treatment has worn or been washed off. They will usually do it for a lot less than you could, and they have the facilities and experience to do a better job, too. If your water-repellent garments are not as dry as they once were, it may be a good idea to send them to the dry cleaners even if they are still fairly clean.

Down Clothing

Use. People have died from not knowing how to use their down clothing properly. Down is one of the most efficient and all-around best insulators available when dry, but when wet it is next to useless—and hard to dry out and restore to usefulness in the field. Therefore, the number-one rule with any down-insulated item is keep it dry. This means keep it dry from external sources of moisture such as rain, open water, or melted snow, and also keep it dry from the moisture that comes from you.

Many winter campers carry a small whisk broom that they use diligently to remove every last trace of snow before entering their tents. This is a good habit to cultivate. Such habits and proper winter camping techniques will eliminate most of the moisture from external sources, but there is little you can do about the moisture your body gives off. The amount of moisture you give off depends in part on ventilation and activity, so keep cool, move slowly, and wear layers for flexibility. Even so, there will come a time when your down gear will be saturated by perspiration, and that is where real trouble begins.

Clothing will often pick up a lot of dirt, body oils, and perspiration from the wearer. If you keep yourself clean, you keep your clothing clean. If you do get insulated clothing dirty, a wipe with a damp (not wet) rag will remove most of it. If it is really stubborn, a small amount of spot remover may do the job. A good trick is to wear an extra parka or windshell over your down gear (make sure it's breathable). This layer takes most of the dirt the world hands out, and is much easier to clean and care for. It will also provide an amazing amount of extra warmth for very little extra weight. You will also find it very practical in bush or forests, where branches can rip open a down jacket in seconds.

When packing your down clothing away, stuff it randomly into a pack compartment or stuff bag. This random stuffing helps break up down clumps and keeps loft longer. The stuff sacks also make excellent pillows when stuffed, and provide convenient handling around camp. They also provide protection when the item is not in use. Remember, down-insulated items are fragile and are in danger any time they are out of their stuff sack or pack compartment. When you intend to use some item, remove it from the stuff sack and shake it out or fluff it up and wait a few minutes. This will give you the most efficient use from your insulation, which must recover from the compression cycle if it is to be most effective.

For extended storage never leave your down gear in an airtight, waterproof, tight little stuff sack. While these sacks are excellent on the trail, if used for extended periods of time they can kill the down, or promote rotting and odors. Always store down in its expanded state if it is to be stored for any length of time. Good ventilation will allow the down and the shell to dry out, and any smells to dissipate. Clothing can be hung in a closet or stuffed in a loose, breathable stuff sack. I prefer the closets, but if you have cats or small children, you may prefer the loose stuff sacks.

Inspection. Since you have no way of inspecting the inside of the clothing to see how the insulation is doing, you have to judge the down from other signs. When your clothes are no longer as warm as they once were, this is a sign that something should be done to get back the loft. If you are still comfortable in them in cold weather, and if they aren't really dirty, then you probably have very little reason for washing them.

After checking over the clothing for down clotting, examine the exterior and interior shells for down leakage, small rips, split seams, etc., which mean repairs are in order. Especially watch the seams, for a loose seam can eventually become a major problem.

Cleaning. Specific instructions for washing down-filled items are given in the section on cleaning down sleeping bags. Basically the idea is to clean the shell and the down without removing too much of the down's natural oils.

TENTS

Use. Read the manufacturer's suggestions for pitching your tent and follow them because he should know what he is talking about. Each style tent will have its idiosyncrasies, but we will follow the common A-frame mountain tent for an example.

1. Find a suitable spot for pitching your tent. This can be simple or difficult, depending. Usually, the more you need a spot, the harder it is to find a good one. If you have time, look around. A little extra effort at this point will undoubtedly pay off with more comfortable sleep.

2. Conscience permitting, clear an area slightly larger than your tent floor of all sharp rocks, vegetation, etc., that can speed up the wear on your tent floor. If you are carrying a ground sheet you can use it under the tent to protect your precious floor. (Ground sheets cost less to replace than tent floors.) If you do use a ground sheet, make sure it is smaller than the tent floor; a ground sheet that sticks out will trap all the rain running off the tent, and direct it under the tent and hold it there. Water beds are great, but leaky tent floors are not. It is a tent, not a life raft. Also remember that tent trenching is for the pioneers, who needed it with their floorless tents. You have no such excuse for desecrating the wilderness.

3. Spread out the tent and stake down the four corners in a rectangle. Try and make it neat; it is the foundation upon which you will build your home for the night. If it is windy, this step can be interesting.

4. Frame up one end with the poles and stake out the first ridge pullout. Erect the other end and stake out the other ridge pullout, but don't overtighten yet.

5. Stake out all other floor loops and pullouts that are called for. This will vary from tent to tent, but put them all out before you do any serious tightening.

6. Fine tune the strings. Make them all tight enough to eliminate flapping or wrinkles without putting too much strain

on any one spot. If you can't do it and you know from experience that a taut pitch is possible with that particular tent, go back to step three and straighten out your foundations.

7. Stake out the fly if rain is threatening. The fly may be staked to the tent pull-out stakes, and usually is, but for maximum strength and efficiency as an insulator, it should be staked out with separate stakes slightly farther out than the pullouts. The fly should not touch the tent anywhere or condensation may leak inside.

Remember, a properly pitched tent is a strong tent; people have weathered out some incredible storms in a little mountain tent with no problem. But an improperly pitched tent, even if it is of the best quality, can flap itself—and you—to death. Seams can split, poles can break, and the whole mess can go sliding off a mountain, so do it right.

If high winds are a possibility, use a shock cord to take up any major stress before it gets to the tent. Almost every book or mountain shop can show you how to rig them properly.

As I said, the floor will almost always be the first to go. Make it an unbreakable rule that no shoes get in the tent unless they are off the feet.

When hauling your tent around in the stuff sack, give a little thought to what a set of sharp tent pegs can do to any fabric they encounter. A set of wire pegs jammed in loose can provide you with a shower stall instead of a tent. A separate stuff sack for pegs is a good idea.

If you are one of those people who has to have a wood fire to wake up to, remember that winds have been known to shift, and sparks have been known to fly, and tents have been known to burn. If you are using one of those abominations

known as a space heater inside your tent, you should know that carbon monoxide kills. If you sleep with one of these oxygen burners going and don't make sure of adequate, night-long ventilation, then you just don't wake up—ever.

Inspection. Watch the seams most of all; a seam that lets go can be a major disaster, and of course it will always let go in the worst possible conditions (blizzards and rainstorms). Next, watch along the bottom for leakage and renew the seam sealant if it seems time to do so.

Tent poles are usually up to the demands placed on them in most quality tents, but if they fail they will usually fail around the joints. Keep a watchful eye here for cracks or fatigue signs, but the poles can fail in windy conditions with no previous sign of weakness. Perhaps you could carry one extra segment that could make do for any failure, but too many tents require different poles for each segment. Watch for burrs or sticky poles, and eliminate them with a file or knife blade.

Cleaning. Tents can rot. Even nylon tents can rot. This means that a clean tent is a healthy tent, so clean your tent before you store it away. Set it up on your lawn, spray it with a hose, and let it dry in the sun. Make sure everything, including the floor underneath, is dry before you pack it away. Repeatedly folding coated materials can fatigue the fold lines and cause separation between the coating and the fabric. Fold loosely with the heavier coated floor fabric to the outside and while you are folding up the tent, take the time to wipe off any sticky vegetable matter (or worse) you find on the floor. Pitch or sap can cause a chemical reaction that can weaken the fabric if left on long enough.

Cleaning for storage is fairly important,

as a lot of people who neglect it find out, but just as important is regular cleaning to prolong life. Dirt or sand tracked into a tent can act like sandpaper on your coated fabrics, abrading them away in no time. For this reason many campers carry small whisk brooms to brush out their tents, which they do regularly. A neat trick to get out all the dirt, crumbs, and ants that come in after the crumbs, spiders that come in after the ants, etc., is to turn your tent inside out before packing, and flap it in the wind for a few seconds. This does an even better job than the whisk broom, and should be part of your prepacking routine.

Tents can be washed, but remember what has been said about warm water, mild soap, and coated or water-repellent fabrics. Washing with a hose while the tent is set up should do a fair job, but you can do a better one by hand in your bathtub. Whatever you do, don't throw your tent into an agitator machine; you can rip out seams and generally mess it up beyond repair.

SLEEPING BAGS

Down Sleeping Bags

Use. A sleeping bag protected by a stuff sack is relatively safe, but a sleeping bag outside its protective sack is fragile. Don't abuse your bag, and it may outlast you. Abuse it and you lose it, maybe even before you finish paying for it. And since a down sleeping bag is a major investment these days, replacing down bags can cost you plenty.

Don't hang your sleeping bag over the tent to air out, then go for a leisurely day-long stroll; it may not be there when you get back. Strong winds can pick it up and carry it far away, or perhaps just far enough to catch it on a branch or something. Getting back all your down after it has been spread all over is not going to be easy. Or perhaps wind won't be the culprit. Sad to say, there are people (and even animals) who want your sleeping bag, so keep an eye on it at all times. Never leave it outside your tent unless someone is there to watch it for you.

If you have your bag laid out, you should be using it or preparing to use it. Before placing it down, carefully inspect the prospective bedroom area for any sharp objects that could pierce the sleeping bag shell. Small branches hacked off just a few inches from the ground are ideal for this job. Sleeping bags can be placed directly on the ground without a pad, cover, ground sheet, or tent floor, but do not do this regularly. Ground sheets are cheap, sleeping bags are not; it makes a lot of sense to use the ground sheets to take the brunt of the abrasion, dirt, and moisture that is trying to get into your sleeping bag and ruin it. A sleeping bag cover is a good investment; it helps keep the bag clean and provides extra warmth with little extra weight.

A few minutes before you are ready to crawl in, take your bag out of the stuff sack or pack compartment, and shake it out or fluff it up by hand to help the down regain its loft after compression. Many people recommend taking it out as soon as camp is set up (they say that down needs a long time to regain its full loft), but you can do a good job in only a few minutes if you put a little effort into it.

Every morning, weather permitting, before you pack the bag away into its tight, waterproof, stuff sack for transport, the bag should be aired out. This will remove quite a bit of the moisture buildup caused by your perspiration during the night, and it should go a long way toward keeping the bag smelling clean, too. I like to use a tent as a clothesline, and usually leave the bag stretched out on top while morning chores take place. Keep a sharp eye on the bag in windy conditions, turn over occasionally, and shake it out a few times to help break up down clumps. Before breaking camp, put the bag back into its stuff sack. This way it is safely stored away while you are tromping around with sharp tent stakes, poles, etc.

After your trip air out your bag thoroughly in the sunlight, which bleaches out smells, but also weakens the nylon fibers somewhat. If you are worried about ultraviolet, then toss your bag into a commercial dryer with the setting on cool or fluff dry, and watch it fluff up like new. Many people throw in a pair of clean sneakers; the rubber-nylon generates static electricity that helps loft, and the pounding of the sneakers helps break up any clumps.

After the bag has been aired out thoroughly you can store it away. Down should always be stored in its expanded state, with adequate ventilation, so don't pack it away in the tight, waterproof, nonbreathable stuff sack you use on the trail. Quite a few people go to the trouble of hanging their bags out full length in some closet; otherwise, use an oversize stuff sack that breathes.

Inspection. When your insulation loses its loft you will get cold. Generally this will sneak up on you so slowly that you won't know exactly when it happens. If your old faithful sleeping bag is not as warm as it once was, the time has come to think about restoring the loft. This should not be necessary more than a few times in the life of a sleeping bag—barring accidents like spilled suppers or tipped canoes—so don't get carried away.

Much more frequent inspection is required in other areas. Since down often mats or shifts, inspect often for these problems and shake or fluff the down back into place, and break up any clumps. On cheaper bags with exposed seams, inspect the seams to see if they have snagged anything and broken, or look for abrasion. If even a slight seam separation starts, it can soon become a major problem; and a small stitching job at the right time could save a major overhaul later. On bags with hidden seams, there is not much you can see, but watch for baffles that are pulling loose (not too likely on quality bags, but still a possibility) and fix right away. Rips or tears in the shell are obvious (down is usually pouring out at an amazing rate), and treatment is just as obvious—sew them up or patch them up fast. Zippers are rarely a problem anymore, but keep an eye on them anyhow. Watch out for tape or teeth wear, and replace if troublesome.

Cleaning. I wash my sleeping bags only when they really need it, as shown by drastic loss of loft, severe clotting, filthy shell that can't be sponged clean, or perhaps a lingering odor. Any one or all of these symptoms means time to wash, but the question now becomes, "How to wash properly?"

I recommend washing by hand, gently, in a bathtub. Take pains to rinse thoroughly; no matter what soap you use (make sure it is a mild one though) and no matter how soft the water in your area, thorough rinsing is of major importance. Otherwise the soap can leave a film on the down and cause clotting or loss of loft. Without thorough rinsing you can actually decrease the loft of the down by washing, so take care.

Just as important as the rinsing is the drying. Bags can be dryed on a clothesline (takes forever) or can be dryed in a large commercial dryer set on low heat. Highly recommended is adding a pair of clean sneakers, which aid in static buildup and which pound out most of the clumps. If your bag is low on loft, or has a lot of clumps, you might try this trick before resorting to washing.

Hand washing is highly recommended, but is a tedious job. Here is how to go about it:

1. Fill your tub with lukewarm water, and add a moderate amount of nondetergent soap. Ivory Flakes, Woolite, or one of the special down soaps are best, but definitely no enzymes or strong detergents; they can strip out too much of the down's natural oils.

2. Very gently, squeeze, knead, and pat the water into the bag. Do not twist, yank, or wring. Once the down is wet, handle with care. Do not try to pick up the bag in this state as the down now weighs enough to rip out baffles.

3. Drain the tub of soapy water, pat out most of the water in the bag slowly and gently. Refill with clean lukewarm water. Rinse thoroughly, slowly, and gently.

4. Repeat step three at least once more than you think you have to. When you get clean water coming out, the rinsing is done; you can't overrinse but you can easily underrinse, which causes clotting and loss of loft.

5. Gently compress most of the water out of the bag. Carefully pick up the entire bag. Put your arms under the bag, support as much of it as you can, and whatever you do, don't grab it by the shell and yank. Several extra hands are helpful here.

6. I recommend a big dryer (a clean one set on low or medium; less than 150°), the tennis shoes again, and perhaps a couple of dry white bath towels to soak up some excess moisture. Open the dryer occasionally and check to see that the bag is actually moving around. If it stays in one place too long the side next to the heat can burn even on low settings. Run it through until the bag and the down seem completely dry. Remember, overdried down will absorb moisture from the atmosphere until it reaches its normal moisture content (12 percent), and underdried down will lose excess moisture slowly to the same point. Don't pack it away when wet for any length of time; wet down can mildew. If it is still damp, or perhaps even if you don't think it is, hang it for ventilation for a few days before packing it away.

7. If a dryer is not available, the bag can be hung from a clothesline, but take care that it gets as much support as possible. Otherwise, the baffles can still rip out. It will be there for days, unless someone comes along and steals it, so I like the dryer better.

That is all there is to it, but it is enough. Some people do use washing machines, but this is chancy. Positively don't use an "agitator"-type washing machine; the agitator style is too rough, it jerks and twists the bag around too much. If you must use a machine, use the delicate cycle of a clean automatic washer. Make sure no one has left bleach or other harmful residues in the machine by first running it through a wash cycle empty. Then fill with cold or warm water, and proceed with care and fingers crossed.

To avoid all of the above hassles and work, dry cleaning from a reputable, experienced cleaner is the way to go. Many experts recommend dry cleaning in any case, but it does have some peculiar hazards of its own. Realize that waterfowl down prefers water to solvent, naturally, but that the right kind of solvents can do an excellent job without much damage. Make sure the operator knows his business; for example, ask him what kind of solvent he will use (he should say petroleum-based solvents).

Certain horrible things (twitching awfuls, brain damage, coma, death) can happen to you from breathing in solvents, so *air out your bag thoroughly before sleeping in it after it has been dry cleaned.* Otherwise your heirs may have a negligence suit against the dry cleaner, but this won't help you any. Incidentally, if you did a quick repair on your bag with sticky ripstop tape, you might be interested in the fact that dry-cleaning solvent will probably remove any such patch. This is annoying both for you and for the dry cleaner, so make sure all patches are sewn on securely. Do not try to save money by dry cleaning at home or in a laundromat; pay the people who know what they are doing and don't begrudge what you have to spend.

Fiber Sleeping Bags

Everything I said about the fragility of the sleeping bag still goes, but fibers have some advantages over down in the field and in the laundromat. While they may give up some loft to down, fibers are going to get more and more of down's market because of one thing—when fibers get wet they still keep a great part of their loft and insulating power. Also, because fibers have long filaments, a torn seam is not necessarily a complete disaster, and when they get wet they may be wrung out in the field, and can be back in service immediately. These points are particularly important to those who need a reliable bag; however, proper precautions and care are still called for. Use a pad, try not to snag the shell, and watch for sparks.

The bags using Fiberfill II or PolarGuard are advertised as machine washable, and of course they are, but read over the instructions that are included with the bag. Most people are given the idea that these fibers are practically indestructible. Compared to down they may seem to be, but never forget that improper washing can still ruin your sleeping bag, no matter what insulation it has. Too many people pushing the fibers don't stress this enough. An agitator-type washer can still rip out seams (the bag may have different design and construction, but the same principles apply; wet bags should be treated very gently). Improper washing can ruin your fiber bag, so read your instructions carefully, follow them carefully, and wash your bag carefully. Dry cleaning is definitely not recommended for the fibers; it may affect the insulation.

REPAIRS

This section will cover only field repairs. Keep in mind that the following repairs are "first aid" only, designed to get you home, where proper repairs should be made. Most of these repairs stress emergency conditions and a minimum of tools, and therefore have a short life expectancy. Proper repairs must follow or else you have merely postponed the problem. Repairs that are done at home, with a full complement of tools and the proper materials, can outlast the rest of the article.

If you use your equipment properly, care for it conscientiously, and inspect it regularly, then you might never need to do any of that troublesome field repair work. Try to cut corners on equipment maintenance, and you will end up with repairs. And of course they will invariably be field repairs, under the worst possible conditions, with improper tools, and a bad temper.

Repair Kit

Some very ingenious things have been done in the way of makeshift repairs using whatever tools and materials just happen to be on hand, but it makes a lot more sense to prepare a small repair kit for such events. With such a kit "impossible" jobs become merely inconvenient, and inconvenient ones become fairly easy. My repair kit is simple, light, and so far it has never let me down. Here it is; expand on it as circumstances seem to dictate.

• Seam ripper—handy to have, does a better job on seams than a blade, faster and easier, too.

• Needle nose pliers—small, good quality pair. They seem to always find something to do. Mine have a wire cutter section, which is a must.

• Safety pins—about a dozen, assorted, rustproof. They are very handy things to have along if a zipper lets go. Pin to the tape, not the fabric.

• Sewing needles—three fairly large ones, stored conveniently in the seam ripper.

• Thread—strong button and canvas type, which will hold up well. Take lots, it weighs nothing and can get used up pretty fast.

• Wire—a small loop of soft wire for almost anything. You can fix or make some really amazing things with a pair of pliers and some wire.

• Ripstop tape—it fixes rips, and it is strong enough to be used for many other things as well.

• Nylon rope—not really a part of my repair kit, but I always take some along. Nylon rope is exceptionally useful for camping, and it comes in handy for repair

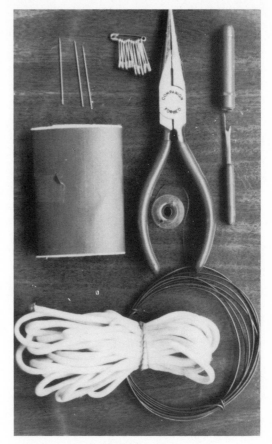

A light, compact, field-repair kit.

work too. The 550-pound-test parachute cord type is probably the best size.

Pack Repairs

Pack bags and soft packs are generally made from the toughest fabrics available, so very little repair work is ever needed here. Any rips that do occur will probably come from climbing through a barbed wire fence, or snagging on some other sharp, tough object. A patch can be sewn on; however, if you have ripstop tape along you can patch with it instead. Put one patch on the inside of the pack, where the contents will help keep it in place.

Then, if you want to, you can put another patch on the outside. The sticky part of the inside patch should help keep the outside patch on, but don't count on it. One trick is to use a hot pot or pan to "iron" on the patches. This helps the adhesive stick, but not too hot; nylon melts at 480°F.

Seams are a likely failure spot on the pack, so be prepared to sew up any of them that let go. If you have been inspecting your equipment regularly you shouldn't have this problem, but if a seam does rip, sew it up with your sewing kit.

If your zipper lets go this can be annoying. You can't just sew it up because you may have to get into the pack for gear. Safety pins (lots of them) can do the trick. The alternative is to sew up whatever part of the zipper went bad and use only the part still working for access. This may or may not work, but it can allow partial use of the pack until the zipper can be replaced.

On cheap packs, which don't bother with such niceties as finished seams around the zippers, a few months of use can fray the fabric enough to seriously impair the zipper's use (snags). Empty out the pack, trim off as much of the frayed fabric as possible, and flame seal the edges yourself. Careful here, a few sticky zippers are better than a burned-up pack. When you get home, do a good job on these areas with some hot object to eliminate the problem properly. Better yet, do the job before trouble develops.

I have yet to tear a web strap, or wear one out in use. The nylon ones are immensely strong and tough, so you will have no problem with them unless they are cut (not likely without you cutting them) or tear loose from the pack seams. Properly designed seams that attach the straps to the much weaker fabric over a large area should last as long as the rest of the pack. See Chapter 4, "Packs," for how to attach a strap properly.

If your frame gets broken, you are in a lot of trouble unless your bag is one of the convertible types that is usable without any frame. If the frame is absolutely shot, don't give up and carry the bag in your arms; this is much more exhausting than trying to rig up some kind of a backpack. You can sew the shoulder straps to the bag and make a rucksack, which will be hell to carry with a heavy load, but still better than carrying it in your arms. Or if you are innovative and know your woodcraft, such an emergency is justification for rigging up some kind of pack frame from natural materials. I have seen some remarkably finished looking, very comfortable pack frames made out of branches lashed together. In fact, up North, many people use such frames extensively with a commercial or homemade pack bag.

If your frame is not totally destroyed, you may be able to repair it. If only one joint or tube is broken, you can fix it by cutting a piece of branch and splinting the break with it. Here is where the wire is helpful, but if you didn't bring any, scrounge around and see if someone left some nearby. Failing any source of wire, ripstop tape is the next best thing. If you don't have ripstop tape, look in your first-aid kit for some surgical tape. In cold weather, either type may stick better if warmed slightly (maybe warm the frame, too). If you don't have tape of any kind, lash it together with your rope. No rope? Then what on earth were you doing out there in the first place?

Clothing Repairs

Sew split or ripped seams or patch them with ripstop tape. Sewn repairs can be permanent—if you have the time and the temperament for it out in the woods—or they can be quickies with large stitches, designed to get you home where you can do a better job.

A lot of clothing gets burned up drying out over a fire, so avoid this. If your boots happen to be the item you've overcooked, you have a problem. To minimize your misery rig up some wrap or something from spare clothing. This will not help much, so don't burn your boots. If you can spare the weight, carry a pair of lightweight shoes for emergencies and for wear around camp.

Tent Repairs

A tent is supposed to provide you with shelter from the sun, rain, bugs, cold, and wind. Sun is no problem; rig up any piece of opaque cloth for a shade. Rain with no wind is easy; all you need is a poncho or tarp, or fly, pitched any one of a multitude of ways. Flying, buzzing, biting bugs can sometimes become a real danger. Fortunately they are easily outwitted. Since they can't really home in on people that well, any shelter that blocks them from three sides means eliminating three-fourths of the bugs. Of course, some mosquitoes are born smarter than others.

Cold is a function of space. Your body gives off heat, and any small enclosure will help retain that heat and help you stay warm. People have lived through blizzards without tents before, merely by knowing this fact. If you have no tent, a snow cave is still a possibility, or anything enclosed that cuts down on heat loss. Remember also that moving air is cold air; make your enclosure as windproof as possible. But don't close it completely or you can smother to death. Learn winter survival techniques, so that if you ever do find yourself in such conditions without a tent, at least you will know how to cope.

Actually, in most conditions, you should be able to get by quite nicely without a tent; pack your ripped tent away and leave it in your pack. Who knows, the fresh air may even provide you with the incentive to give up tents altogether. Many backpackers scorn tents; they use only a tarp, a poncho, or nothing. They claim they get closer to nature without the tent, so try and look at the good side of the experience if you ever lose yours.

A tent that is ripped should never be left up in high winds, unless there is a genuine emergency. Otherwise, what started out as a small rip or perhaps a split seam that could be repaired soon becomes a major repair or perhaps even a completely ruined tent. Once a rip starts, take down the tent and do not use it until it is properly repaired. In most cases this will mean only minor hardships. However, in some special cases you are now endangering your survival. You will have to make the decisions: is it better to wait out the blizzard and try to stay warm in a snow shelter, or should you hope that the rip will weather the storm?

Sleeping Bag Repairs

Sleeping bags can burn up, get ripped up, or if down filled, they can be effectively ruined by water matting the down. All of these are to be guarded against constantly, but the time may come when you have to do a field repair on your sleeping bag. Then you will take much better care of your bag in the future.

First of all, rips are best fixed with a patch of ripstop tape over a sewn seam. If you merely sew up a rip, down will often leak no matter how diligent you are, though this is a partial cure. The ripstop tape by itself does a fair job, but if the patch pulls off then the stuffings are still free to get lost. Use both for security, at least until you can get home and do a proper repair with a machine and fine stitching.

Open zippers should be pinned together with safety pins or the zipper can be sewn completely shut. Many sleeping bags don't have a zipper anyway; it is mainly a convenience item, and you can get by without one by wriggling in and out from the top. Stitch or pin to the tape or else you will leave needle holes that may leak down forever.

If your bag gets burned, you get little sympathy from me. There is no real excuse for such accidents. Open fires should not be necessary for warmth. If you are cold eat something, do isometric exercises, put on more dry clothing, or get a warmer sleeping bag. As for those who get their bags wet and are tempted to dry them over an open fire, I think it only fair to warn you that the shell burns a lot faster than the down dries.

Keep your down bag dry. Down bags that get soaked are a major problem, in some conditions a potential killer. If you are involved in some activity that seems like it could lead to a wet sleeping bag, consider using a fiber or foam-insulated bag. These bags can be used when wet with little or no loss of warmth. If your down bag does get thoroughly soaked through some accident, then you may be in real trouble.

I can't think of any way of drying out a down sleeping bag in the bush that doesn't involve a lot of trouble and patience. In above-zero weather you can hang the bag out to dry, shaking it often to break up down clots. In below-zero weather I would suggest you forget about sleeping and immediately find some place warm (like home). If this is an impossibility, you have problems. So far I've never had to try and dry out a down sleeping bag in below-zero weather, and I really don't want to. If you have, and know some trick that works, I'd be glad to hear of it.

Index